CORNFLAKE CRUSADE

By *GERALD CARSON*

"He that witholdeth corn, the people
shall curse him; but blessing *shall be*
upon the head of him that selleth *it*."
—PROVERBS XI: 26

RINEHART & COMPANY, INC.
New York   Toronto

PUBLISHED SIMULTANEOUSLY IN CANADA BY
CLARKE, IRWIN & COMPANY, LTD., TORONTO

© 1957 BY GERALD CARSON
PRINTED IN THE UNITED STATES OF AMERICA
ALL RIGHTS RESERVED
LIBRARY OF CONGRESS CATALOG CARD NUMBER: 57–9631

To My Mother

ACKNOWLEDGMENTS

THE author acknowledges with a deep sense of obligation the assistance received from individuals, general and special libraries, universities and other institutions mentioned below. If any name should appear below, and does not, it is through inadvertence. Some who rendered substantial assistance have passed on while the research and writing was in progress, suggesting how late the hour is for capturing this particular segment of the American story.

The manuscript owes so much to Mrs. Stanley T. Lowe and Forest H. Sweet that it is doubtful if the book could have been completed without the encouragement, help and candid criticism of the text which each provided. I have also to thank Dr. Benjamin Ashe, A. L. Miller and Dr. Mildred S. Titley for reading the manuscript, and for their valuable suggestions and criticisms. None are, of course, responsible for any errors of fact or interpretation.

Various libraries and repositories which were visited generously made their resources available. The author wishes to thank Miss Margaret Scriven, Librarian, and Miss Elizabeth Baughman, Reference Librarian, of the Chicago Historical Society; Mrs. Ruth P. Braun and her staff, The Catlin Memorial Library of *The Detroit News*; the Reference Division of the Forbes Library, Northampton, Massachusetts; George H. Fairchild, Librarian, the Historical Society of Pennsylvania; Charles R. Green, Librarian, the Jones Library, Amherst, Massachusetts; Dr. F. Clever Bald, Assistant Director, Michigan Historical Collections of the University of Michigan; Miss Janet Doe and staff, the New York Academy of Medicine Library; the New York Bar Association Library; the staff of the Reading Room at the New-York Historical Society, and especially Mrs. Bella C. Landauer; the Reference Division of the New York Public Library and the expert and gracious staffs of Rooms 300, 308 and 328; The Philadelphia Free Library; Mason Tolman and Miss Edna Jacobsen, The New York State Library; Harold Swart, Chief of Readers' Service at Printers' Ink Publishing Company; the Quincy, Illinois, Free Public Library; Mrs. Frances H. Morgan,

Librarian, the Scoville Memorial Library, Salisbury, Connecticut; Miss Doris K. Meyerhoff, United States Trade Mark Association; Fred Dimoch, the University of Michigan General Library; Miss Helen L. Warner and staff, the Willard Library, Battle Creek, Michigan.

Thanks are due also to the following for their varied contributions—answering queries, double-checking an elusive fact, providing photostats, making suggestions, preparing bibliographies and reference materials, making available inaccessible periodicals, pamphlets or books and unpublished material through interlibrary loans: Miss Florence Rowley, Librarian, the American Association of Advertising Agencies; Mrs. Ruth M. Yakel, Executive Secretary, The American Dietetic Association; the Armed Forces Medical Library; Norman Draper, Director of Public Relations, American Meat Institute; Charles C. Colby, Reference Librarian, Boston Medical Library; Andrew Duncan, President, The Cereal Institute, Inc.; Charles T. Smutney, Librarian, *The Chicago Tribune*; Miss Margaret Rose, Reference Librarian, The City Library Association, Springfield, Massachusetts; Colonel Arthur P. Long, and Lt. Colonel Stanley J. Weidenkopf, Office of the Surgeon General, Department of the Army; Mrs. Elleine Stones, Chief, the Burton Collection, Detroit Public Library; William Henry Harrison, Director, Fruitlands and the Wayside Museums; Illinois State Historical Library; John H. Berthel, Librarian, The Johns Hopkins University Library; Mrs. Helen M. McFarland, Librarian, Kansas State Historical Society; the Library of Congress, especially David Chambers Mearns; Stephen T. Riley, Librarian, Massachusetts Historical Society; Mrs. Evelyn Hunter, Librarian, the Millerton Library; R. W. Thomas, Curator and Librarian, New Haven Colony Historical Society; Richard N. Wright, President, Onondaga Historical Association, Syracuse, New York; Miss Dorothy Stuart, Assistant Librarian, The State Historical Society of Colorado; and the University of Chicago Library.

Also assistance was generously given by: Roy V. Ashley, Miss Edith and Miss Mary Barber, R. Habermann, Secretary, Battle Creek Chamber of Commerce; Professor Adelia M. Beeuwkes, August F. Bloese, Miss Helen M. Bramble, Frank Briscoe, Henry D. Brown, Miss Leta Browning, Ralph Starr Butler, Earnest Calkins, the late Professor A. J. Carlson, Walter N. Chimel, Ross

Coller, James C. Colvin, Miss Lenna F. Cooper and Dr. J. E. Cooper.

Timely help of an unusual kind was forthcoming from Mr. and Mrs. George Degener, Jr., who loaned their fireproof chicken house for the storage of the manuscript. I also am indebted in various ways to R. O. Eastman, Dr. Moses Ehrlich, Miss Ruth Enlow, Dr. Morris Fishbein, Dr. Jonathan Forman, Chester Foust, the late Earle J. Freeman, Mrs. Regina G. Frisbie, Mrs. Martha Brockway Gale, Parker Gates, Harry Gilbert, Professor Carroll W. Grant, Mrs. Helen B. Green, Putney Haight, Burritt Hamilton, Ray B. Haun, Dr. David D. Henry, S. N. Holliday and Mrs. Ernest L. Ives.

I levied upon James A. Jackson for contributions which were of great assistance, as well as S. E. Jennings, August Johansen, Miss Elsa Johnson, Dr. Norman Jolliffe, Dr. Louis C. Jones, Clarence Jordan, Dr. George L. Kaeur, Mark W. Kiley, K. H. Knowlton, Sidney Kocin, Dr. Hedwig Koenig, G. H. Lauhoff, John C. Lippen, Joe Lynch, George C. McKay, Dr. Douglass Miller, Mrs. Dorothy Mongan, Frank W. Northrup, Thomas C. O'Donnell, George Oliva, Ralph Olmstead, James O'Shaughnessy, Arthur Osterholm, Stuart Peabody, Miss Dorothy Potter of the *Daily Hampshire Gazette*, Northampton, Massachusetts, Horace B. Powell, Wilfred J. Rauber, Historian of the Village of Dansville, New York, and Professor Warner G. Rice.

Francis Robinson has a share in what follows, as does Mrs. Grace C. Rose; the late Andrew Ross, too, for his invaluable recollections of W. K. Kellogg and early food merchandising, also Mrs. Ruth Schaefer and the late Edgar F. Schaefer lent a hand, as did John Sickles, Mr. and Mrs. Wendell Smith, L. E. Stacey, Henry M. Stegman, Colton Storm, Mrs. Bertha B. Stump, Mrs. Forest H. Sweet, Miss Marguerite Swallen, Mrs. Fanny Sprague Talbot, R. R. Thomson and Miss Cynthia Walsh.

Roswell Ward provided information about the Centennial Exposition of 1876 from family sources, Professor Luther S. West prepared a helpful memorandum on Dr. John Harvey Kellogg and Battle Creek College. George Whitsett wrote me a letter, an important one, and Don Wright introduced me to Whitsett. This book, and I, owe much to Willis Kingsley Wing; and to Professor J. Harvey Young, who generously provided a copious flow of citations and suggestions for further investigation.

x   *Acknowledgments*

To Ted Amussen and his associates at Rinehart, who with taste and enthusiasm turned a typescript into a book, I am deeply and admiringly grateful. Permission to reprint portions of the book which first appeared in magazines was kindly granted by *American Heritage, Michigan History, New York History* and *Sales Management*. The book owes much to Miss Louella F. Still for her copyreading and her full and careful subject index.

From my wife, Lettie Gay Carson, who typed the first draft and brought taste and judgment to bear upon each problem as it arose, I have had faith, hope, charity and unfailing good counsel.

PREFACE

THESE last words, which appear first, constitute a kind of hail and farewell to the diet revolt of the past century, and to a group of characters richly endowed with singularity.

The fantasia of our food reform has not hitherto been set down as a consecutive narrative. Out of it came, on the one hand, an insatiable popular interest in "scientific" eating, and more food cultists, faddists and kelp wizards than any other civilized nation has ever known. And on the other hand we have the enterprising ready-to-eat cereal industry which, with its "built-in maid service," its eye-filling packages and massive advertising, has influenced importantly both what we put in our stomachs and our minds. The "world" laughed at "the food protest," but succeeding generations ate corn flakes and philologists could not but observe that the word "dyspepsia" had disappeared from common speech.

For some twelve years I have been pursuing the social history of American eating, the food reformers and the cornflake kings, trying to sift fact from folklore and get the storyline straight in my own mind. A chronology which has been helpful to me and may assist others appears in the back of the book. I have tried to tell the truth—what happened, and why—as I encountered it, recognizing these limiting factors: the historian is human and has his own point of view. "Truth" is shaped primarily by survivors and by those who leave the fullest records. Half-truths are probably the only kind we know, and sometimes the fraction is even smaller.

"As it is the commendation of a good huntsman to find game in a wide world," says Plato, "so it is no imputation if he hath not caught all." Other hunters are welcome in this public domain. There are no "no trespassing" signs.

There has been no attempt made to underline the applicability of this chronicle to our own times. But it does have latent topical elements.

Some of the more durable members of the living generation may yet encounter the problems of compulsive vegetarianism. Food experts agree that present surpluses will tend to become shortages. This possibility, many call it a probability, has tremendous implications in relation to our present dependence upon meat vis-à-vis the cereal diet. Current farm methods of food production will not be "sufficient to feed our children and grandchildren as we are being fed," declared Professor Sleeter Bull of the College of Agriculture, University of Illinois, at a dinner in Chicago last year.

And lastly, it has been pointed out by a scientist in the field of nutrition, Dr. Glen Charles King, that twenty million Americans still do not know how to eat intelligently.

"Courageous nonconformity, whatever its purpose," says Whitney R. Cross, "ought of itself to constitute a precious heritage to the twentieth century." With this reminder I hope to elicit from the reader a measure of charity and tolerance toward some very cranky people who figure in this account of "philosophers" and folkways.

G.C.

Millerton, New York
May 15, 1957.

CONTENTS

CORNFLAKE
CRUSADE

Foodtown, U.S.A.

Miss Daisy Buck, who used to preside over the newsstand in the Michigan Central depot at Battle Creek, Michigan, in the early years of this century, patted up her back hair, the way women do when they feel themselves in command of the situation.

"Battle Crick," she told an audience of visiting drummers, "is the best-advertised little old town in the whole United States."

During the years just before and after 1900, Battle Creek had turned away from the Arcadian life of a Main Street town and entered the industrial age with something of a bang. Named for a ruckus between two Indians and two surveyors, one of the world's most minuscule Indian affrays, in which no wounds worse than a broken head were inflicted, Battle Creek developed slowly around a water-power site. The "crick" turned the wheels of village industries —saw and flour mills, broom factories, planing mills; later joined by furniture works, agricultural-implement and steam-pump factories.

What really gilded the town, though, and gave it boulevard lights, a first-class hotel and its first multimillionaire, was the invention locally of a whole category of dry breakfast foods, precooked, ready to eat. The crinkly Battle Creek foods proved to be a spectacular contribution to kitchen convenience in a servantless world. They helped to keep down the High Cost of Living, raised the national consumption of fluid milk, added a bright new variety to a monotonous and heavy diet.

Millions of dollars' worth of advertising and billions of breakfast-food cartons made the good name of Battle Creek a kitchen-and-pantry word from one coast of continental North America to the other, carried it across all oceans and seas, hypnotically repetitive, impressing daily upon the mothers and small fry of the world the health message of the Cereal City, which marketed food and philosophy together. By 1911 there were 108 brands of corn flakes alone being packed in Battle Creek.

That is what Miss Buck meant.

The breakfast that required no cooking, that would keep indefinitely, that poured crisply out of a cardboard box, was as American as beans or baseball. Yet two other countries were soon eating more corn flakes per head than the U.S. did. Within less than a generation, the crackling foodstuffs invented in this small Midwestern city were munched daily in most of the world's countries, colonies and dependencies. Although the peoples of all nations have ever remained stubbornly nationalistic in their food preferences, the American "health foods" proved to be the exception to the rule.

Ingenious cookers, heavy steel rollers, running at differential speeds, and the inherent virtues of the small grains did the job for Battle Creek; though some observers of the burgeoning Michigan metropolis have said enviously that it was done with mirrors. This grudging compliment referred to a certain virtuosity in the use of salesmanship which Battle Creek demonstrated in persuading the world to drink "coffee" made out of wheat, eat a "chop" based on macerated peanuts, or breakfast on crunchy flakes instead of fried ham, hot biscuits and boiled coffee. There were moral, sumptuary and even religious overtones to the cornflake crusade.

At any rate, Battle Creek grew and prospered upon the technology of mashing and mauling wheat, bran, corn, oats and rice into entrancing, dainty new foodstuffs. The new foods, the "scare" advertising and the health preachments by which they were sold, changed profoundly the world's eating habits and brought to Battle Creek new energy and wealth, new citizens, an unquenchable booster spirit. With the food factories came maturity, sophistication, social complexities—a carriage aristocracy, an Entre Nous Pedro Club, an interurban, sin, and the best opera house between Kalamazoo and Jackson, its stage large enough to handle a Ben Hur race with two chariots and four horses.

"The World's Cereal Bowl," "The Cereal City," "The Health City," "Foodtown," "The Biggest Little City in the U.S.A.," "Cornflake Capital of the World," and "A Little Chicago" were all sobri-

quets which newspaper paragraphers applied to Michigan's most celebrated small city. Battle Creek was acknowledged to be "a pretty smart town."

What other small city has exerted so great an influence upon the character of our civilization as Battle Creek? A fair case could be made out for Durham, North Carolina. Known as the "Town Renowned the World Around," Durham sent out upon the world its celebrated Bull Durham Smoking Tobacco. But Battle Creek, with fervor left over from its "underground railroad" days, set a higher moral tone. Its aim was no less than to save the race from its physiological sins, and to get well paid for its good advice. Only Battle Creek offered solid sustenance and a vision of the Edenic life in which the soybean vied with the wheat germ, and the acidophilus washed down "All the Wheat That's Fit To Eat."

"The health food business is one of the Lord's own instrumentalities," proclaimed Mrs. Ellen G. White, priestess of the Seventh Day Adventists, who made their world headquarters at Battle Creek.

No other industry could make *that* statement!

"Battle Creek has twenty-one thousand people," said a Chicago visitor in 1902, "all of whom are engaged in the manufacture of breakfast foods." Another commentator remarked, "Cascarets are unknown in Battle Creek. They can't 'work while you sleep' here, for nobody sleeps—excepting, of course, the policemen."

"A cablegram from anywhere in the world addressed 'Battle Creek,' will be delivered," exulted Charles W. Post, the Postum and Grape Nuts pioneer. There was a sense of urgency and destiny about the billboard erected opposite the Michigan Central depot— "Better Yourself in Battle Creek."

It was, indeed, a pleasant little city of square, white houses placed well back from the street among oaks and maples, with twelve-foot ceilings, grandmother's mirror with gold-leaf frame brought from Connecticut; and mother in the parlor accompanying herself as she sang "The Blue Alsatian Mountains." Shaded avenues were arranged on a rectangular grid pattern in the gentle valley of the Kalamazoo River. It is a gracious land of low hills and pretty lakes, the southern Michigan hay and fruit belt. Smokestacks, water towers and shining rows of huge grain elevators rose from the floor of the valley, symbols of the opportunities developing in Foodtown, while outlying "string" streets reached toward Kalamazoo, Bellevue, Athens and Marshall.

By the 1940's, some hundred million spoons clicked rhythmically against brimming bowls of breakfast food every morning in the United States, with the grains preferred in this order: corn, wheat, oats, bran and rice. The discovery of America added to man's food supply the potato, white and sweet; the tomato, pumpkin, squash; the many varieties of beans, peppers; eggplant, watermelon, rhubarb, the turkey, crabapples, the berries—black-, rasp-, cran-, straw-, blue- and goose-; also corn and peanuts. The peanut, under various coy disguises, was the dining-room staple at the Battle Creek Sanitarium, while flaked corn became the aptest symbol of the revolution at the breakfast table. Though wheat has a longer history and enjoys a greater prestige with Western man, it was corn which nourished the American pioneer. Easy to cultivate, able to multiply itself 250 times in a single harvest, the corn plant is a food source of marvelous efficiency. Corn quickly became the true American staff of life, the inspiration of artists, of literature, its influence transcending all the wealth of the Incas or the dreams of the Spanish conquerors. Corn-fed hogs provided the meat on the settler's table three times a day; corn also appeared seven days a week as meal, syrup, bread and pones, Indian pudding. Corn whiskey supported the frontier economy, passing easily as money, while the "hominy man" and the "hot corn lady" cried their wares picturesquely on city streets.

It is no wild fancy to suppose that corn, as meal and as meat, as a liquid source of warmth and courage, has been a prime source of American enterprise and optimism. The broken endosperm of delectable, botanically fascinating *Zea mays*, cooked in retorts, rolled into flakes, toasted to a crisp brown and hauled out of cereal factories by the trainload, is merely the latest in a long series of distinguished services rendered to man by this versatile grass.

In 1952, Canadians ate even more poundage per capita than did U.S. families. The Australians munched almost twice as much grain in the form of flakes, shreds and granules as we did, even though 50 per cent of Americans eat an ounce or so of cereal every day. Today, Battle Creek optimism and salesmanship push on toward limitless goals. The pace is always quickening. In 1956, the

United States alone scooped up 1,233,000,000 pounds—the largest tonnage ever, and the highest per capita—of prepared breakfast foods that had been rolled, baked, ground, flaked, beat up, exploded and extruded; worth $379,000,000 at wholesale prices. The advertising expense in connection with distributing breakfast cereals in 1956 amounted to around $41,000,000, and the cereal factories are also enormous users of cardboard, printing and premiums such as nylon stockings, eighty-two-piece silver-plate sets, space helmets, atom-bomb rings, plastic boomerangs, voodoo papers and cowboy regalia. The horse-opera trappings are, incidentally, quite passé now. Ever responsive to the shifting interests of their young public, the break-fast-food companies have now tackled the problems of interplanetary navigation. They are today the principal source of equipment for pre-teen-age space-flight men.

The cereal premium is an ingenious device of American merchandising designed to satisfy the inborn urge to get something for nothing. Both the American Mom and the Space-Helmet Set respond frenetically to the lure of an added extrinsic value like cat's-eye marbles in six assorted colors, or a poinsettia costume pin. In the form of "gifts," either packed in the carton or obtainable in exchange for boxtops or coupons and small amounts of cash, the breakfast food, soap, tobacco, home-appliance makers, and other premium promoters spent more than an astronomical one and a half billion dollars in 1955 on premium merchandising. It is an old idea. Paul Revere, as a silversmith, distributed fancy "trading cards" —premiums—to prospective customers. B. T. Babbitt, of cleanser fame, offered colored lithographs in exchange for soap wrappers. Elbert Hubbard, the Sage of East Aurora, N.Y., once a peddler of Larkin's Soap, gave a brass kerosene lamp with each case; button-hooks for high-button shoes, perfume and celluloid collars. One of the dicta of the old Roycrofter was: "The premium method of merchandising will live as long as trade itself, because it moves with the tides of the human heart."

A six-year-old consumer-trainee recently assured his mother that he didn't mind getting his own breakfast and eating it by himself.

"I *like* to eat alone," he explained. "I can just sit and think, and read my cereal boxes."

Once, one chose a cereal food for happy breakfasting with the feeling that what would fatten a hog or strengthen a horse was good for humans, too. "Now," says a disgruntled oldster, addressing the editor of *The New York Times* under the nom de plume of "Kicker," "I find that Cereal A is especially made for children who play hard, Cereal B is for nursing mothers and Cereal C is what makes champions.

"I am not a child, a nursing mother or an invalid, and I think it smacks of professionalism to be a champion.

"I have just bought a pound of rice and am looking for old-fashioned oatmeal in bulk and will hope to find some packaged cereal free from thiamin or vitamin B or tin whistles and silverware."

"Kicker's" views will not be taken seriously. The cereal makers know who their best friends are—and where they are. For them, skilled students of mass behavior—Elmo Roper, A. C. Nielson, the advertising agencies—examine with anxious solicitude our breakfast habits, our preferences as to grain-types, our taste in premiums, tabulated by age group and sex, by season and the day of the week, by family size and geographical region. People eat more dry cereals in the summertime, less in the winter; but the difference is not great. The cereal folks know how many of us eat eggs in the morning, or pancakes, or bacon, or sweet rolls; and how many follow the "basic breakfast pattern"—orange juice, cereal-and-milk, buttered toast and coffee—recommended by the Cereal Institute, Inc., a research and educational endeavor supported by the whole industry.

Average eating time: twelve minutes, daily except Sunday. Girls eat more cereals than boys, ten-year-olds than teen-agers. One out of three cereal eaters adds fruits or berries. The detail in which this kind of information exists is astonishing. A cereal sales manager can know, if he wants to, how many redheaded, car-owning, employed bran eaters there are in Columbus, Ohio, or any other city, whether each one is a union man or not, member of a lodge, what kind of house he lives in, how many kids he has, even his average weekly grocery bill.

When grandpa fed the stock and milked the cows before breakfast, when the children trudged a couple of miles to the little unconsolidated red schoolhouse, the only question about the adequate breakfast was—was it adequate? There has been a certain amount of retrogression. The "Breakfast Question" of today revolves around the light eater, the coffee-and-rolls bolter, or—even worse—the breakfast skipper.

The breakfast-food industry still meets the problem of breakfast delinquents with an historic versatility. It has ranged widely, from Arthur Godfrey to Harvard University, in its search for potent co-adjutors in the cause. Mass-feeding tests have demonstrated the importance of eating from one fourth to one third of the day's food at the morning meal. The bicycle ergometer, with the hungry subject pedaling madly, has determined Maximum Work Output. Mental alertness, the magnitude of neuromuscular tremor have been related to the cereal breakfast, the bacon-and-eggs breakfast and the no-breakfast.

What of the "coffee only" husband, who wonders why he feels so hungry and dizzy at midmorning? What about the woman who dreams of weighing one hundred and twenty-three pounds once more? What about the thirteen million Americans who are over sixty-five today and who will number seventeen to twenty million by 1975? The Cereal Institute has looked into all these matters. It has verified by scientific procedures what the breakfast-food folks always suspected—that the fat and the thin, the young and the old, feel better and thrive better with an adequate breakfast under their belts.

Let us not overlook the commercial significance of these discoveries. One family of four, well indoctrinated and convinced of the superiority of a single cereal brand, if each member lived to the Biblical threescore and ten, could conceivably be worth around two thousand dollars, over a lifetime, to the favored brand. Corn flakes, it has been amply demonstrated, can easily become familial.

Why, particularly, did one town in Michigan become the home and center of breakfast foods, of the national hunt for the better life?

Was it geography or something about freight rates? No.

Skilled labor force? No.

Local source of grain? No. Calhoun County, in which Battle Creek is located, produces a mere driblet of the wheat needed by the cereal plants, only nominal amounts of the other grains used.

Battle Creek's special asset has been its human resources. The

•

names of three men stand out, all great persuaders: Dr. John Harvey Kellogg, surgeon, health evangelist, food inventor; Charles W. Post, shrewd capitalist and hypnotic advertiser; Will Keith Kellogg, Dr. John Harvey Kellogg's younger brother, a dour, moody genius of finance and exploitation, who inspired a sales force with an almost religious sense of dedication as they fanned out over the grocery trade of North America. The seldom-compatible Kellogg brothers, lowering and tilting at each other for fifty years and more, so different and so alike, together made Kellogg the greatest name in cereals; and W. K. Kellogg went on to establish one of the largest charitable foundations in the United States.

In the comfortable 1880's, Battle Creek had some seven thousand democratic residents and not a single millionaire. The town rocked along, making threshing machines and pumps, milling flour, weaving knit goods, building wagons. It was just another provincial burg of which the drummers quipped, "I spent two weeks there one day," with a German band, an old opera house, Vaporium ("the great $1.50 catarrh remedy"). The community was still rural in atmosphere, the trading center for the county farmers who drove in on Saturdays, put their teams up at the tie-barn, and talked about the crops: "Terrible weather for hay, aint it?"

Those were halcyon days, or so they seem now, when a country-bred youth went courting with a bag of peppermints and wrapped the lines around the whipsocket on the way home. A lad could leave his Columbia chainless bicycle in front of Charles Austin's elite grocery or Minty's Cigar Store without lock or guard. Sometimes the entire force at the Nichols & Shepard thresher works, with wives and shoe-box lunches, would pile into a Grand Trunk Special, drawn by the pony engine, to spend a bright August day in the blackberry patch near Olivet.

What gave the city its special flavor was the religious-health-medical doctrine of the Seventh Day Adventists. For fifty years, Battle Creek was the world headquarters of this aggressive, fundamentalist society of the faithful, who observed their Sabbath on Saturday. Devout believers in the Second Coming, convinced vegetarians, the Adventists followed Genesis literally where it says, "Behold, I have given you every herb bearing seed, . . . to you it shall be for meat."

The Advent folk were steered into the health reform by an astute prophetess, Mrs. Ellen G. White, who supplemented her religious message with instruction in elementary physiology and washing up, and tried to put an end to piggery at the dinner table.

There was a remarkable dynamism about this calling out of a whole church against dietetic error. Revivalistic, tub-thumping in character, the early Adventist agitation over food provided an effective propaganda background for the commercial breakfast-food industry. Gifted in oratory, piety and business administration, Sister White called the signals in matters of faith, dress, decorum and diet as well as Biblical exegesis.

The pioneer residents of Battle Creek brought with them from humble Eastern homes the religious experience of camp and grove meeting. The Inner Light guided them on their way—and often caused a peck of trouble, too. Battle Creek went in for table tipping, mesmerism, phrenology, and heard distinctly the knocking of the spirits. The Methodists and Presbyterians, meanwhile, made no distinction between criminals and Universalists, while the Progressive Friends found the Universalists too stuffy. Above all, the Seventh Day Adventists flourished like Jonah's gourd. Theirs was a workingman's literal creed, filled with horrid-looking beasts and images of splendid thrones. It was a viable program for the rural areas *circa* 1880.

You might think that Old Splitfoot wouldn't have a chance in Battle Creek. But ornate dress, sybaritic living, worldliness slithered into the Michigan Eden from nearby Kalamazoo, or arrived on the Detroit Accommodation. There were local quacks to prey upon the gullible. Shady visitors worked the town, unloading lightning rods, gold-mining stocks, an inside interest in a perpetual-motion machine.

Crystal gazers, hypnotists and neuropaths, mental healers made themselves as cozy along Battle Creek's Main Street as a boll weevil in a cotton bale. Travelling doctors put up at the Potter House, some of whom could diagnose disease just by taking one look at the patient. The ineffable Bernarr Macfadden twice muscled in on Battle Creek's fame, swinging along the streets of the Health City in bare feet and shorts, chest up, stomach in.

The crank element is no longer conspicuous in Battle Creek.

Many years ago it folded its tents and moved to New York City, Florida and Southern California. The modern breakfast-food executives and the California kelp wizards have common ancestors. But they parted company long ago by a process of divergent evolution. The breakfast-food processors of today are interested in the breakfast nook of the normal family. The food cultists are throwbacks, Indian medicine men, with a slicker routine.

What was called "The Battle Creek System" radiated from the Battle Creek Sanitarium, headquarters for the vegetarian attack on pork. It was the home of health congresses and strange theories. There was enough of an air of fanaticism about its corridors and walks to produce a mild form of genuine persecution. Hoodlums and urchins invaded the West End, where the "San" was located, to frighten the Adventists' horses, snatch at their bridles, chant "bran eater" and "Gizzardite" around the purlieus of the Tabernacle. Sometimes a comely lady Adventist in her Bloomer-type uniform was forced to hide in a nearby store until rescued by an elder.

To Dr. John Harvey Kellogg, superintendent of the Battle Creek Sanitarium, the medical Kellogg brother, more than to any other individual, Battle Creek owes its initial fame. Gifted and versatile son of Adventist parents, Dr. Kellogg expanded a struggling little medical boardinghouse run by the Adventists in the 1870's into the vast institution of the 1900's; and it still flourishes. Kellogg drew well-to-do Americans with the leisure to worry about their insides to Battle Creek for an expensive turn at "getting the stomach right." The "San" is a phenomenon not immediately understandable to those who never saw it in its days of glory. Here was refreshment for body, mind and spirit. It was hard to get one without the others, but easy to get all three. The vast resort offered the combined features of a medical boardinghouse, hospital, religious retreat, country club, tent Chautauqua, spa, all carried forward in an atmosphere of moral reform and asceticism.

Ripples from Battle Creek washed all distant shores, modifying over the span of two generations our ideas about food, physiology, nutrition, fresh air, physical culture and the Good Life. In the early days of radio, Battle Creek had a muezzin of the kilocycles, who called upon the faithful to do their duty, every hour on the hour from station WKBP, whose call letters stood for "We Keep Breakfast Popular." Even now, throughout the day, the announcer of a local station, successor to WKBP, intones, "This is station W-E-L-L, Battle Creek."

There was just one trouble with the Sanitarium diet. It was remarkably dull. To keep his hungry guests from breaking training, Dr. Kellogg invented some eighty new grain- and nut-food products, including peanut butter and the flaked breakfast foods. Imitation was inevitable. C. W. Post had a spectacular success and it was later duplicated by W. K. Kellogg. Each one of the trio was as smart as a traction lawyer. Together, they kept Battle Creek in an uproar for more than a lifetime, the two Kelloggs breaking ninety before they slipped their moorings. The time-spirit worked in their favor. The United States was just entering into a kind of life which did not require a strong back or pork three times a day. But millions of city dwellers ate as though they were still plowing between the stumps. Gastric troubles prepared the way for the "health foods," while "cholera morbus"—the collywobbles—the consequence of eating contaminated food, underlined the urgent need for better technology and higher standards in food processing.

So far as the distinctive food products of Battle Creek were concerned, a mechanized agriculture provided an abundance of grain at low cost; and the women's magazines educated each new crop of brides in the uses of the factory-processed "patent foods." The public wanted "pure food." Battle Creek produced it by the trainload, packaged in the new consumer-unit cartons, uniform in weight, precooked, even "predigested" they said, though that was neither important nor true, and Untouched by Human Hands. "Or feet," one wag once observed.

Breakfast-food tonnage still goes up year after year. And so does meat consumption. What has happened is that, in general, the whole population is eating better than our grandfathers did.

The Battle Creek contribution, in addition to the invention of a whole new class of foods, has been to increase the stature of the cereal grains, widen our knowledge of their nutritional values, point the way to a lighter and more varied diet, provide maximum convenience: slit, tilt, pour.

"The grains are great foods," said W. K. Kellogg, the cornflake man who acquired and then gave away fifty million dollars. Or, if the uncommunicative founder of the Kellogg Co. didn't utter this pithy maxim spontaneously, it was got up for him by some advertising man. Those of us who are alive around 1975 are likely to consider the Kellogg saying with a more than academic interest. Americans may someday become compulsory vegetarians. "It is possible that meat production, a relatively inefficient form of agriculture, may not keep up with the expansion of population," says Norman Jolliffe, Director of the Bureau of Nutrition, Department of Health, New York City. "Towards the end of this century," Jolliffe continues, "assuming the present rate of population growth, the United States will have to divert a large proportion of cereal grains from animal feeds to direct human consumption unless the problem is otherwise solved by science." When grain is passed through the stomach of an animal and we eat the meat, it takes about eight acres to produce as much food as we could get from one acre, if we ate the vegetable food directly. And so, the traditional high-protein diet of the U. S. may be succeeded through sheer necessity by a high-grain diet.

Saints, backwoods visionists, inventors and dreamers, creators of industries, are seldom well-adjusted people. In these pages, then, appear much singularity, a passionate attachment to truth and to half-truth, many instances of vanity, high and low motives, the will to power, the urge to improve the erring brother even if it kills him. Many in the cast of characters were called cranks. But rather than settle down with a permanent, marbleized list of American heroes, is it not far better for us to revise the canon and enrich our social history with new personalities, as we are able to find them? Here, at least, are some new faces—food reformers and cornflake kings. If there is a thesis to be demonstrated, it is that error binds the present to the past and promises to enliven an infinite future. The cause of Right Living is never lost, never won. Its advocates left a heritage of broad social significance, and some memories not without their entertaining aspects. The story begins with a provincial English curate who was in a quandary.

I I

The Landing of the Vegetarian Pilgrims

TOWARD the end of the eighteenth century, the Reverend William Cowherd was in a dilemma that was likely to cost him his living. Cowherd felt himself slipping into heterodoxy, and had good reason to suppose that the Reverend J. Clowes, rector at St. John's in Manchester, England, would not long be in need of a curate who had an inclination for anatomical studies and Emanuel Swedenborg's conception of the soul. As the troubled cleric moved away from the safe anchorage of the Thirty-Nine Articles, he found his difficulties compounded in another way. He was also getting queasy about the propriety of eating meat. He turned to his Bible for guidance. It clearly told him, in certain passages, to eat the grains and the fruits. The grasses were for cattle. The herb was ". . . for the service of man." The prohibition as to eating flesh was clear: ". . . meat commendeth us not to God." If meat make the brother stumble or offend—and it did, it did—the injunction ran, "I will eat no flesh while the world standeth." And, again, "Be not . . . among riotous eaters of flesh."

There were other considerations which touched Cowherd closely, the moral obligation to be kind to animals, the sacredness of all life. Again, there were texts: "They shall not hurt nor destroy . . ." "He that killeth an ox *is as if* he slew a man." Any loophole, ambiguity or opportunity to escape the intent of Holy Writ was removed by the Sixth Commandment: "Thou shalt not kill."

The consequences of dipping into the fleshpots were immediate ". . . ere it was chewed . . . the Lord smote the people with a very great plague"; which, being interpreted, might refer to

15

any one of several unpleasant contingencies, trichinosis, maybe, or to use an old-fashioned word which will appear frequently in this chronicle, dyspepsia. And so, the Reverend William Cowherd was resolved. He left St. John's. For a time he held the church-living of Beverly, in Yorkshire, and taught—possibly chemistry, since he was a chemist—in Beverly College. Finally he broke cleanly with the Church of England, with cassock and chalice and reredos and the familiar and well-loved ordinances. He became Incumbent at the New Jerusalem Chapel in Peter Street, Manchester, teaching New Church doctrine to chapel folk. With the Bible his authority, and wide latitude in interpreting it, Cowherd eventually found Swedenborgianism too shackling a creed. So he started a church of his own. Vegetarianism was its cornerstone. Here, in a loose-fitting religious garment of Bible literalism and easy Christian association, in an atmosphere of social reform, the Reverend William Cowherd felt for the first time genuinely free from the tyranny of sectarianism.

It was in 1800 that Cowherd established his own church. He called it the Bible Christian. The chapel was in King Street, Salford, Manchester. Here he preached W.O.C. (without compensation), supported himself by practicing medicine.

"Christ's followers," he said, "should heal bodies as well as souls, after their Master's example."

Some letters which Cowherd had written, touching upon vegetarian diet and the evils of tippling, powerfully affected William Metcalfe, also a Manchester clergyman and homeopathic doctor. Metcalfe, too, held New Church views, had taken up vegetarianism on moral and religious grounds. On September 1, 1809, Metcalfe renounced forever the roast and the bottle; and in 1817, as pastor, led a hardy flock of primitive Christians from Manchester to Philadelphia, where he became "the first public advocate (of vegetarianism) in America." The company embarked from Liverpool early in the year in the ship *Philadelphia Packet*, Captain Singleton. The congregation endured a tedious voyage of eleven weeks. All came through safely, though there were several cases of apostasy. The bracing salt air put a keen edge on appetites. Only about half of Metcalfe's followers arrived in port as virgin-pure vegetarians. The lure of the meat tubs had proved too potent.

Metcalfe established his vegetarian church in a little frame building made over from a Lancastrian school, later replaced by a modest sanctuary of brick, on North Third Street, above Girard Avenue. Metcalfe, like Cowherd, served without compensation. For his support, he opened a day school and academy, and advertised for patients interested in homeopathic treatment. In 1890, the Bible Christians erected a stone church, at Park Avenue, above Montgomery, back-to-back with Russell Conwell's Baptist Temple. Here the primitive Christians raised their voices to sing:

> No flocks that range the valley free
> To slaughter we condemn;
> Taught by the Power that pities us
> We learn to pity them.

At this time Metcalfe had long been dead. It was just as well, considering the circumstances of the removal from the old North Third Street Church. Here the fundamentalists had worshipped for more than a generation. Here the American Vegetarian Society had met. Here, with flowers and merriment, the church body had gathered to dine on vegetarian "mince pies" under the banners and slogans of their faith. Then the church had fallen upon evil days. A pleasant neighborhood of open fields had become a city slum. Next door to the church was a sausage factory, its engine disturbing the worshippers, its steam discoloring the tombstones in the churchyard. When the body decided to move, their agent promptly sold the property to the pork packer. Soon the sanctuary was just a storehouse for hams, which the Reverend William Metcalfe had called "the Brandy of diet."

The Bible Christian church in Philadelphia struggled along for about a hundred years. Early in the twentieth century it quietly expired. The group initiated the U. S. vegetarian movement and shaped its thesis. Metcalfe gave the cause moral and religious arguments, tended his pastorate, founded the first vegetarian society, edited its magazine, *The American Vegetarian*, and died in 1862 with full confidence that asparagus seed had a bright future as a coffee substitute; "already in many places," he said, "becoming such a favorite, as to threaten wholly to supplant coffee at the breakfast table."

It was in the spring of 1850 in Clinton Hall, New York City, that the American Vegetarian Society came into being. It was the first of a long line of similar idealistic efforts in a meat-eating world. "Father" Metcalfe represented the Philadelphians. Doctors Russel T. Trall and Joel Shew spoke for the New York City water curists. Professor R. D. Mussey of the Ohio University at Cincinnati, formerly of Dartmouth College, joined the gathering. Sylvester Graham, the brown-bread man, signed in. An absent stalwart, Dr. Isaac Jennings, sent greetings from Oberlin, Ohio, an oasis of hope in "the flesh-eating West."

A Connecticut Yankee who had enjoyed a snug practice in Derby, Dr. Jennings had lost his medical faith. He began to prescribe placebos of wheat bread and cochineal, and solemnly, a few drops of *aqua fontana pura*; pure spring water. Worse still, Jennings admitted his deviation from conventional practice in a book with much color and charm of expression, *Medical Reform* (1847). For his honesty he lost his friends and his practise. Jennings fled Connecticut for "the fenny atmosphere of the West." There Charles Grandison Finney, revivalist and president of the Collegiate Institute in Oberlin, gave the troubled doctor asylum.

Oberlin stood for the earnest reform outlook. No chess, no checker games, no "tight dressing." Oberlin passed through the water-cure mania, embraced mesmerism, had its own phrenological society for studying amativeness and other interesting faculties of the brain, and was reviled for its abolitionist stand with the libel that the Colony preached "amalgamation." Like Battle Creek a generation later, Oberlin was a wind harp, swaying and tinkling in every new breeze.

The vegetarian clique met again in the fall of 1850 with Dr. William A. Alcott announcing from the chair, "A vegetable diet lies at the basis of all reform." Orson S. Fowler, the phrenologist, was there and Bronson, Dr. Alcott's cousin with his lean face, gray, worn temples and glowing eyes. Bronson Alcott was a vegetarian because Pythagoras was, because of Cousin William and "by instinct." Thomas L. Nichols, advocate of bloomers, free love and spiritualism, sent his greetings from the Erie County (New York) jail where he was a temporary lodger. Nichols played his fiddle in the Buffalo lockup, read Gil Blas and his fan mail from Alice,

Rosalie and Julia, and received a visit from a brunette who was so prettily his champion that, before he knew it, he had slipped his arm around her and had his first kiss in jail.

A little magazine was launched by the Vegetarian Society to print didactic fiction, testimonials, homilies and gruesome stories about butchers. And so, through the 1850's, meetings were held, communications considered. Dr. Russel T. Trall, who ran his own medical college, vigorous publicist for all health fads of the midcentury, announced an extreme position on milk and sugar. There was a great vegetarian feast, with Horace Greeley presiding, and among the honored guests on the dais were Mrs. Lucy Stone, T. L. Nichols, after he was sprung from the Buffalo calaboose, Mrs. Amelia Bloomer and Susan B. Anthony. Dr. James Caleb Jackson, of the Glen Haven Water Cure at the head of Skaneateles Lake in New York, proposed a toast in a bumper of well water, "Total Abstinence, Women's Rights, and Vegetarianism." A Mr. Booth brought fraternal greetings from Wisconsin.

Greeley suggested that a good vegetarian ordinary was urgently needed in or near Beekman Street in New York City. The convention heard a report that food would yet be made of wood. And there was a petition from the printers about their pay.

In the autumn of 1854 the printers continued to be unpaid. And so they ceased to print. Fourteen years and two innocuous pastorates after Metcalfe's death, the Reverend Henry Stephen Clubb succeeded to the leadership of the Bible Christians. Clubb was able to put together a new national society of vegetarian buffs. His new group was called the Vegetarian Society of America. Clubb was its president, edited the official organ, *Food, Home and Garden*, and enjoyed long hours of contemplation under his own vine and fig tree. At least, he had a fig tree.

Like his predecessor, the Reverend William Metcalfe, Clubb was from Manchester, a dreamer and nonconformist. Clubb had arrived in this country in June, 1853, and formed connections quickly with the leading radicals in the health reform movement; Dr. Trall, a real ultra; Dr. William A. Alcott, the leading popular writer on hygiene; Orson S. Fowler and his brother, L. N. Fowler, publishers of semiscientific, pseudophilosophical works on popular psychology, temperance, and Woman. Like the Fowlers, Clubb was filled with a mass of undigested information, extravagant theories. Greeley gave Clubb a job and the columns of Fowlers' & Wells' *Water Cure Journal* were also open to his busy pen.

During the debate on the Kansas-Nebraska bill in the long session of 1853-54, Clubb covered Congress for the *Washington Union* and acquired an enthusiasm for Kansas which led him into a picaresque venture. He became founder of an Edenic colony on the Neosho River, near Fort Scott in Kansas Territory. For Henry Clubb the venture proved to be an embarrassment; for his followers, a disaster. From Kansas came in distressing detail the answer to Clubb's rhetorical question propounded from the pulpit, "Is Edenic Life Practical?" The answer was negative.

Capable of forming "original plans," the Reverend Henry Clubb possessed, in an odd and explosive combination, high courage and an inadequate theory. A true empiric, Clubb resembled valiant Cerdon in Samuel Butler's "Hudibras"—ingenious in constructing an argument which did not correspond with the facts. Clubb even had the phrenology of a reformer. His head (width by the calipers, 6"; length, 7½") showed "unique organization." The head was peculiar in shape, almost square. The faculty of conscientiousness was extraordinarily developed. If the head looked a little flat on top, that was because of the strong development of Benevolence and Firmness.

The year 1855 was a busy one for Clubb. He had, first, his studies and meditations. The plain fact pressed sorely upon him that the early Church was vegetarian, later corrupted by Constantine. He dreamed of someday completing a vast historical work, the definitive history of vegetarianism, for which he scribbled out notes and cobbled his ideas as he could find the time. He was in the thick of the Kansas affair. He dashed off a circular describing the "Octagon plan" for the Kansas paradise, in which we may see the influence of Orson Fowler, inventor of the Octagon house. The odd layout of the Settlement was to prove strange indeed among the regular quadrangles of Kansas sections and quarter-sections. Clubb preached, wrote, edited. He drew up a model bill for Congress designed to suppress the liquor traffic in the District of Columbia. And he was in love.

The girl was Miss Anne B. Henderson, a Michigan farm girl of

Allegan County, who had been drawn to him by a vegetarian circular. Anne's letters to her future husband still exist, an idyllic reflection of a reformer's courtship. She warned Clubb that she was no beauty, just a very ordinary Scotch country girl, "a *brunette*, with raven-black hair, blue eyes, and red cheeks to match." She was a Whig, she told him sternly, never read novels, knew nothing of the latest polka, but delighted in lectures, would like to learn to set type. She hoped to attend the Female College on which the Michigan legislature had passed a bill. She read the *New York Tribune* and the *Water Cure Journal* for Henry's sake, and was studying shorthand too. She would be useful to a husband who might happen to be a town supervisor in, say, Kansas. She also could wash, iron and make shirts, sewing them so fine they would last twice as long as the "boughten" kind. "There is a woman's rights advocate in Allegan," Anne once wrote, "who Advocates Free Love and believes a girl may have twenty or thirty beaux! . . . I hope none of these Free Love Advocates will go to Kansas."

Some sixty colonists joined in the Octagon Settlement scheme, only about a third of them practical farmers; and the farming they knew was that of the forested northeast, not the plains country. The rest gave their occupations as blacksmith, tailor, librarian, widow, printer, hairdresser, tinsmith, colporteur, professor of music and water-cure doctor. All who joined before the end of January, 1856, were called Founders.

The end was failure and it came with merciful speed. Clubb and his associates promised too much, performed too little, though Henry must have cut quite a dashing figure, looking quite like a "Border Ruffian" himself in his red shirt, a big Colt revolver slung at his hip. There was one plow for all. The company built no mills, set up no Scientific Institute, no agricultural college, no Museum of Curiosities and Mechanic Arts. But the "whereas" of the Constitution declaring that meat and rum were abolished in the Kansas fairyland was rigidly enforced, adding greatly to the misery of the shareholders. The whole wild scheme was dauncy. The farms were too small, the capital inadequate, the emigrants not adapted to the life. Kansas was a legal no man's land. There was no resort to the courts because they didn't exist. The time Clubb put in on writing his book of this period, *The*

Maine Liquor Law, might better have been spent in getting his hands on some quinine, or hanging a door for the "large central Octagon building," a log cabin sixteen feet square.

Clubb's own quarters were "made of an old Indian wigwam and tenting," reported a disillusioned survivor. On one occasion Mrs. Clubb shared her bed, briefly, with a Kansas rattlesnake. That's the way things were.

Despite the mosquitoes, chills, fevers and drought, thieving Indians and Missourians, short rations and even death, the Reverend Clubb escaped from this fiasco without any particular afterclap. The Clubbs returned to Anne's home state, settling at Grand Haven in the next county north of Allegan. Here Henry published a newspaper. He later served in the Union Army during the Civil War. He was knocked off his horse in the battle of Corinth by a rebel Minié ball; but a more serious service-incurred disability was his case of piles, so bad—it said in his pension application—that Mrs. Clubb had to get posted up on their treatment in a home handbook.

Clubb enjoyed a modest career in Republican politics in Michigan, rising from alderman of Grand Haven to state senator from the Twenty-ninth (Ottawa and Muskegon) District. But in 1876 he returned to his pulpit in Philadelphia where he remained until his death in 1921. Mrs. Clubb wrote little *pensées* on "Women's Rights," "Louis Kossuth," and "Allegan." Clubb pottered around with his omnium-gatherum on vegetarianism, jotting down what Herodotus said, the opinion of Philo, the meaning of the Psalmist and Josephus. The author got as far as a heading for Chapter XIII, "Vegetarian Principles and Practises Among the Apostles and Early Christians," living to be over ninety, writing, preaching, wrangling, editing and doing a preface for Sylvester Graham's *Philosophy of Sacred History.* But he never did unfold his grand design of showing that the proper food of man is that "obtained in a direct manner from the vegetable kingdom."

Henry Clubb stood midway between the early planting of vegetarian thought in the U. S. and its harvest time at Battle Creek. He was in touch with Dr. James Caleb Jackson, who in 1858 created at Dansville, New York, the prototype for the Adventist Sanitarium at Battle Creek; with Alexander Ross, the Toronto reformer; with Dr. J. H. Kellogg, the father of ready-to-eat breakfast foods, and Uriah Smith, the Adventist elder and editor of Battle Creek. They all shared common vegetarian ground. Interesting subgroups emerged. Some vegetarians wouldn't eat tubers, but only foods grown in the light of the sun, the "aspiring" vegetables. Some would eat only herbaceous plants grown in virgin soil. Others put their faith in nuts and milk. One species would take raw food only. Fruitarians abstained from all food obtained by inflicting pain. Some permitted fish, if netted. Certain persons of great goodwill and tender conscience would not wear leather shoes, because they were made from the skins of animals, sending off for wooden footwear to the Dutch emigrants at Holland, Michigan. Some emphasized the moral and ethical basis of their creed, others stressed the scriptural authority, still others the sentimental imperative— the way a pig looks just as it is stuck, the brutalizing effect upon the butcher of his coarse occupation.

A good man felt his kingship more truly when he could walk among his cows in the cool of the evening without their casting a suspicious glance at him. Like Shelley, who took his constitutional with a volume of the Greek tragedies in one hand and a bit of fruit in the other, the American vegetarian-humanitarian dreamed of a new Golden Age. It was an eclectic vision in which classical mythology was mingled with the Garden of Eden story, seen through the eyes of romantics with grave doubts as to the value of civilization. Ovid, Rousseau and the Old Testament seem strangely assorted. But each contributed something to the idea of innocent nudes, of vegetarian lions and grass-eating tigers. Sensibility had overcome sense.

"Just as it takes an excessively rich diet to make one appreciate bran," wrote Hoxie N. Fairchild in *The Noble Savage*, "so it is in slightly over-ripe stages of culture . . . that one yearns for simplicity."

All vegetarians, whether Adventists or not, yearned for the day to come when man would curb his longing for beef and bacon, acquire the higher wisdom of the gorilla and realize Shelley's prophecy:

> No longer now
> He slays the lamb, who looks him in the face,
> And horribly devours its mangled flesh

Which, still avenging Nature's broken law
Kindled all putrid humors in his frame.

The sentimental argument against killing our four-footed, furry friends is unanswerable—if that's the way one feels about it. Recognizing that the cult has a strict if slightly addled logic, the skeptical gentile only stiffens the will of the meatless gourmets by opposing them. The refutation of odd notions is always an item of unfinished business.

It was from Philadelphia that the doctrine had spread originally, and Philadelphia continued in the early 1890's to be the vegetarian city. But the cause was gaining. A Missouri Society maintained a Vegetarian Room in Kansas City. Interest was stirring in St. Louis, Minneapolis and Pittsburgh. Washington was expected to come in soon. Boston was active, and Oregon was suggested by a correspondent in *Food, Home and Garden* as a good place for a new try at vegetarian colonizing. But the objection was raised that salmon and venison were too plentiful there and the going would be rough for those who wished to avoid temptation. This view carried the day.

"The vegetarian craze has struck Chicago," observed *The Inter Ocean*, "and bids fair to become a fashionable fad." The Chicago coterie attended lectures on Thought-Force, held *soirées*, read up on constipation. They subscribed to the Chicago *Vegetarian* and dined at the Pure Food Café ("No pork in our beans"). The Café was on the corner opposite Marshall Field's and Carson, Pirie, Scott & Co. A violin and piano duo provided an agreeable musical background, while Chicago's "higher-thought organizations" lunched and supped on "progressive dishes to match the progressive times," and carried home a parcel of Battle Creek Sanitarium health foods.

A particular point was always made of the conversion of celebrities. A news flash came through: "Rider Haggard has become a vegetarian." George Meredith was reported as taking up the idea. Clubb welcomed him warmly, but expressed the hope that Meredith's books would become "less fleshly in tone." Edison, it was said, turned to the progressive dietary when his liver and kidneys kicked up, but returned to his former habits when they calmed down. This was a frequent complaint made against temporary comrades, frightened by a bilious attack but inadequately prepared on the philosophic level. Wendell Phillips, Emerson, Thoreau, Margaret Fuller and Dana were all claimed for the cause by a retrospective Adventist writer, at least "in their early years."

The name of Battle Creek appears frequently in Clubb's magazine. Reference is made to the work of the Sanitarium, the Adventists and their Battle Creek College, the busy bakeries of the Sanitarium Food Company. There were numerous items about Dr. J. H. Kellogg and *his* magazine, *Good Health*. In turn, the Battle Creek folks gave their hearty support to the national society. On one occasion they staged a benefit for the Vegetarian Society of America, featuring a vegetarian juggler. Fresh from his triumphs at the Opera House at Grand Rapids, where he had been booked in for a solid week, he broke the jump to western Canada by putting on a free performance at the "San." Elder McCoy, the chaplain, spoke on disease. Then the stage was cleared and Will K. Kellogg, the useful handy man, the shy, dogged, younger Kellogg, the man who balanced the books and discreetly carried out the dead, showed a series of stereopticon slides.

The vegetarians were conscious that they were near in position to other reform groups—to the "Band of Mercy" movement, to the Society for the Prevention of Cruelty to Animals, to their theosophic friends. Mrs. Annie Besant, author of *Vegetarianism in the Light of Theosophy*, and assorted mahatmas and swamis who came over to take in the Columbian Exposition in 1893, had shown that the vegetable philosophy and occult thought were like the hand and the glove. Meatless eating attracted the modern Man of Feeling. It was a blend of home-grown spiritualism with doctrines derived from the Brahminic and Vedic literatures of India, plus the writings of Madame Helena P. Blavatsky. Oriental thought gave a theosophic fillip, a mad incoherence to the more pedestrian ruminations of the belly vegetarians. The New Thought recruits joined up about 1900. They learned to hold the health-thought and say, "I am well." They returned to nature, wrote books which were bound in limp leather and read Emerson in extract. They smoked New

Thought cigars—no nicotine; and quoted the Bhagavad-Gita. With the help of Yoga they learned how to breathe, how to chew, how to sit, how to keep still, and did it all portentously.

And so to those vegetarians who were in spirit Essenians, anchorites and flagellants, glorying in their ground-up nut butters, Mrs. Besant brought the subtle astral world. Hers was an attractive vegetarian *mystique*. It was a different approach; as when she told how on one occasion she was coming into Chicago on the train and a profound sense of desolation oppressed her spirit. This, of course, has happened to others. But in this instance, Mrs. Besant was able to search out a theosophical basis for her melancholy. She was getting astral messages, the reproaches of the thousands of slaughtered beasts from South Chicago, suspended between the material and the thought world. It is not easy for the uninitiated to follow the path through occult and cabalistic literature of an intellectual nomad like Mrs. Besant, or to understand exactly how she came into rapport with the American current of diet reform. One may understand her sufficiently, perhaps, in remembering Carlyle's remark upon John Stuart Mill's lady: "Mrs. Mill has the most *unwise* appetite for knowledge of any woman I know."

Long after Henry Clubb's energies had spent themselves, his little magazine lived on in one form or another. It became the *Vegetarian-Humanitarian-Fruitarian*. It moved to Los Angeles and gathered to itself *The Character Builder, Dr. Gifford's Journal of Hygieo-Therapy, Prof. M. Tope's Phrenological Era, W. E. Brokaw's Equity, the Science of Right Human Relations*, and *Zion's Young People*. Mrs. Besant and Graham were often quoted. Material clipped from T. L. Nichols was placed before a new generation. A Nature Doctor wrote on "How I Cured Myself of Cancer"; while the advertising pages offered The Grape Cure. The more we see of change, the more it is the same thing. Vegetarianism remains endemic.

Among the reforms of the yeasty mid-years of the last century, the diet reform is explicable as a reaction against gluttony, against the frontier's "hog and hominy," against the frying pan; against drunkenness and against an orthodox medical practise which relied upon bloodletting and ipecac.

Many physicians knew little, cared less, about the alimentary tract. Yet "dyspepsia" was a word on every tongue. "All classes and all ages suffer from its attacks," said the *Encyclopedia Americana* in 1830. "Few are so happy as to pass through a life of ordinary duration, without undergoing a protracted struggle with this malady."

The victim nibbled cassia and took dyspeptic bitters. Drank Epsom salts. Put mustard on his meat. Drank brandy and water with his meals. Gave up meat. Gave up vegetables. Tried starving. Then stuffed himself. Dressed his food with cayenne pepper and horse-radish. Tried the regimen of arrowroot, gumwater and rice water. Had flaxseed poultices laid on. Was leeched around the region of the stomach, and took the blue pill, the dandelion, the bismuth. He turned to Kickapoo Sagwa, the great "stomach restorative" of herbs, barks and roots, put up by Doctor Prairie Wolf and Doctor Laughing Dog, according to ancient tribal secrets of the plains Indians; but distributed, oddly enough, from New Haven, Connecticut. The victims of "dyspepsy" tried also, in contemporary phrase, "Thomsonianism, Quackism, Regular-ism and all." Is it surprising, then, that the sufferer subscribed for *The Water Cure Journal and Herald of Health Reform*, learned something of the revolt known as "Grahamism," and finally took tickets for Dr. Graham's lecture course? Or, in desperation, began to board at a Graham hotel, a fugitive—the phrase is Lydia Maria Child's—from "gravies and gout, dainties and dyspepsia"?

The moral conviction, Christian ethics, tender emotions and gastric experiences which fostered vegetarianism all came together in "The Battle Creek Idea." The repentant glutton, full of "uric acid" and remorse, checked in at the Sanitarium and began to take a respectful interest in "the body's kitchen." He read Dr. J. H. Kellogg's books, ate the Kellogg special foods. The Holy Bible and the torpid liver, to sum it up, created the opportunity for cornflake imperialism.

Those social habits which caused "the risings," the furry tongue, which explain why the bowels so often failed to "exonerate themselves," appear in the next chapter, as recorded by contemporary witnesses.

The Great American Stomach Ache

ALBERT WHEELER, a Massachusetts man taking the cure at Dr. James Caleb Jackson's sanatorium at Dansville, New York, shortly before the Civil War, munched his graham cracker as he sat on the second piazza and looked out calmly upon a mad world.

"Everyone," he declared, "is jostling his neighbor, and his mouth is filled with pork, rum and tobacco."

In his native New England, Wheeler had seen what a breakfast of pork and beans and pie could do to the parishioners of the Congregational Church on a hot summer Sunday morning. The effects were so stupefying that the minister preached, in effect, to tons and tons of pork and beans. Wheeler knew well the salt-fish diet, too; had seen countless little girls hand up a "store order" to the clerk: "please send by the bairer six pounds of codfish." He knew the molasses, flour and condiments, the ginger and the bags of black pepper that went into the salt-box houses of eastern Massachusetts—and the nostrums that followed to repair the damage.

A New Englander in revolt against the traditional sentiment expressed in Emerson's remark upon pie at breakfast—"What's pie for?"—found at the Dansville "Cure" a broad opportunity for acquiring a rounded view of mid-nineteenth-century American dietary transgressions. There, the Kentuckian reluctantly gave up lard and redeye. A descendant of the Palatines of Schoharie County, New York, might turn up, the victim of long overindulgence in square potpie, Middleburgh bologna, Schnecken, Roeliches and long blackberry grunt.

Cooper, in *The Chainbearer*, has a frontier housewife say:

"I hold a family to be in a desperate way when the mother can see the bottom of the pork barrel." The reliance upon pork was even more complete, if that was possible, in the Western country. A York-state man wrote back home from Camp Point, Illinois, "The living in this western country is not at all to my liking. Everything tastes and smells of 'hog's grease. . . .' It is no wonder that the West yields a golden harvest to the Doctors." Another Easterner, G. Waterman, wrote to *The Graham Journal of Health and Longevity*, of the corn bread and pork he encountered at Pekin, Illinois, the vegetables saturated with still more grease. Westerners dined on coffee, hog and hominy three times a day, the *Graham Journal* editor observed; and kneaded their corn bread with grease and eggs. As a consequence, "bilious complaints are now all the fashion at the 'Great West.'"

Giles Jackson, a son of the medical-reform Jackson, went to Nebraska Territory for a change of climate in 1857. Giles's letters back home recorded the emotions of one brought up on the shores of beautiful Skaneateles Lake, in finding himself on the far side of the Mississippi, with nothing between him and a harsh reality but a volume of Miss Martineau's "Travels" and a mosquito bar. Almost all the men on the boat, as the *Ogden* steamed up the Missouri River, were smoking and chewing and spitting, and making "a great stench of tobacco in the cabin." As for food, "We got soda-crackers (poor), rolls (poorer), and corn cake (poorest) to eat. Salt and pepper, with pork fat reign supreme." Condiments, it should be mentioned, were on the forbidden list of most food reformers of the time. Giles reported finally that he was able to eat a "reform" Thanksgiving breakfast of baked potato and brown bread "with a thankful spirit."

Horace Greeley had an intimate knowledge of the bill of fare in the Far West, for he made the journey overland from New York to San Francisco in 1859 and boarded for a while in Denver. The staples were bread, bacon and beans, one meal like another. But the times, he said, were improving. The hen population within five hundred miles of Denver, formerly four or five, had recently risen to twelve or fifteen and egg prices were falling.

To James Parton, the trans-Mississippi country was an uncivilized wilderness. Leading biographer of his generation with his popular lives of Franklin, Jefferson, Greeley and others, a bit on the ultra side himself in matters of smoking, drinking and eating, Parton wrote that travelers who headed west from St. Louis would "strike a region where the principal articles of diet are saleratus and grease, to which a little flour and pork are added." The mixture would not sustain the natives, he said, except that they carefully "preserve" their tissues in whiskey.

From prehistory down to the colonization of America, man was principally interested not in choosing foods which contained the essential nutrients, or even the foods he particularly liked, but in getting enough of *something* to eat. The Scotch who flowed into Philadelphia, the Irish "b'hoys" who built the canals and railroads, and all the immigrant arrivals representing other national strains, joined with the resident American farmer in the ingestion of a God's plenty of food, eating, for the first time, above a ton of foodstuffs per person per year, with heavy emphasis upon meats. It was the hunger approach to diet.

A cheap, abundant food supply and a robust habit of life sent our ancestors off on a gigantic gastronomic binge which knew no limits until modern urban living modified the prevailing idea of what constituted three square meals. In our rugged democracy all classes could for the first time acquire the palpitations, nightmares, obesity and eructations formerly the exclusive perquisites of the higher orders of society. Those who could afford it took the waters at Saratoga or Ballston Spa, or turned to a convalescent home for a discipline of compulsory fasting and internal bathing. Those with limited funds could try the extract of colocynth and aloes, or dine penitently when *in extremis* on oatmeal gruel.

When the American freeman in a normal state of health sat at table, his elbows worked like a fiddler's. When he had finished, he departed. That was etiquette. To linger, to chat, meant that the meal had not been sufficient. "The ordinary mode of eating," said Mrs. Trollope, "is abundant, but not delicate." "How do you do?" was not a conventional greeting but an anxious inquiry.

A native writer, Robert Tomes, author of *The Bazar Book of Decorum*, a popular book on American manners, which ran through nine editions between 1870 and 1878, confessed that "there is no country in the world where there is such an abundance of good raw material for the supply of the dietetic necessities of man, or where there are so many people with the means of obtaining it, as in the United States . . ." and yet "there is hardly a nation that derives so little enjoyment and benefit as the American from its resources. We are . . . too carnivorous . . . the national stomach is kept in a constant state of active assault." The result: "atonic dyspepsia."

Edward Hitchcock (1793-1863), geologist, Congregational clergyman and President of Amherst College, had his attention drawn to the diet question in the 1830's by problems of an urgent personal nature, he having been low in dyspepsia. President Hitchcock estimated that people ate about twice what they needed. Even the poor expected to sit down to two or three major dishes at each meal. In professors' and ministers' families, far removed from the world of fashion, midday dinner consisted of two meats, gravies, pickles, vegetables, condiments, cheese, bread and butter. Then they polished off a pudding or pie, with perhaps fruit to fill in the chinks.

If company came to dinner there was a third meat on the table, more pies and custards; if there were supper guests the hostess put out dried beef, beef tongue, pastry, preserves, custards, two or three kinds of cake. At seven or eight o'clock there was tea, very strong, with fruits, nuts, jellies and trifles. Guests were expected to eat some of each dish, while the lady of the house was required by *politesse* to press the cake, the sweetmeat, the cheese upon the foundering visitor. And so, there was an incessant inviting.

"Will you have some butter?"

"Will you take fish or meat?"

When one was out among company, there was scarcely time or opportunity to carry on a connected conversation.

"Will you have pickles?"

The pickle bottle is offered from the left. The person opposite presents the pickle bottle; again the servant "shoots the pickle bottle in between you and your conversable neighbor." One became quite overcome by the pickle persecution.

A ceremonial dinner party in Boston society of the 1850's was ideally designed to bring on bilious spells and the lack-lustre eye. There was a formal affair at William Appleton's, for example,

served "by three blacks and our two servants." It consisted first of
"cold Oysters, Oyster Pates, Hock wine offered; boiled and baked
Fish, Pass the wine; next, boiled Turkey, roast Mutton, Veal with
Peas and Ham; Sweet Bread and Croquettes; then Wine and
Roman Punch. After Course, two pair Canvas-Back Ducks, two
pair Grouse, Wood Cocks and Quails, with Salad:—Blanc Mange,
Jelly, Baked and Frozen Pudding, etc. etc. with Ice Cream, Grapes,
Pears, Apples, Oranges & Ornamental Sweets from the Confec-
tioner." If any good thing was said later in the Appleton drawing
room, it is doubtful if it was heard by the liverish company who
had far more need of Huxham's tincture, of quassia or a mechanical manipulation of the epigastrium, than of an epigram. It was a
triumph merely to survive through the tureens, the meats, relevés,
removes and game, to the tipsy cake. No wonder Appleton's doctor
put him on a diet of "dyspepsy crackers and milk."

It was a peculiarity of the American breakfast that it equalled
in quantity the European dinner. A neighbor dropped in on a
Colonel in Alabama just as he was breaking his fast.

"Well, old fellow," said the Colonel, "how goes it"; shaking
hands cordially. "How do you do? Come, Sir, sit down, and take
some breakfast with us—(Maria, bring a plate, and knife and fork)
—Come, Sir, take a dram first—(Hand a glass, Maria).

". . . Let me help you to another piece of steak. Have some
gravy, Sir . . . who do the people talk of voting for—(Take some
butter, Sir)—in your part?

". . . (Maria, set that decanter on the table).—Take some
whiskey, Sir. But tell me, who do you intend to vote for?"

President Hitchcock, lecturing to the young "literary gentlemen" of Amherst College, reminded his hearers that the usual
breakfast of a sedentary man, not a farmer or backwoodsman, consisted of two meats, bread and potatoes, salt, pepper, pickles, sometimes eggs, toast, hot cakes, biscuits and butter. A bit of cheese
made a tasty finale.

In the same decade, the 1830's, when Hitchcock was trying
to interest the young men of Amherst in the temperate life, the
Boston Moral Reformer stated that overeating killed twice as many
as Rum, a strong statement in view of the Reformer's high esteem
for the lethal effects of brandy and water. The New England Maga-

zine offered satirical proposals for a Society for the Suppression of Eating, and the Female Moral Reform Society, meeting at Utica in 1839, a real bluestocking group, included in their resolutions that it was the duty of mothers and teachers to know physiology so that they could avoid high living and come nearer to the mark of a sober, temperate Christian life. Also they commented that overeating was an incitement to venery.

To the easy availability of U. S. foodstuffs was added another peril: poor preparation. The campfire, the cabin, the exigencies of the scout and trapper, produced a national taste for frying-pan cookery. In a time of few utensils, one could always tote a pan. In went the pork and the flour, and the cook could turn out hot corn pone while he broiled a rasher. Many unpleasant sensations in the upper gastric region were simply due to a long devotion to the frying pan. The trapper, the squatter hoeing his corn patch, ate his wild game as he could get it, enjoyed a squirrel broth as much as the next fellow. But, day in and day out, he depended upon thick pieces of salt pork as his breakfast staple. Hunks of white side meat were broiled for noon dinner. Supper saw the pork served again with a white flour gravy and molasses as a sop for corn bread and biscuit. On this monotonous dietary the rural American managed to conquer a continent and produce a posterity to inherit it. The hog of the period was the long-legged "rail-splitter," fast on his feet, tough to chew. Meal, mush or hominy made the side dish. When the meal sack was low, the housewife extended the meal with dried pumpkin and got along.

Around Civil War times a lecturer upon food and cookery appeared from France, M. Pierre Blot, who tried to elevate the American cuisine. Blot got a stony reception. A few in the small, rarefied world of the bon ton imitated the French with their ices and ice creams, their green vegetables and salads. But the cits refused to surrender their skillet, spider bread and dried-apple pie for Frenchified fruits, pot herbs and foreign sauces. The craving for variety could be met only by using a comparatively small number of food materials in a large number of different ways. Thus the good wife set her table with a profusion of preserves and pickles to perk up the appetite; and flour took the form of an infinity of cakes and pastries. During 1878 one Vermont housewife made 152 cakes,

421 pies, 1038 loaves of bread, 2,140 doughnuts. Some in the popular health movement, making a virtue out of an unavoidable necessity, agreed with a crotchet of Hitchcock's that the less variety at a meal the better. For this rationalization the Amherst President rested upon classical authority. Hippocrates, he pointed out, said that a variety of dishes produced a "commotion" in the stomach.

Wolfing down the meal has a long history in North America. In stagecoach days, when the tavern keeper rang the dinner bell, the customers rushed from the washing pump to long tables, just as they later learned to slide on and off the stool of a railroad café in fifteen minutes. The rule at an American inn was, eat all you want. Price: 25 cents, whiskey 5¢ extra. The mode of eating was, as has already been noticed, "not delicate." The pattern was "gobble, gulp and go." The American gentleman, whom Mrs. Trollope characterized as "George Washington Spitchew," ate with blinding speed, shoveled his victuals in with his knife and swore while he did it. Afterwards and briefly, he cleaned his teeth with a pocketknife. The traveller went right to the point, like Dr. Samuel Johnson, who plunged his fingers into the common sugar bowl until Mrs. Thrale ordered the bowl to be taken away.

These deficiencies in diet, these graceless manners had almost as disastrous an effect upon the nation's teeth as upon its stomach. They did, at least, stimulate American eminence in the field of dentistry, and provide unusual opportunities for an interesting practice.

The Western trader followed his calling even as he stowed away his meal. He would notice if his neighbor dined on pork, and invite him to join in a speculation in hogs. Meanwhile, "The waiters drop fatness, literally," wrote J. Milton Mackie, a Yankee professor from Brown University.

"The only difficulty is in getting little enough of anything you may call for," continued Mackie. "Just a bit of a thing—*un morceau*—is an impossibility. A thin cut can't be had . . . when I came down in the evening, to get a cup of tea and a bite at a biscuit, I never could escape the everlasting, "Have a beef-steak, Sir?' of the waiters. 'Tis a great country out West, and the men who live in it are feeders to correspond."

A visitor to Chicago when it was an "upstart village," when a lady could get stuck in the mud at the corner of Randolph and La Salle streets and sometimes extricate herself only by leaving her shoes behind, found there the "usual American celerity in eating and drinking. No change of knife or fork, or plate; no spoon for the sugar-basin; no ceremony whatever observed; every man for himself, and none for his neighbor; hurrying, snatching, gulping, like famished wild cats; victuals disappearing as if by magic."

Were these the manners only of the untamed West? Here is a breakfast table scene at Niblo's Hotel in New York:

"Here was no loitering . . . nor lounging . . . no intervals of repose in mastication; but all was hurry, bustle, clamor, and voracity, and the business of repletion went forward with a rapidity altogether unexampled." Diners ate and departed abruptly. "The appearance of the table under such circumstances, was by no means gracious either to the eye or the fancy. It was strewn thickly with the *disjecta membra* of the entertainment," pieces of fish, chicken bones scattered in disorder, eggs and shells deposited in wineglasses.

The vegetarian paladins were not always objective reporters. Strong on theory, they saw the world from a particular point of view. It is surprising that the prophets of the future sciences of nutrition and public health hit the nail on the head as often as they did. The absence of a common body of verifiable knowledge, and of experimental techniques, left the early propagandists open to vagaries and idiosyncrasies.

Even Hitchcock, a trained scientist, exhibited peculiarities of view. He was tepid on the subject of eating fruits. Salads were permissible if eaten sparingly. So were carrots. Radishes, hard on the stomach. Peas and beans, definitely unwholesome.

"The process of digestion seems to be partly chemical," Hitchcock said, "partly mechanical, and partly mysterious." A stomach was neither a mill nor a fermenting vat, nor a stewpan. "A stomach, gentlemen," he told the scholars of Amherst, "is a stomach."

Dr. Alcott considered baking powder and all alkalis to be "rank poison." A. J. Bellows, author of *The Philosophy of Eating*, was a phosphorus man. Clergymen used up their phosphorus on

Sunday, lawyers on court day. They should give up their fat pork and white bread, eat more fish, unbolted bread, vegetables and fruits. Empirical judgments, but, in this instance, good advice, too.

"Scientific" eating and its reassurances did not come forward prominently until the end of the nineteenth century; and the characteristic Battle Creek foods were the beneficiaries of the newer knowledge of nutrition, as the milder word "indigestion" replaced the harsher "dyspepsia." It was about then, approximately 1900, with the popularization of the calorie as a unit for measuring the energy values of foods, that the first U. S. woman was heard to say in a public restaurant as she extracted the meat from a lobster claw and dipped it lusciously in the melted butter, "I shouldn't do this, but I'm not counting the calories tonight."

Bellows in his *Philosophy of Eating* was no vegetarian, but he drew a picture of the American farm family worthy of the most pessimistic Edenist. He found our farm population almost as feeble and sickly as city people. Rural Americans were giving up their bran and buttermilk to the cattle and the pigs, losing the wheat germ through new flour-milling procedures. The immigrants, the Scotch and Irish, turned from their old-country oatmeal and barley cakes, the buttermilk and cheese, and "soon fall into our starch and grease eating habits . . . their children become as pale, puny and toothless as pure-blooded Yankees." Some few clung to their whole-meal bread, ate the vitamin-rich organs as well as the muscle meats, brewed and drank their spruce beer, chewed twigs as they ruminated, and munched dandelion greens in the spring. Whether they did these things to thin the blood or for whatever old wives' tale, some did retain their older culture, to the lasting benefit of their teeth and general well-being.

An inventory of the foodstuffs which rural Americans bought for home consumption emerges from an examination of the account books of crossroads stores. They stocked beef in brine. The rafters were hung with hams and shoulders of smoked meats. There was pork in the meat box, salt mackerel by the barrel. Hogsheads of New Orleans or Porto Rican molasses lay on a stout cradle. Condiments, spices, pepper and mustard were bought in large bulk packages, and the dried codfish lay in stiff piles like lumber.

Saleratus, the old word for baking soda, came in kegs. It was the active principle in raising bread and biscuits—"the grandest word in the trapper's very abridged dictionary." Sister White, the Seventh Day Adventist seeress, who frequently struck out against prevailing American mores in food and drink, had especially harsh things to say of saleratus. "Yellow saleratus biscuits, and heavy clammy bread are breaking down the digestive organs of tens of thousands," she said.

A roll of the states and regions reveals few variants from the common pattern. The Battle Creek "health foods," when their hour struck, had a whole continent to reform. The first settlers of Michigan, in territorial days, put down their baked potatoes, johnny-cake, pork from a shoat so lean it wouldn't fry; so they boiled it, and added flour gravy. They gathered wild berries, ate game as they could get it. Their sauce was what was jocosely called "the Michigan appetite." Michiganders could eat anything, it was averred, even a "boiled Indian."

During the first five years that the first generation of Kelloggs lived in the Michigan clearings, "Our morning meal," recalled Merritt G., the oldest son, "was almost invariably hot pancakes with bacon fat and molasses; our dinner was, in part, of pork cooked in some of the various ways, fried, baked or boiled." Dr. John Harvey Kellogg used to say that he grew up on corn-meal mush and very little else, which undoubtedly contributed to his contracting tuberculosis at an early age. The father had a chronic diarrhea which lasted ten years, inflammation of the eyes and was nearly blind for weeks on end. These symptoms were almost certainly due to dietary deficiencies; but what the doctor did was to put, first, a fly blister on father Kellogg's neck. It made a fearful sore. Next came the calomel in such massive does that Kellogg's "tongue was so swollen that it protruded from his mouth."

U. P. Hedrick, the horticulturist, who combined literature and pomology in such agreeable proportions, has left a vivid boyhood recollection of W. E. Parker's store at Harbor Springs, across Lake Michigan's Little Traverse Bay from Petoskey. There in his boyhood—the 1870's—he saw the barrels of salt meats, the crates of cod and mackerel, barrelled wild pigeons in good pigeon years, prunes and dried apples in boxes. How farm boys felt about dried-apple pies may be inferred from this verse which Hedrick remembered:

I loathe, abhor, detest, despise
Abominate, dried-apple pies.
I like good bread, I like good meat,
Or anything that's fit to eat.
The poorest is dried-apple pies.
Give me a toothache or sore eyes
In pref'rence to such kind of pies.

Dr. Gabriel Miesse, a picturesque medical quack of Ohio, and something of a phrasemaker, once said, "You can't put down men who are un-put-down-able." So it was with our great-grandfathers. They had the Michigan appetite; they ate Michigan-style grub, whether they hailed from Michigan or not. They swallowed Hostetter's Celebrated Stomach Bitters, Warner's Safe Cure, and Castoria. Despite such instances as that of the Ann Arbor child who was dosed with eighty-seven bottles of Mrs. Winslow's Soothing Syrup, the population more than doubled in the 1830-50 decades.

The food of the city man in modest circumstances was not greatly different in character from that of the farmer, though it might be staler. The five-hundred-dollar clerk, employed by a New York wholesaler when Pearl Street was the country's great jobbing center, ate with fifteen or twenty others like himself at a four-dollar boardinghouse where the lady of the establishment got her living by stinting. Dr. Asa Green, a former clerk himself, described the table fare of such a house under a cloak of humor in saying that the beefsteak had been dried, not broiled over the coals, that the sausages were stale, the pork oversalted. The harridan of the house purchased only what could be bought at half price. Eggs, fowls and oysters were never seen, but there was plenty of dry bread. No toast, buckwheat cakes or hot rolls. The butter was oversalted to make it s-t-r-e-t-c-h. The coffee was based on the principle of the "Manhattan hydrant." The grounds in the pot were from damaged beans, burnt crusts or roasted rye. With milk added, it looked like "ashes and water." At dinner the meat was dry as a chip. The butter boat contained grease, water and salt. The gravy boat was empty. The potatoes were watery; likewise the beets and cabbage. The crust of the apple dumplings and apple pies—to end this chronicle of misery—was like sole leather when a tired clerk put his teeth to it.

The mechanic or artisan ate cabbage and salt pork, turnips and beets. The source of "cholera" and most other ills had not been identified; but there was a dim awareness that people ate and drank unwisely, that those who moved from farms to live in cities couldn't with impunity eat the same fare as they used to do. Pamphleteers wrote of the merchant "breaking down at his desk," the minister collapsing in his pulpit, the merchant bringing home from his countinghouse an outraged stomach, "his head a mere furnace of red-brains, and his body a heap of burnt-out cinders."

A man of consequence in his business or profession faced a special hazard to his health: the "established barbarisms of a public dinner." Parton recalled with distaste an occasion in New York where he saw "a half acre of doctors" gorging themselves on indigestible foods in indigestible quantities. And he mentions one dinner where the guests were five hours at table.

It took ten courses to celebrate properly the opening of a small railway, the Massawippi Valley: after the soup the meats—five kinds—from baked trout to the red meats, boiled, cold, roasted, making up seven different kinds of entrees. Six relishes whipped up flagging appetites, and after ample vegetables came pastries and puddings with brandy and wine sauces. There were four kinds of pies. *Dessert* came later, the nuts, the charlotte russe, raisins, fruits and slabs of ice cream.

But what am I saying?—this was only frugal Vermonters' idea of dining spaciously. It took twenty-three meats, twenty-four vegetable items, four kinds of pickles, four breads, five condiments in the castors, an even dozen of pies, tarts, cakes and puddings, and ten liquors for the citizens of Chillicothe, Ohio, to extend a proper gastronomic welcome to Governor De Witt Clinton of New York when he visited their city.

The five-o'clock ordinary at the St. Nicholas hotel in New York City served up eleven courses every day. The palace dining cars on the Chicago & North-Western Railway offered a meal of oyster soup, entrees hot and cold, choice of roasts, game, vegetables, pastry and puddings, then "small pastry" and dessert. Back East, at Harvard, a dinner at commons was a pound of meat, boiled Mondays and Thursdays, roasted the other five days. It took seven courses to set out a proper senior-class supper at Cambridge. After the main repast, the waiters brought on cold meats, anchovy toast, calf's-foot jelly and nine kinds of puddings to remove any anxiety which might remain among the young gentlemen that they might need something to sustain them through the evening.

There is a literature which contradicts the general tenor of what has been said here of American food during the nineteenth century. It is derived usually from the memory of a happy youth, or from farm-bred fancies recalled in later life. Mark Twain, on a tramp abroad, 'mid pleasures and palaces, wrote nostalgically of the Missouri food of his youth. H. L. Mencken carried through a long and eventful lifetime the genial recollection of stewed blackberries, spread while still warm on homemade bread, also warm. The bread and the spread were, according to the Baltimore sage, "bursts of complete felicity." Christmas was a Lucullan feast, until the family doctor came, looked at their tongues and plied the Mencken boys, Charlie and Henry, with *oleum ricini*. The science of metabolism of the period said that the stomach couldn't digest well at night. But the Mencken boys upset the theorists and usually escaped the ipecac.

A comfortable middle-class kitchen of the 1870's must have been a pleasant place, with its six-hole Windsor range and well-scrubbed poplar floor, gray walls, red-checkered curtains and cupboards to hold the frying pans, cake griddle and gray enamel saucepans. The teakettle was of iron, the coffeepot, tin. Homemade soap was handy by the tin washbasin; or, on Sundays and holidays, "boughten" Pear's Soap. Everyday dishes were of white stonewear. The salt box hung on the wall beside the spice cabinet, the coffee mill attached to the door trim nearby. An almanac hung from a nail near the stove, beside the slaw cutter and fly swatter. At the center of the kitchen table stood a five-bottle castor, a spoon holder and covered butter dish.

It was around such a kitchen in southern Michigan that life revolved in the Elijah Thompson family, as described by Della ("Delly") Thompson Lutes. Father felt keenly about all garnishes; "weeds," he called them. Mr. Thompson required that noon dinner be "fillin'." Doughnuts were a daily affair. Fried mush was seasonal.

It ushered in, and out, the winter solstice and the buckwheat-and-sausage breakfast. The mid-century father and indubitable head of the family didn't want pap. He wanted *breakfast,* and would have scorned in astonishment the breakfast of "The Coming Man," a cant phrase of the 1870 decade, the standardized meal of orange juice, cereal, toast and coffee. Father liked pink slices of home-cured ham, smoked with corn cobs, served with flour gravy. And potatoes, boiled with a milk gravy and creamed codfish. And two or three eggs.

Life is too various to be divided into neat epochs and eras. Let it be said, then, only that in the latter part of the nineteenth century a gradual change could be observed in the day's first meal. There was more mush and porridge bubbling on the back of the wood range, less meat swimming in the frying pan. It was a slow and straggling movement, a turning toward a diet which was to be lightened still further through the ministrations of Battle Creek. A time came when even oatmeal was considered "heavy," when Dr. John Harvey Kellogg attacked it as enthusiastically as his precursors had ever denounced the "false state of society" which gorged on a steak-and-pie breakfast. Oatmeal and cracked wheat, Doctor Kellogg wrote, taken with cream and sugar, become a combination well calculated "to create a magnificent dyspepsia." At any rate, the sedentary American, the man behind the roll-top desk, started the day so often with a sour stomach that one compiler of cookbooks, Marion Harland, rechristened dyspepsia "Americanitis." "Man," said the Battle Creek *Health Reformer,* sadly, "is growing weaker."

Elder J. N. Andrews, one of the early Battle Creek Seventh Day Adventist saints, was brought up on mince pie, sausages, cheese, baking-powder biscuits and melted butter, doughnuts, pork, pickles, tea and coffee. He didn't see the connection when his stomach went on strike. A man of his times, he assumed that his heartburn was "something ordered by God's hand." A man in such a fix was ripe for the teachings of Dr. Graham, who had shot up spectacularly into public view as the most influential of the food reformers.

"The fiend Infidel is to be put out of the way," mocked the *New-York Review,* "by nothing less than spare diet and a course of vegetables." Grave and dedicated, like an old Roman Censor, Father Graham admonished his age for its excesses, held high the hope of a day when all North America would eat like Christians instead of boa constrictors. A formidable crusader, Graham took on not only the butchers in a finish fight, but the commercial bakers as well; and, as will appear shortly, got mobbed for his pains.

Sylvester Graham Watched America Starve

SYLVESTER GRAHAM (1794-1851) was a fluent, verbose, contentious clergyman and self-styled physician, an original, who without giving up his Bible faith, added on the consolations of brown bread. Both vain and able, Graham advocated his dietary theories upon Scriptural authority, and his own. The Reverend Graham denounced baker's white bread as the starvation diet of a declining nation, in language which recalled the prophets of the Old Testament. His image of himself was indeed that of an Elijah or Isaiah ". . . and other true prophets of God." As to liquor, Graham was "a tee-total fanatic." Also on his list of abominations were feather beds—they induced unchastity—pork, tobacco, salt, condiments, tight corsets, heavy clothing, Brandreth's pills and hot mince pie.

Graham was being much heard of in the middle 1830's. The newspapers discussed his theories, not always gravely. But he was a celebrity and a force, directing public attention sharply to the intemperate eating of those crapulous times. He was able to point convincingly to the unpleasant consequences of excessive drinking and the high-protein diet. Long after his death in 1851, Sylvester Graham's fame was carried on in the survival of "graham bread," a generic name for any coarsely ground whole-wheat bread, and in graham crackers. His influence persisted in a lurking prejudice against the very whiteness in bread which was once prized and admired. The lectures which Graham delivered and the ponderous, repetitious books which he made out of them, are still reverently kept in print by food faddists, naturopaths and lacto-ovo-vegetarians (use milk and eggs) as well as the simon-pure vegetarians (no foods of animal origin permitted except possibly honey).

The name of Graham and the physiological views associated with it are still venerated by the promoters of papaya juice, herb therapy, various mucins for colitis, and mung-bean sprouts.

During the years of the last century when Americans began to gather in cities, Graham's health precepts helped the digestive system of the nation to adjust to the new age. It was time for a change—and for Graham. James Parton, the biographer, a follower or at least a sympathizer, wrote of Graham that he "arose and lectured and made a noise in the world, and obtained followers. The substance of this message was that Wc, the people of the United States, are in the habit of taking our food in too concentrated a form. Bulk was necessary as well as nutriment; brown bread is better than white. Graham was a remarkable man . . . one of the two or three men to whom this nation might, with some propriety, erect a monument."

Graham was led to the study of diet, hygiene and moderation in the broad sense of *mens sana in corpore sano* through a professional interest in topers and rakes. Son of two generations of Connecticut clergymen and physicians, youngest child of an old man of seventy years, Graham, as a boy, was passed from hand to hand among numerous relatives, and came about as close to being a child of nature as was practicable in nineteenth-century New England. Later he worked as a farm hand, clerk and teacher. But ill health hung at his heels, the classic experience for producing a health reformer.

Young Sylvester's education was sketchy. In 1823, at the late age of twenty-nine, he entered Amherst Academy. President Heman Humphrey already had his hands full. He was in the process of abolishing the misses' department, fighting for a college charter, worrying over rumors of gay oyster suppers among the young "literary gentlemen," of card playing and conviviality based upon the ingestion of cherry rum. And then came Graham. He quickly showed himself to be "an ardent and eloquent speaker, arrogant and forceful"; in short, a nuisance. Graham was expelled upon a trumped-up charge sponsored by his classmates. No favorite with the faculty either, he was remembered as a copious talker, a "stage actor" and a "mad enthusiast." The Amherst episode was followed by a nervous breakdown and marriage to his nurse, a Miss Sarah Earl, who brought him a small dowry.

Despite his pinched life as a quasi-orphan, his father dead, his mother gone mad, despite a patchwork education, incipient tuberculosis, a late start in life, the burden of a wife who sometimes took a little wine or gin for her stomach's sake, and a brood of children, Graham tackled life confidently with the forces at his disposal. He was himself the leader who in his estimation could bring men to a hygienic millennium, and joined in happily with the medical levelers who were raising a hue and cry against calomel and the lancet.

Graham had a flow of words that could not be stanched. He was a born fighter, with a lively sense that he had been, or was about to be, persecuted. Opposition only hardened his resolve, as it did that of the *Sibyl*, organ of the ladies' dress reform movement, which sang:

> And Persecution's lowering storm
> May gather thick around
> But still we'll cry 'Reform, Reform',
> And hold our vantage ground.

Graham was one of the un-put-down-able men.

Ordained in 1826 as a Presbyterian minister, the Reverend Graham became connected with the Presbytery of Newark, New Jersey, preaching at Berkshire Valley and Bound Brook in Morris County, until a larger opportunity arose and he became General Agent for the Pennsylvania State Society for the Suppression of the Use of Ardent Spirits. While he searched for an explanation of the perplexing fact that great numbers of his fellow citizens liked to get squiffy on brandy-and-water, Graham came under the influence of the teachings of the Reverend William Metcalfe. He may have been a practicing vegetarian already. A personal expense book from the Bound Brook days shows that Graham bought wheat by the sack from local millers. It records no bills for meat. But there was, astonishingly, some wet goods, Holland gin at eighty-eight cents a gallon. "All against my remonstrances," wrote the diarist, but "Mother said it must be so."

About this time Graham's platform appearances began to cause a civic commotion. His lecture on cholera was widely attended and discussed. He was among the first to offer Advice to Young Men, and got up a frightening lecture on the subject in which appeared striking textual resemblances to an earlier treatise, Simon André Tissot's *Onanisme*. With "Chastity" and "Diet Reform" added to his repertoire, Graham was soon in demand up and down the Atlantic Coast, drawing fees of two hundred and three hundred dollars a night in Philadelphia, New York and Boston.

"No man," Graham boasted, "can travel by stage or steamboat . . . or go into any part of our country . . . and begin to advocate a vegetable diet . . . without being immediately asked . . . 'What! Are you a Grahamite?' . . ."

The Reverend or Doctor Graham said he never read a book. He made quite a point of it. But he purchased, if he did not read, Broussais' *Physiology*, Meckel's *Anatomy*, Dunglison's *Physiology*, Paxton's *Anatomy* and he had a copy of Paris on diet. Graham knew the Bible well, could read the Greek and Hebrew texts. He was undoubtedly aware that the kind of bread to which his name became attached was as old as the hills. Hippocrates recommended unbolted wheat-meal bread "for its salutary effects upon the bowels." The Greek wrestlers ate a coarse dark bread. Pliny said that the Romans subsisted upon it in the days of their greatest glory. And, to come down to nearer times and circumstances, the British regiments who fought the Revolution here complained of their coarse "Brown George"; and Baron von Steuben told Judge Richard Peters of Philadelphia that the German soldiers owed their good health to their brown "ammunition bread." Good Father Graham knew these things, one believes; but, if he did, he wasn't saying so. Not out loud. But he could have said, with his hand over his heart, that he did not know Claude Bernard's work, or the German school of physiologists; for neither did anyone else in North America at the time.

It was an aspect of Graham's vanity that he stoutly maintained the pose that he owed no debt to any one. There were others, he acknowledged, "who can expatiate on the benefits of a vegetable diet and a correct general regimen." But he, only he, Graham, especially equipped by Providence, was the one who could perceive and bring out "the correct constitutional principles in the nature of things." He felt himself inspired: to a confidant, Gerrit Smith, he wrote, "I *feel* that I know the mind of God."

Graham acknowledged that Pythagoras had taught that man ought to confine himself to foods of vegetable origin; but his own arrival at similar conclusions was entirely independent. Friends and followers read the classical authors and modern authorities, sometimes sent him excerpts from their works. But his own method was observation.

"I must frankly acknowledge," he said, "that I have had much less to do with books than with bodies."

The Reverend William Metcalfe said mildly that Graham came in contact with the vegetarian faithists of Philadelphia in 1829, and "the probability is, that his introduction to a knowledge of their dietetic views led him to study, and subsequently to lecture on the physiological portion of their doctrines." There was also correspondence at this time between Graham, Metcalfe and Dr. Alcott, the Boston educationist, who broadened the ideal of dietetic simplicity to include other factors that influence health.

Graham's own account of his interest in food was that he developed the Spartan diet to eliminate the craving for whiskey. This attracted attention, since the liquor traffic was one of the pressing questions of the day. So, with intensive study of animal and vegetable "economy," working while others slept, lecturing and talking all the while, Graham worked out to his complete satisfaction a theory of diet in which bread occupied a central position.

In Graham's view, the real decline and fall came when men "began to put asunder what God joined together"; *i.e.*, to refine the bran out of wheat flour. "Every farmer knows," said the *Graham Journal of Health and Longevity*, "that if his horse has straw cut with his grain, or hay in abundance, he does well enough. Just so it is with the human species. Man needs the bran in his bread."

For commercial bread and the "public bakers" who made it, Graham had little use. Bread should be made in the home, not by servants but by the wife and mother, with her own hands, in the tradition of the good old New England mother of early Federal days who stood long over her dough trough, kneading the dough and forming the loaf, watching the baking as anxiously as she would the cradle of a sick child. In this high employment, to the Reverend Sylvester Graham a sacred office, the housewife attained something of the dignity of a noble matron of republican Rome as she busied herself about the cool, airy "meal room" and the spotless bread trough. Let Dinah do something else. Manda could mind the flies. But mother should make the bread. As for the commercial bakers, they might not be worse than other men, Graham conceded, but they were in business for profit, not for their health. The temptation was always present to use inferior materials, to produce a loaf as large, as white and as heavy as possible from a given quantity of flour.

Between Graham and Dr. Alcott there existed a slight difference of opinion upon the ideal bread. Graham countenanced the use of yeast. Alcott recognized only the completely unleavened loaf of whole wheat. Either way, it was practically unsalable. The bakers found that they couldn't make an attractive loaf with the coarse unbolted flour. So they made their dark "health" breads by using white flour for its adhesive qualities, then added cracked wheat and coarse flour for flavor, with molasses for color. This dough was heavy. So they worked in large quantities of saleratus or pearlash to sweeten the dough. Alcott emphasized the "poisonous" character of the alkali. Graham dwelt upon the miller's bolting cloth as the shroud of the American people.

The bolting of Graham's day took out much of the bran, but not all. The white flour which he knew was "specky." It was not until the 1870's, and Sylvester Graham long in his grave, that improved steel rollers made flour really white, exaggerating the nutritional deficiencies which Graham had dramatized earlier. Bread should be eaten only when it was at least twenty-four hours old, the master advised, spread with butter only when stone cold. Hot bread was almost as bad as hot mince pie. The Graham program, with all of its oddities, does represent a striking triumph for empiricism, since it did retain the whole-wheat values of the minerals and vitamins.

As Graham acquired a following, he not only became the philosopher of "the good brown bread" but also took the broad vegetarian position. He developed his argument from scientific grounds, compared man's eight incisors, four eyeteeth, eight small cheek teeth, and twelve large cheek teeth, with the similar equipment of the panther, the camel, the orangutan. Unlike some of his colleagues, Graham granted that man was capable of eating meat. This was hardly a major concession, since he could see it done three times a day, on a panoramic scale, by stepping over from his New York headquarters at Fowlers & Wells' publishing house to the dining saloon of any Broadway hotel.

Graham assured the timid and the devout that there was no conflict between sound dietetic principles and the Bible; and even called upon phrenology for support. He never entirely swallowed this fashionable pseudoscience, though there were many links and sympathies between the food reformers and the professors. To the extent that he was a scientist, Dr. Graham suspected that the phrenological theory was a crackpot venture. As a Protestant clergyman, he didn't like phrenology because the zones and bumps on the head were deterministic. They encouraged fatalism, weakened man's sense of awful individual responsibility. As a lecturer with bookings to think about, he did not favor rival attractions.

Dr. Graham had numerous reasons, then, for disapproving when Boston turned out to hear a popular lecturer who exhibited, like a sacred relic, an ear of Johann Kaspar Spurzheim, the fashionable philosopher of craniology, neatly preserved in alcohol. And yet Father Graham did not hesitate to use phrenological arguments. His justification was no doubt that of the evangelist who uses any rope to truss up a sinner. And so phrenology took its place in his *armamentum* of arguments. Proof was adduced from the organ of *alimentiveness* "or the instinct that prompts us to take food." It was supposed to be situated before the ear, just under *acquisitiveness*, about where the sideburns are worn.

Graham recommended fruits and vegetables, to touch briefly on some other aspects of his dietary, either fresh or "preserved in their own inspissated juices." All food should be cool, chewed slowly and thoroughly, with abundant salivation. Since the Grahamite was required not to drink water with his meals, and precious little at any other time, it must have been an interesting spectacle to see a disciple down his graham crackers. Graham constantly weakened his case by overstating it. Condiments caused the blues and led to insanity. Meat eating inflamed the "baser propensities." Tea led to delirium tremens. Because of the so-called progress of civilization, the Yankee, that is, American, race had been deteriorating for three generations. Chicken pie produced cholera morbus. Another predisposing cause of cholera was "excessive lewdness." That explained why, when cholera was epidemic in Paris, the fancy ladies dropped off by the hundreds.

A slender, wiry man, active as a pea on a hot skillet, Graham was remarkably excitable. He combined "reformatory" convictions with a certain rusticity of manner and delivery, so that his lectures produced the effect more of sermons than of secular addresses. "Mr. Graham's manner is rather fantastical," said a contemporary newspaper. "He made great use of the screw-augur gesture," boring into the left palm with the right forefinger. Then he would fling both arms upward and outward in a sudden, expansive gesture. He was often tedious and prolix, with his General Introductory Explanations, his reasoning upon Philosophical Principles (finger bores into palm), and his animadversions upon The Nature and Attributes of God (arms flung up and out). Only an age devoted to the lyceum could have taken the punishment.

During the winter season of 1835-36, Graham arrived in Boston. There was to be a series of lectures upon American malnourishment, each opening with prayer. Well-known now at the Franklin Institute in Philadelphia, and at New York's Clinton Hall, 131 Nassau Street, the home of Fowler & Wells' Phrenological Cabinet, where the vegetarian comrades often yarded up, Graham came to Boston trailing triumphs at the Baptist Meeting House in Mulberry Street; at Providence, Fall River and New Bedford.

There were also unpleasant recollections. A portion of the press had tagged the food reformer a "Peristaltic Persuader" and a crank. On the happier side, Graham had heard glowing testimonials delivered by ardent converts. A certain W. T. said he ate according to the Graham gospel, stayed in New York City all summer and didn't catch the cholera. The New York followers also presented him with a set of resolutions and a silver pitcher.

In general, Graham found Boston more congenial than New York. Boston was peculiarly susceptible to reformers. The way had been prepared in a measure for the "food question" by Dr. Alcott. Dr. R. D. Mussey of Dartmouth had lectured in Boston on temperance and tight lacing. Graham himself had dropped off at Hanover in a successful effort to line Dr. Mussey up for his program.

Out of Graham's labors in Boston came, in 1837, the formation of the American Physiological Society, which maintained a reading room, listened to lectures and held meetings with all of the ritual typical of nineteenth-century reform movements. The members were laymen, just ladies and gentlemen, many "more or less feeble." For some it was "a last resort." Reverend Fitch of Boston told how he had been cured of whatever he had, by practicing Grahamism. Dr. Mussey seconded a resolve that the vegetable diet would cure consumption. The subject was vigorously surveyed, "Should physiology be introduced into our schools and colleges?" A glance at the Millerites was contained in a resolution "That the millennium, the near approach of which is by many so confidently predicted, can never reasonably be expected to arrive until those laws which God has implanted in the *physical* nature of man, are . . . universally known and obeyed."

When the topics were too delicate for mixed company, the ladies had "for women only" sessions. Later there was a collation of wheat-bran tea and milk toast. One would give much to see the reaction to some other aspects of the Graham practice; such as when S. G. told his followers to laugh and sing, to leap or hop occasionally, for the sake of the thoracic viscera. This was in the Boston of which the *Hampshire Gazette* in Northampton said, "The Bostonians are a dyspeptic variety of the human family, and the man who professes to cure or prevent that direful disease takes them on the weakest side. The surest way of approaching most men is said to be through a dinner, but you must secure a Bostonian by telling him how to digest one. No doubt Mr. Graham can do it scientifically."

Graham reviewed with condescension the most notable experimental study of the digestive process made in his time, Dr. William Beaumont's famous observations at Fort Mackinac upon the digestion of Alexis St. Martin. St. Martin was a French Canadian who unluckily received a load of duck shot at close range in his left side, and lived out his years with a lid on his stomach. Graham, possibly jealous that another than himself was privileged to peer into St.

Martin's fistulous stomach and interpret the phenomena which took place when a square meal, or a slug of bourbon, hit the gastric membrane, gave Dr. Beaumont a quick brush-off. He was not "a profound physiologist of enlarged views."

The Boston Grahamites, as a matter of fact, tried to steal St. Martin, a simple *habitant*, away from Dr. Beaumont. It was their one effort to substitute experimental evidence for "philosophy." But Beaumont had his singular prize tied down by an agreement as tight as a Chautauqua contract; and anyway, St. Martin, suspecting that he would be made a public show, obstinately rejected the whole idea.

The Physiological Society became in time simply a Grahamite coterie. When it ran out of testimonials, with nothing new to talk about, the Society folded up. Its members found Graham finally to be tendentious and long-winded, as many had secretly known all the while.

There was a theatrical quality about one of Graham's exploits. The bakers of Boston were enraged by his assertions that they used alum and sulphate of zinc to make light, white bread out of poor flour, and often extended it with bean flour, peas and potatoes, chalk, pipe clay and plaster of Paris. The butchers were equally inflamed by the lecturer's unappetizing descriptions of local abattoirs. Such threats were raised against him that the proprietors of Amory Hall closed the place to his lectures. The owner of the new Marlborough Hotel, the first "temperance hotel" in the U.S., re-established the position. The building was still not quite finished. But the proprietor offered Father Graham the use of the dining room, though the Mayor of Boston said that his constabulary could not protect the meeting. So the Grahamites handled the police work themselves. The lower floor of the building was boarded up, the upper stories equipped with quantities of slaked lime and manned by a shovel brigade. When the lecture hour arrived, the hotelkeeper took his stand at his door and parleyed with the mob in the street. The situation was touch and go, recalling an earlier Boston commotion on a more famous occasion, in King Street, when someone ordered the main guard of His Majesty's 29th Infantry to fire upon the town-born. And so again there was an order

given, and a second massacre. The vegetarian bullyboys clobbered
the meatcutters, dumped their lime on the bakers until they were
all floury; "whereupon the eyes having it, the rabble incontinently
adjourned."

Before the enthusiasm for Graham's doctrines had run its
course, health societies appeared from Bangor to Oberlin. They
met. They prophesied. They collected books for collateral reading;
Dr. Mussey on tobacco, Doctors Trall and Joel Shew on the water
cure, Alcott's tome on the vegetable diet, and the tough, wordy
volumes of the old master himself. Graham boardinghouses sprang
up. Boston had one at No. 23 Brattle Street. There was even a provision store, forerunner of today's health-food stores with their car-
rot juice, mineral salts and theosophy.

Mrs. Mary Sergeant Neal Gove, hydropathic physician, later
the consort of Thomas L. Nichols, the kinetic reformer, ran a
school in Lynn, Massachusetts. There she introduced the bloomer
and the brown-bread supper, hard beds and the "wet-sheet" treatment. Mrs. Gove talked and talked—of mesmerism and the occult,
of "individual sovereignty" (*i.e.*, free love). Mrs. Gove became
founder and editor of the *Health Journal and Advocate of Physiological Reform*, a little David of a magazine which took the field
against overeating and pointed out the evil effects of corsets upon
the thoracic cage. Lynn must have provided a salubrious climate
for remarkable women, since Mary Baker Eddy and Lydia E. Pinkham subsequently flourished there.

Horace Greeley was, in the main, faithful. He dined at a Graham
hotel in New York (morning bell, six A.M., curfew, ten P.M.). It
was a sort of Club des Jacobins where the radicals of the day assem-
bled over a convivial cup of cold water and planned the coming of
their kingdom. The boarders, said Professor William S. Tyler, a
young tutor at Amherst at the time, were "not only Grahamites but
Garrisonites—not only reformers in Diet, but radicalists in Politics.
Such a knot of Abolitionists I never before fell in with . . . Arthur
Tappan, Goodell . . . of the *Genius of Temperance* . . . Dennison
of the *Emancipator*."

In this high-minded atmosphere Greeley met and fell in love
with his future wife as they shared their beans, boiled rice, graham

bread and puddings. The Lowell Bloomer Institute entered the movement with a vegetarian debate. Rochester, New York, had a Graham house. Boarders at Wesleyan University, Middletown, Connecticut, commenced eating on the Graham system. The idea reached Williams College, too, which established its own Graham Club.

The Grahamite meals turned out to be too meagre for active people. The restaurants and clubs petered out after a time, to rise again later in the century with a religious sanction as Seventh Day Adventist cafés. In time, only those "of a dyspeptic constitution," the chronics who enjoyed the distinction of delicate health, remained to eat the farinaceous meals, sleep on the hard mattresses and investigate the meaning of the big words in the doctor books, such as "crepitation" and "carminative."

In his last days, Graham retired to Northampton, Massachusetts, "a fine-looking old gentleman," said the local *Gazette*, "egotistical and scholarly." Northampton was a congenial setting for the old firehorse of reform. The area was a center for the water-cure treatment, with several establishments in the vicinity emphasizing the simple diet, improved hygiene and gymnastics. Harriet Beecher Stowe and Catherine Beecher returned to Nature at Northampton. Major Thomas J. Jackson of Virginia came for the treatments, and Jenny Lind, too. Lydia Maria Child and her husband, David Lee Child, valiant abolitionists, lived in nearby Florence in a transcendental community, the Northampton Association of Education and Industry. The community was devoted to labor, self-improvement, free conscience and interminable discussion. Garrison and Wendell Phillips visited there. Henry C. Wright, the blond Englishman who awoke Mrs. Mary Neal Gove to the larger life, addressed the group at Florence under a venerable pine tree. The social life was unconventional and free, "running to the verge of propriety," says an annalist of Florence, "but never beyond"; a nice adjustment!

Here lived, for a time, under Lydia's sponsorship, that picturesque wanderer on the face of the earth, the African sibyl, Sojourner Truth, very black, with strong cheekbones, brooding eyes, a native dignity and flashing wit. Sojourner was a laundress on weekdays. On Sunday, she stood before the assembly—Garrison, Lucretia and Lydia Mott, Wendell Phillips, whoever was there—tall, gaunt, a bright Madras handkerchief worn as a turban, and sang:

> I'm on my way to Canada
> That cold, but happy land.

Sojourner also spoke on "women's rights and niggers," handed about *cartes de visite* bearing the legend, "I sell the Shadow to Support the Substance." She once rebuked the Seventh Day Adventists for fanaticism and spent her last years, by what seems an incredible coincidence, in Battle Creek. There she was a sort of ward of Dr. John Harvey Kellogg at the "San." She spoke occasionally in the Sanitarium parlors and sold copies of her life story along the shady streets of the old "underground railroad" town. When the aged ex-slave came to the end of her long "sojourn to preach truth," she was buried in a spot now shadowed by the great marble mausoleum containing all that is mortal of another great publicist, Charles W. Post, the breakfast-food multimillionaire. The imposing Post mortuary structure serves a useful purpose today as a landmark pointing the way to Sojourner's modest stone.

As his last years approached, Sylvester Graham told a Northampton neighbor that people would come someday to see the peg on which he had hung his hat, and the building, he said, would be carried off stone by stone by relic hunters. This was pure rhetoric since the house was of frame construction. It is still there, a convivial gathering place known now as Young's Café, on Pleasant Street, where the food philosopher once cultivated his vegetable patch, pondered the depravity of the Whigs and accumulated a large corpus of melancholy poetry.

In one of his poems Graham argued that the coldness of the hearts of the dead did not match that of the living. There is reason to believe that Father Graham referred to an unhappy domestic life. The converts to Grahamism were generally men, just the reverse of the response to dietary novelties today. Mrs. Graham sniffed at her philosopher-scientist-moralist husband's system, a particular grief to a man who sensed that he belonged to history. Mrs. G. spread a luxurious table, possibly relishing the role of temptress. A sympathetic contemporary, Dr. Russel T. Trall, mentioned that Graham had lapses—an "occasional deviation from his own standard of physiological living." This placed the philosopher in "very peculiar circumstances," for any grossness in dining would, of course, open the way for charges of hypocrisy.

Sometimes, in moments of agitation, the old gentleman went out upon the town abstractedly. Clad in his dressing gown, fretful, anxious, he trumpeted in the very streets, throwing out dark hints of family cabals against him. Madness, the subject of one of his poems, seemed a nearby thing, lurking in the alley ways, keeping pace with the poet as he prowled among the shadows of Northampton's Shop Row.

Graham occupied himself with letters to the editors of the local newspapers, promising "Communications of Moderate Length." He worked fitfully at a book on meat and wine in the Bible, bathed in Mill River every day in the year. Once upon his recovery from an illness he published an apology for having been sick. No one felt more keenly than he how unsuitable it was.

Like Hippocrates and Galen, Dr. Graham stressed exercise as an antidote to disease. He is undoubtedly responsible in part for the modern "apotheosis of muscle" which produced the gymnasium, weight-lifting and Indian-club drills. Graham gave new hope to all spindly youths with acne and headaches, constantly feeling their biceps and dreaming of trouncing the school bully; such as small, insignificant George Winship, of Boston, who eventually, with his yoke, succeeded in lifting 2,750 pounds, and hoped—*ad astra per aspera*—to make it an even 3,000 pounds.

Thin, eccentric—with his morning ice baths, his Indian samp and cold, dark bread, his habit of ceaselessly talking, his censoriousness, his inability to keep his nose out of any local occurrence— Graham lived out his time, a fiery champion, looking for a recreant upon whom he could prove the true doctrine. Few men were less fit to bear ridicule or had more of it to endure. Some wag was always printing a scrap of verse suggesting that when a Grahamite died, he should be buried with a loaf of graham bread, because there must be dyspeptics in heaven. The *New-York Review*, referring to digressions and wanderings in one of Dr. Graham's lectures, printed a malicious report quoting Graham himself. According to the canard, Graham explained his incoherence by saying that he had taken an extra slice of graham bread, and got high on it. When the infirmities of his last illness were upon him, Graham was trundled in a wheelbarrow from the Pleasant Street house to the shop of a "professor," the local barber. The incident made a juicy conversation piece and got into print.

Like Dr. J. H. Kellogg, who came after him, Graham expressed the hope that he would live to be a hundred. Dr. Kellogg made a near miss. He lived to see the parish buried three times over, and crossed the bar himself at ninety-one. Graham didn't come near the century mark. On September 11, 1851, the old food fighter died triumphantly on a rice diet of his own choosing, after a dose of Congress water and a tepid bath.

Graham lived in the romantic mode, with singularity a proof of superior endowments. If his posthumous fame had been less than his own expectations, it has exceeded what most of his contemporaries would have allowed him. Dr. Kellogg was always conscious of a direct link with Graham's views. The founders of the Michigan water cure "were influenced by the teachings of Graham," Dr. Kellogg declared.

"The Battle Creek food business began in New England nearly a hundred years ago," said Kellogg, referring to Graham's advocacy of whole wheat. He also noted that Graham had made a visit to Michigan on a lecture tour and had had contacts with John J. Shipherd, the cofounder of Oberlin, who moved to Michigan and established a second center of reform at Olivet College. Many a pioneer Michigan farm wife, Graham found, knew how to grind whole wheat in her hand mill and make a shortcake from the unbolted flour. But her reliance upon the "Grahamish cake" did not rest, in most instances, upon principle. She ate unleavened bread because the pork barrel was empty and the potatoes had run out. Likewise, when there was no tea to be had, the Michigan wives used "tea weed," a kind of wild Bohea of the woods. They made a coffee substitute from caramelized bread. Or they browned wheat, bran and molasses for the same purpose, not because they were bilious but because they were poor.

Dr. Kellogg recalled that barrelled graham flour was a well-known commodity in the grocery trade, freighted to Battle Creek from a small mill in New York state, either at Lockport or Rochester, The Doctor wasn't sure which. But the real impulse which made Battle Creek a health center came when Elder James White, J. N. Loughborough and other Adventists "adopted Graham's ideas, which he elaborated in a work entitled 'Ten Lectures on the Science of Human Life. . . .' Graham's idea of eating scientifically, physiologically, was well planted and this was the real foundation of the Battle Creek food business." Dr. Kellogg described Sylvester Graham as "a scientific man, a college professor and a lawyer"; which shows that he remembered the old gentleman favorably but not well.

Good health habits and the sparse diet alone could not, of course, guarantee general well-being. To say so was to overlook many other factors—inheritance, history, environment, a possible psychological fixation upon one's "weak" stomach. The reformers looked for a catholicon and often found an -ism. One thinks inevitably of Graham in this connection. Yet despite all faults and frailties in character and doctrine, Graham exerted a telling influence. He made vegetarianism pandemic. He was a catalyzer of his period and made a substantial contribution in forwarding the most important medical principle established in the nineteenth century, the *vis medicatrix naturae*, the healing power of nature. Graham was a dissenter, and so in the main stream of American history. He emphasized sentimentally the influences of a "false" civilization, mixing elements of the ancients' Golden Age with the Hebrew story of man's idyllic life before the Fall. Graham, being no great reader, may never have heard of Rousseau's paradox of the superiority of the savage over the civilized state; but he shared the ideas nevertheless of the *Discours sur les arts et sciences*.

The empiricists made a substantial contribution in emphasizing the importance of whole-grain foods, cheerful meals, slow eating, thorough chewing, occasional fasting, the cautious use of fats. Their warnings against fried foods and overeating were timely. It may seem at first glance that all of Graham's sound and fury ended up as no more than a muffin pan or porous-knit underwear. But the impact of the old argufier was more significant than that. Between 1830 and 1890 no less than eighty-five popular health magazines appeared in the United States, many with Grahamite affiliations. Sylvester Graham's dietary laws, his reliance upon regimen, his reformer's attitude toward strong drink and tobacco, were all taken over by the Adventist church and by the Shakers, who, like the Adventists, combined Grahamism with hydropathy.

The great cataclysm of the Civil War diverted public attention from the contemplation of the alimentary canal. The advance of scientific nutrition disintegrated the movement. But the earlier concepts persisted in the daily bath, the lighter diet, in more liberal attitudes toward exercise and the outdoor life.

Among contemporaries not already mentioned, Graham extended his influence through Philo Penfield Stewart, inventor of the "Oberlin" stove and cofounder of the celebrated Oberlin Collegiate Institute, Charles Grandison Finney, the Grimké sisters, Theodore Weld. Gerrit Smith was a close confrere. Fruitlands, too, Bronson Alcott's experiment in co-operative living at Harvard, Massachusetts, was touched by Grahamism, as were Brook Farm and the Oneida Community. Mrs. Asenath Nicholson was so enthusiastic about "Mr. Graham's rules" that she wrote a book to express the boundless overflowing of her own vegetarianism. In *Nature's Own Book*, a queer, cranky volume about carrots and parsnips, Mrs. Nicholson out-Grahamed Graham: for while he grudgingly allowed some meat, and fish at times (fresh water only, broiled), Mrs. N. never gave an inch on proteins of animal origin.

A widow of long standing, originally a schoolteacher and Vermont Baptist, Mrs. Nicholson pulled off the most incredible mission of her generation. She travelled to Ireland to bring Protestant "Bible reading" to the Irish poor; and no explosion followed her ministrations. With her tracts and her Testaments, her parasol, a kind heart beating behind a bearskin muff, Mrs. Nicholson sat in the thatched cottages and gave Bible readings in exchange for Irish music, laughter, dancing and a hand over the stile.

"I will not leave you comfortless; I will come to you," quoted the New England woman in the prim American bonnet, while the potatoes bubbled over the peat fire, and the cottagers listened in polite wonder.

An especially effective transmitter of Grahamism was Dr. James Caleb Jackson, abolitionist, water-cure doctor, lecturer and popular writer upon regimen. At Dansville, New York, Dr. Jackson founded a resort which became famous for bringing together the Graham diet, the Preissenitz hydropathic methods and the "let alone" system of medicine. Vincent Preissenitz, an unlettered peasant of Silesia, having treated himself successfully after an accident with cloths kept wet with cold water, developed a system of treatment replacing the heavy medication in general use during the first half of the nineteenth century. Perspiration was followed by copious applications from the mountain spring at Graefenberg, where ice-cold douches fell sixteen or eighteen feet upon the hardy patient, who also took the water internally—twenty to thirty glasses a day. It was sometimes difficult for the invalid, shivering beneath his clammy sheet to know which was the more rugged, the old routine of mercury and antimony, or the shock treatment of the cold plunge. During the middle years of the century, the methods of Preissenitz became popular in North America, along with the hygienic reforms then current. Dr. Jackson took a leading part in developing the hydropathic concepts here. To him came the weary Adventist pioneers, exhausted fishers for men's souls, Sister Ellen G. White and Elder James White, and young Dr. J. H. Kellogg. They found at Dansville, as will be seen shortly, a blueprint for what they built on a larger scale and at a later date at Battle Creek.

V

Bloomers and Bread Crumbs

DR. JAMES CALEB JACKSON was a York-state farmer and son of a farmer, born March 28, 1811, in Manlius, of Massachusetts stock. His father wanted him to be a doctor. It was his mother's hope and prayer that he might go as a missionary to the heathen. Both parents got their wish, in a sense. Largely self-educated, James Caleb was so apt in the classics that by the time he was twelve, he could handle both Latin and Greek like a college senior. With no taste for the plow or grub hoe, farmer Jackson was led into the antislavery cause at an early age by his warm humanitarian feelings, his desire to be "a public man," to wake up society, to "overthrow effete institutions," as he said, "and build up better" [ones]. With encouragement and assistance from Gerrit Smith, the patron and protector of New York State reform, Jackson escaped from the backwoods. He edited several "reformatory papers" devoted to temperance and abolition, acquired a reputation about the state as an orator and debater.

Poor health intervened in 1847—heart, dyspepsia, right kidney —to interrupt Jackson's career. He became a patient of Dr. S. O. Gleason who had fitted up Greenwood Spring at Cuba, New York, as an establishment run on the principles of Preissenitz. Gleason had been diplomaed by the Castleton Medical College in Vermont. Thereafter he organized a lecture tour with a small manikin, and not having much success, moved on into the field of water cure, which wasn't crowded. With Gleason, Jackson regained a measure of health and found his lifework.

Gleason, Jackson and a Miss Theodosia Gilbert, who had a little capital, started up a hygienic institute at the head of Skaneateles

Lake near Scott, in a building originally intended for a Fourierist phalanx. The place was christened "Glen Haven Water Cure." Jackson attended to the business affairs of the Cure while he "read" medicine and spent enough time in Syracuse to receive the diploma of the Medical Eclectic College there. Three years later, Dr. Gleason withdrew from "the Glen" together with most of the patients. But Jackson cured a schoolteacher of her brain fever without the use of medicines. A half-dozen patients at the Clifton Springs Water Cure promptly moved over to Glen Haven. Dr. Jackson sent an agent around central New York, with copies of *The Water Cure Journal* under his arm, to point out the Glen Haven advertisement, and staged a great "hygienic festival," attended by a hundred and fifty editors and reformers, including Mrs. Elizabeth Cady Stanton, Mrs. Amelia Bloomer, a sprinkling of old antislavery comrades and the clergy. After this well-publicized event "the Glen" never lacked for patients.

Even in his early, tentative days at "the Glen," before the institution at Dansville, New York, was thought of, Dr. Jackson showed qualities of leadership. The experience of the patients at Glen Haven was enriched with communal and sentimental associations. Guests remembered and treasured every facet of Dr. Jackson's personality, his fearlessness, his novel medical doctrines, the evening he gave that unforgettable reading from "Hiawatha." They remembered the buckets and tubs of the old bathhouse, the congeniality which drew together the fellow searchers for the better life, the winter they sleighed three times to Homer.

It was all very much like getting a degree from a cherished alma mater. The "Home" kept alive the sense of affiliation in *The Letter Box*, a kind of alumni publication. In this chatty little promotional paper it was noted, for instance, that "Mr. G. was of the class of 1852-53, a very sick man." Now once more at home and in health, G. writes back wistfully of how he "longs for Graham crackers," and would "rather have the family of 1853 gathered together at the 'Glen' than be a dignitary at the wedding of the Princess Royal." *The Letter Box* printed newsy items about "alums": "Saw Sallie Sleeper in Philadelphia; she looks well." Former patients, indeed, spoke of themselves as "graduates" and spoke up for Dr. Jackson in the vigorous vocabulary of vegetarianism, referring to "swine poisoning," scoffing at the practice of regular medicine—"She had swallowed a hogshead of doctor stuff."

Then there came a break—the death of Miss Gilbert and the inheritance of her interest by a husband with whom Dr. Jackson found himself unsuitably yoked. The unsatisfactory relationship and a fire which destroyed the main building combined to turn Dr. Jackson's thoughts in other directions. In 1858, having disposed of his interest in the Cure on Skaneateles Lake, he went to Dansville and rented a ruin. There he developed his own institution, known as "Our Home on the Hillside" and later as the Jackson Sanatorium.

Before Dr. Jackson's arrival, a little hydropathic resort near the village had struggled along precariously for some six years. Each manager seemed more feckless than the one before. It was not an engaging prospect, as the energetic new doctor, with a faithful little band—his immediate family, his staff and a few rugged patients whom nothing could dismay—looked up at a rambling, windowless, leaky, rotting rookery in the fading light of an October evening. Striped by four piazzas one hundred feet long, decorated by the indefatigable jigsaw, the hotel looked like a wedding cake that had been left out in the rain. But there was a splendid view from the upper piazza, and everyone tried bravely to ignore the weeds and underbrush, the rats, the bugs and the bats, and to think of the desolate spot as "Our Home." It was, at least, above the malaria belt. Dr. Jackson's heart leaped. Ever the classicist, he whispered fervently, *"una spes, unaque salus ambobus erit"* (one hope and one health shall be to us both), and silently vowed that the new venture would soon have a winding carriage road right to the door, a good head of water and a grapery.

Meanwhile, there was cleaning to be done, scrubbing and scouring. Dr. Jackson hammered and sawed, took his turn at washing dishes, curried the horse, filled the position of physician-in-chief, and rose at four A.M. to start it all over again. Dr. Harriet N. Austin, James Caleb's adopted daughter, who possessed the diploma of the T. L. and Mary Gove Nichols medical college in New York City, bought the carpeting. It was a day never to be forgotten in Dansville when Harriet, with short hair and wearing the sanatorium bloomer dress, jaw set and color high, faced George Woods in his hardware store and asked to see his carpets.

"Wilkinson . . . a woman dressed like a man, who does business just like a man! I never would have believed it," Woods exclaimed later as he dashed upstairs into Lawyer Wilkinson's office. "Look out your window, you can see her."

Harriet, having purchased fifty yards of carpet, laid down the money and asked in level tones for a receipt. Now she was swinging easily along Main Street, her Turk-satin tunic looking very rich in the late, slanting sunlight. She turned into Chestnut Street, then Elizabeth, continued until she came to Perine Street, and so went on up to the Cure. There was not a grocery, not a milliner's shop that day but whose clerks and customers rushed to the door to see the marvel. Dansville suppers were well chatted *that* night.

Up on the Hill, the work went on. Sheets were hemmed, ovens stoked for baking bread, wooden tubs constructed for the inunction, the pail douche, the popular sitz bath, in which the patient sat in a tub, his legs dangling over the sides. The road connecting the Cure with the village was renamed "Health Street." Markers were set for each eighth of a mile, so ambulatory guests could measure their achievements when they went for a stroll. Dr. Jackson prescribed walks, high up into the woods on the hill back of the Home, as far as the All-Healing Spring or the D.L. & W. railroad tracks. When the patients got up there, they were instructed to turn toward the west and look at the sunset, turn away, and then back to look again; the second time—between their legs. This gave them a new point of view on the Genesee Valley, and got them to bend over double.

Dansville was a live town. It had fine water power, a seminary, flourishing churches and stores, honest lawyers and a daguerreotype gallery. There was a literary society, the Coterie, and a public meeting place, Canaseraga Hall; and there Miss Doctress Austin, her hair bobbed to avoid congestion in the brain, spoke on dress reform for woman, and Reverend George Trask, editor of *The Anti-Tobacco Journal*, lectured on his specialty.

Dr. Jackson issued tracts upon health and dietetic subjects: "The Whole and the Hulled Wheat," "The Weak Backs of American Women." Though the terminology which the doctor used is long outmoded, the emphasis which he placed upon the mind in treating the body has a brisk, contemporary sound about it. He was remarkable in his ability to invoke the will to believe in favor of the treatment. The regimen consisted mostly of pleasant walks, graham bread, subacid fruits, sun, sleep, parlor talks and a sleigh ride.

Recreation was prominently emphasized at "Our Home." Dr. Jackson himself would close the day by giving a reading from "Mazeppa." Come spring, all patients who were on their feet piled into Captain Henry's omnibus for a May-day ride and a dining out. Toasts were gaily drunk in cold (soft) water, to Dr. Jackson, to the "Dinner of Herbs" and to Miss Doctress Austin's fetching costume, "May her shadow never be shorter, nor her skirts any longer."

A Chinese gong summoned all to Liberty Hall when there was to be an entertainment. Liberty Hall! Did Dr. Jackson, with his depth of literary culture, intend to call forth all of the associations which the name suggests? There is in it something of Rabelais's House of Free Will or Pleasure, where the Thelemites lived in accordance with their rule, *Fay ce que vouldras*: and of Shakespeare's "Twelfth Night, or What you Will." Liberty Hall must, then, have been a place of licensed saturnalia, of quite circumspect, quite Victorian orgy, with beaming Dr. Jackson in "high fantastical" humor as Master of the Revels, evoking a mood of relaxation and gaiety. Liberty Hall, at all events, made its own special contribution to "Our Home's" curative agencies: "A merry heart doeth good like a medicine."

On New Year's Eve the "family" played charades. On lesser fete days Miss Austin might recite. Or there would be a concert, with a trio by Balfe, Arditi's *Valse Brilliante* and excerpts from *Norma*. When an interesting patient arrived, he was invited to lecture: a judge, for instance, recently returned from Cairo, who discussed the situation in Egypt. It was confused, and the British had sent ironclads. There had been a light bombardment which, there was every reason to believe, would recall the natives to a sense of their own best interests.

When Dr. Jackson was to speak, a triangular signal was raised on the flagstaff, a colored "J" on a white ground with red border. The "family" lectures were often scheduled for seven in the morning when heads would be clear. The ill were wheeled in on "hand chariots" to hear of "The Constitutional Degeneracy of American Women" with their wedding-ring waists, gros de Naples gowns, whalebone stays and "water falls" of false hair—and everything at sixes and sevens with their poor insides.

Blue-eyed Mrs. Amelia Bloomer, temperance and women's rights advocate, editor of *The Lily*, occupies a niche in our social history which must be embarrassing in a posthumous way, her name forever associated with the costume which she wore but did not originate. Others who became "Bloomers" were Mary Gove Nichols, Lucy Stone, Susan B. Anthony, the Grimké sisters, Mrs. Lydia Sayer Hasbrouck, editor of the *Sibyl*, "and many patients in sanatariums [sic]."

Dr. Harriet Austin designed a bloomer-type outfit which she called the "American Costume." Tall women with large feet, it is true, didn't find the dress becoming, though many farmers' wives appreciated the freedom of the loose tunic and baggy slacks. To all the new dress was symbolic. Male editors hooted at it. But the Reverend Henry Ward Beecher approved bloomers for country wear; while Theodore Weld and Gerrit Smith, always for striking off shackles, liked them anywhere.

Miss Austin saw a bright future for her own trim suit of decent broadcloth. Lola Montez could scoff at the short petticoats, but Harriet vowed she wouldn't be caught dead in a long dress. Some wore the dress privately, just around the house. Some went out on the street in high physiologic fashion. But hardest of all for a womankind reared upon the maxim "Always go to church—especially when you have some new clothes," was the dull standardization of the coat and pantalettes. Harriet exhorted the fainthearted in all earnestness: ". . . for Christ's sake let them wear the American costume when they go to church."

Patients at "Our Home on the Hillside" were not required to wear the American costume, any more than they were required to eat the vegetarian diet. Meat was served to those who, Dr. Jackson conceded, would find the shock too great if they did not get it. But in either case medical and social approval was heavily weighted toward compliance with reform principles.

The diet was arranged on the Graham plan, plus a notable addition, a discovery of Dr. Jackson's which he originated around

1863, called "Granula." Granula was, in a way, bread crumbs. To make Granula, a mix of graham flour and water was baked in brick ovens in thin sheets until it was hard and brittle, then broken into pieces averaging an inch square, ground through a grinder into coarse pieces, the size of large beans or small cherries. These were again baked. After the second baking, they were ground again, coming out finally about the size of Grape Nuts. The baking was done in a very slow oven. It was rather a kind of oven-drying.

"To serve Granula," says James A. Jackson, great-grandson of Dr. James Caleb, "it was necessary to restore the moisture before it could be eaten without consequences similar to eating dried apples and drinking water as a 'chaser'. Therein, of course, lay the weakness in later years, as housewives began to demand instant breakfast foods. The minimum time to soak it up was twenty minutes, but the preferred method was to put about one-third glassful of Granula into a water glass and fill it with whole milk, then set it in the icebox overnight. In the morning, the glass was completely full of soaked Granula, and the top section was largely risen cream. This glassful was stirred and put into a cereal dish, then served with sugar and cream to taste."

Granula made history. It was the first cold cereal breakfast food. Granula was in Dr. Kellogg's mind when he became chief physician at the Adventist water cure in Battle Creek. By a line of descent which can be traced clearly, Granula was the prototype for Grape Nuts. With Granula we leave the prehistory of ready-to-eat breakfast foods and find, at Dansville, New York, the first articulated concept of a processed dry cereal, twice-baked, partially dextrinized, served up with health preachments and a modicum of mystery. Granula, Dr. Jackson advertised, was "prepared by a peculiar process original with us, embracing the use of all the constituents of the grain, which is the best white winter wheat grown in the famous Genesee Valley country." Granula was in composition slightly superior to a good flour, but it cost the consumer roughly ten times as much as flour. The pricing of Granula was an instance of raw courage which was later noted with admiration in Battle Creek. To accompany Granula, Dr. Jackson added Somo, a "health coffee." A company was formed, Our Home Granula Company, to manufacture the products. They were packaged, trade-marked and advertised—"Eat Granula, Drink Somo."

The vegetarian frame of reference included agitators and fighters in all the liberal causes which stirred the social conscience of idealistic men and women. Dr. Jackson was in the thick of it with most of the aspiring people of his day. Clara Barton recovered from her exhausting labors in the Franco-Prussian War under James Caleb's care. She became the "Clara, Beloved" and he the "Father" of a long and affectionate correspondence. "It was, I think," Miss Barton once said to Dr. Jackson when he was an old man, "worth all my illness to have known 'Dansville.'" James Caleb was in touch with Clubb and the Philadelphia Vegetarian Christians. Greeley came to see Dr. Jackson. Robert Dale Owen was a Dansville guest, as was Bayard Taylor, who lectured on a subject of perennial interest—"Moscow."

Antivivisection societies and the enemies of compulsory vaccination worked hand in hand with the vegetarians, conscious of related ideals and objectives. The American Society for Promoting Observance of the Seventh Commandment had to deal not only with human waywardness but also with Lucina Umphreville, "Miss Anti-Marriage," a female incendiary who valued female virtue only in proportion to temptation; a certain prescription for living dangerously. There were all manner of eccentrics with an *idée fixe*. Dr. Mary Walker campaigned for the right to wear men's pants. At Fruitlands, where Bronson Alcott sowed his "Transcendental wild oats," the Alcott ladies wore bloomers of linen. Cotton was forbidden because it was the product of slave labor; wool because it deprived sheep of their property.

At one time the "Our Home" circle and the Oberlin group launched a joint venture, a Christian Health Reform Colonization Commission, to settle bands of health reformers in remote locations. The Reverend H. S. Clubb and his troop of Kansas vegetarians had felt the same impulse to escape the world and "the contamination of old cities." There was in the idea, too, a Puritan inwardness, a deep-seated preoccupation with the salvation of the individual, with one's own personal holy living and holy dying. Colonization was an expression of this turning away from the world to seek some inner Holy City. So it was with the vegetarians.

So too with the Seventh Day Adventists who found that even in Battle Creek the world was too much with them.

The nineteenth-century crusaders were often persons of abounding goodwill and generous instincts, but tedious. A broader culture, the gift of geniality, would have made them better company and perhaps more effective propagandists. However, warmth and the joy of living were not lacking in Dr. Jackson, who showed the world a cheerful countenance and must have had a twinkle in his eye when he diagnosed Sister White's *nostalgie de la croix* as a case of hysteria.

Dr. Jackson, a nexus for so many reform impulses, was responsible to a substantial degree for their transmission to Battle Creek. The first Seventh Day Adventist to imbibe health principles at Dansville was Joshua V. Himes, who entered "Our Home" in 1861. Himes was a born agitator and superb press agent. He had been No. 2 man in the Second Coming excitement with William Miller twenty years earlier. In 1864, when the Adventists were firmly established at Battle Creek, but before they had taken up health as a matter of church discipline, an Adventist physician, Dr. Horatio S. Lay brought his wife, Julia, to Dr. Jackson. She recovered, and Jackson persuaded Lay to remain and join the staff. Lay was an allopath who had "got up" on Preissenitz. This modest, diffident Lay enjoys whatever small place he occupies in history for his positive act of directing a stream of careworn Adventists to Dansville.

When Dr. Lay bundled the elders off to Dansville, of course Ellen White went, too. Sister White was not unprepared for the interesting time she had with Dr. Jackson. She had already had a nocturnal conference with an angel about the two-meal-a-day system and graham crackers. As a consequence of the impressive physiological repairs made by Jackson on his ministerial boarders, the Advent pythoness received a heavenly message instructing the Adventists to duplicate the Dansville setup. The next year, in the fall of 1866, Dr. Lay resigned, and went to Battle Creek to open the first Seventh Day Adventist water cure, the Western Health Reform Institute. Dr. Jackson arranged to go to Battle Creek to deliver a series of lectures. The torch had been passed to a new runner.

The therapeutics of Dansville, the positive results, the twice-baked Granula and healthful Somo would have been completely familiar to any Battle Creek patient or bath hand. But the vitality in the Battle Creek principles, the dazzling subsequent career of the "patent foods," were not mere carbon copies of James Caleb Jackson's early work. They rested on a firmer foundation than copy-cat imitation—upon the insights of a seeress and the creations of a promotional genius—the combined operations of Sister Ellen G. White and Dr. John Harvey Kellogg.

In both were united, to an unusual degree, the good and the clever.

The Grains, the Nuts and the Second Coming

IT was sundown on a June evening, by the calendar, Friday, June 6, 1863. The Seventh Day Adventist Sabbath had begun. Sister Ellen G. White was on her knees, a characteristic position. The occasion was a season of praise and prayer, held during a camp meeting at the modest home of Aaron H. and Lydia Hilliard, New York State Adventists who had emigrated to a farm about three miles out of Otsego, Michigan, and some thirty miles north of Battle Creek. Those were dark days of struggle, for the country and for the pacifist Advent band. Anxious over the plight of members drafted for the Civil War, abused for their noncombatant principles, the scattering of prime individualists was trying, hesitantly, to organize into a church body.

All present in the farmhouse were deep in prayer, Brother Hilliard, Ellen White and some of the other sisters, Ellen leading, when she uttered and repeated in a clear voice the word, "Glory, glory, glory." At first she spoke loudly. Then her voice would die away to a whisper. She seemed to be in a state of suspended animation. Her eyes were open. No breath was apparent. Shoulders, arms and hands moved in time with what she saw.

Thus in vision, probably in Hilliard's old-fashioned kitchen, her hand resting on James White's shoulder, Sister White was "taken off," and the great subject of health reform was opened to her. Under "the Spirit of Inspiration," she spoke on the importance of eating only two meals a day; a consequence no doubt of the physiological belief held at the time that the stomach required five hours to digest a meal. A message to avoid meats came through. Light was given to her to say that meat eating strengthened "the animal propensities" and brought on an overpowering desire to drink whiskey.

The notion that eating animal tissues produced animal characteristics in meat eaters was a modern instance of primitive sympathetic magic, the belief that the heart was the seat of courage, that eating venison would produce a fleet runner, that because of its phosphorus content fish, or even Grape Nuts, was of particular value as "brain food." The theory was an old one but rested upon a misapprehension. Why are tigers fierce? Because they are tigers!

As the revelation on diet unfolded, the Adventists were instructed to rely on graham bread, fruits and vegetables, little salt, no cake, lard or spices, and only water to drink. The trance lasted about an hour. Afterwards Sister White was limp. Her face was pale, body temperature low, pulse rapid but weak. The prophetess had to be helped to a chair. But the dream of the Adventist ecstatic brought great joy to the ranks of the faithful. It was electrifying news that the will of heaven, which they had read about wistfully as making itself known directly to men in the prophetic ages, should be heard so clearly, so specifically, on a Michigan farm.

Next day Sister White, who preached a Creator standing above the laws of Nature and intervening directly in the affairs of men, wrote out her recollections of the occasion. The result was a sixteen-page manuscript for the guidance of the church. From this time on, taking care of the body temple was enjoined upon good Adventists as a religious duty.

After the light was given at Otsego, the Whites ate breakfast at seven A.M., dinner at one P.M., and went to bed without their supper. For Mrs. White this was a real sacrifice, as she was a heavy feeder. When the couple set forth on the steamcars they broke out their stale graham bread and apples at one o'clock sharp, rejoicing "that we were not obliged to carry a popular grocery with us." Sometimes, it is true, Mrs. White did use a shot of cream or take a portion of butter the size of a walnut. Under emergency conditions, she would accept a helping of meat. It was part of the strength of her position that she avoided extremes in applying the health tenets to her own case.

The health work prospered. By 1870, Elder White was able to assert that Adventists' tables were clear of tea and their clothing free of the "stench" of tobacco. Along with Dr. Benjamin Brandreth's Universal Vegetable Pills, along with cigars and plug cut, went alcohol in all its forms, even mince pie; although it is difficult to imagine that any of the flock ever got shiny on spiked mince meat. It was a turning point. The Second Coming people were to recognize the body as the sacred habitation of the soul. Here at last was positive hope of saving for the cause those valuable wayfarers whose digestive tortures inclined them towards cutting judgments and a rough tongue. It was the beginning of a unique Christian health movement.

A couple of weeks after the Otsego revelation, Mrs. White received a medical opinion evaluating her dream. The Whites were taking the air in a carriage with Dr. Lay, the Adventist physician. Sister White repeated the substance of her "testimony" to Dr. Lay. He assured her that all she told him agreed strikingly with scientific principles. She on her part declared that she got it all, not from books or doctors or laboratories built with hands, but from the Author.

As Sister White travelled about expounding her hygienic ideas, people often said to her, "You sound just like Dr. Jackson"; so that she was put to some pains to explain that she had never heard of Dr. Jackson's health magazine, the *Laws of Life*, which succeeded *The Letter Box*, until *after* the revelation of June, 1863, nor had she read any of the other works of Dr. Jackson. This may have been the truth without being the whole truth. Mrs. White undoubtedly knew of how Dr. Jackson had put Elder Himes back on his feet. And in January, 1863, when two of the Whites' children caught diphtheria, Elder White most fortunately happened upon a letter of Dr. Jackson's printed in the *Yates County Chronicle*, at Penn Yan, New York, giving his methods for treatment of diphtheria, adapted for home use. Impressed, the Whites applied them and the children recovered. If Mrs. White seems reluctant to acknowledge a debt, we can only reflect that so were Father Graham and Dr. Alcott. And Mrs. White was consistent. She carried the same policy over into her literary labors, which later caused much rancor, and the use of harsh expressions by her critics, such as "literary kleptomania."

The immediate problem after the health mandate was for the

Whites quickly to get up to date. They were not doctors, James White said, but they would assemble the facts "for the common people." A letter went to Dr. Jackson, asking if they could come to "Our Home" and study the therapeutic methods employed there. Would Dr. Jackson be good enough to forward an assortment of health works to cost not less than ten nor more than twenty-five dollars? The day of lush royalties from Sister White's exegetical writings, the day when, as the Adventists' official visionist, she moved with a retinue of assistants—parlor, kitchen and sewing maids, lady stenographers and research aids—on the deferential arm of her eldest son, Elder W. C. ("Willy") White, still lay in the distant future. At this time the couple lived frugally and precariously. Genial Dr. Jackson replied that the whole family could come to Dansville for board, lodging and treatment at "our clergyman's price," which would be two dollars and a half per head a week. Or they could, if they wished, lodge outside the home. That would be a dollar and a quarter.

The Whites spent three weeks at Dansville. They heard Dr. Jackson lecture, admired the general excellence of the institution, but deplored its worldliness in permitting checker playing. There was, however, a smart sprinkling of good Adventists on hand: Dr. Lay and his wife, old J. N. Andrews, Elders Edson and Hall.

Sometimes Sister (or Mother) White—both appellations are good Adventese—went to extremes not only to forbid but to frighten. In such language as a medical quack might have employed—but justified by the urgency of the situation—she counselled that pork was the cause of scrofula, leprosy and cancer. Just recently, she observed, a horrid pork parasite, *trichina spiralis*, the hogworm, had been identified by a German physician. At the very moment New York City was experiencing an outbreak of muscle-worm of epidemic proportions.

Often during the years which followed, the Adventists grew weary of vermicelli and canned tomatoes, zwieback and dried corn. It was a bland and monotonous way of feasting. "Let the people complain of the vegetarian diet, if they will," mused the priestess of the crumb eaters. "The Israelites always complained of Moses and God."

At "Our Home" Mrs. White also had an opportunity—which

could hardly be avoided—of inspecting the reform costume which Miss Doctress Austin wore. Sister White saw merit in it for the Adventist ladies. She had long deplored fashionable dress as a prime cause of the American woman's ill-health. She disapproved also on the ground of modesty. For what traveller who had seen ladies enter their carriages, the omnibus or the steamcars, could not but know that the hoop skirt was immodest?

The principal objection to the short dress in Ellen White's eyes was not its ugliness but its shortness, and the fact that dress reform had been taken up by women who were suspected of being no better than they should be; or, as she put it, "brazen-faced and doubtful female Spiritualists."

"Miss Austin of Dansville wore her dress very short," Mrs. White said one time when the Elder was also present, and pointed at her thigh to show how short.

"Six inches above the knee," said Elder White promptly. He had always been a good judge of distance.

"I think it is about that," his wife agreed.

Miss Austin, when acquainted with this slander, hotly denied it and said that it wasn't the first time that Elder and Mrs. White had made misstatements about her.

"We shall never imitate Miss Doctor Austin," Mrs. White vowed. She was then meditating upon the design of a dress of her own. It was autumn, 1864. Ellen took pains to get the Dansville patterns so that she could be sure to avoid copying the American Costume. In vision she saw three companies of ladies clad in reform dress: one too long, one too short. The third was just right; hers.

The knee skirts and pantalettes for the sisters of the remnant church emerged from Mother White's atelier the following autumn. Since all of the variations upon the basic bloomer costume looked more like a feed bag than anything else, the finer points of difference are apt now to be lost. Mrs. White sold patterns for the new costume at a dollar each. She warned the sisters against trying to make the dress without using the official patterns that God had ordained; and many a poor disciple who could ill afford it paid out the simoleon and obediently put on the tunic and "trou" while the craze lasted. For a while Mrs. White wore the sacque and pants when she preached. But the church found the odd costume hard to swallow. It was too much. When she went to California in the '70's, Ellen White quietly dropped the bizarre jacket and roomy trousers.

At the time when Mrs. White emerged as a couturière, the Elder had had a stroke and Mrs. White found herself on the opposite side of the argument with Dr. Jackson about his treatment. She gained the distinct impression that along with the good things at "Our Home" they were getting some chaff in the wheat. She no longer attended Dr. Jackson's lectures in Liberty Hall. It was too distasteful to hear him speak of the theatre, of dancing, or throwing a card as therapeutic measures. Three times a day the Advent band held "prayer seasons" in James White's room. This, too, led to some asperities. For it was the opinion of the doctors that too much religion was the cause of the Elder's affliction in the first place.

On the evening of Christmas Day, 1865, Ellen White received a "message" to the effect that the Seventh Day Adventists ought to have a convalescent home of their own. The location was pinpointed—Battle Creek, Michigan. Mrs. White could not lay this urgent matter before the elders right away. So many of them were prostrated at the time that they couldn't get up a quorum. But at the General Conference of 1866, she presented the idea that tired, dyspeptical Adventists who could afford it should be treated in an institution of their own faith. Official approval was immediate. The delegates asked Brother H. S. Lay to write a series of articles on health, which developed into a magazine, *The Health Reformer*. The ministers filled the journal with articles about their own aches and pains. Mrs. White contributed admonitions, exhortations and excerpts from her latest visions.

Like Jackson's *Laws of Life*, *The Health Reformer* was a coterie publication until some eight years later when Dr. John Harvey Kellogg assumed the editorship. He changed the name to *Good Health*, broadened the appeal, played down Old Testament hygiene in favor of reports on German bacteriological research, articles on world-wide developments in surgery, nutrition and physiological chemistry. The tenets didn't change but, under Doctor

Kellogg's hand, the religious-medical-popular health movement brought forward a different kind of evidence.

Mrs. White and the Elder left Dansville armed with the new health-reform issue they had found, while the Adventist publishing office back in Battle Creek was stocked with the works of Doctors Jackson, Russel T. Trall, Joel Shew, Graham and Alcott, Ellen's dress patterns and a supply of baking irons for making graham gems.

Both of the Whites came out of the same cultural environment as that which produced Jemima Wilkinson, the Fox sisters and their rappings, Joseph Smith and Wahoo Bitters. Ellen Gould Harmon was the daughter of a Maine hatter. She fought her way through ecstasy and despair to find a kind of religious climax in accepting the doctrine of the imminent return of Christ to earth, as taught by William Miller. It was in March, 1840, when Ellen was twelve, that she heard Father Miller deliver a course of lectures in the Casco Street Christian Church in Portland; and again in June, 1842. From then on she gathered with the Second Advent people of the city.

Around the end of 1844 or early in 1845, Ellen had her first vision. She saw the 144,000 saints who were scheduled to be saved enter the temple of the new Jerusalem. Every Adventist got a crown with his name on it. Each saint carried a harp and received the ability to carry a tune, a gift which had been denied to many in their earthly existence. "Come in to supper," the Lord said, and they entered to find a banquet of manna, fruits and nuts, laid out on a table of pure silver. Ellen was pleased to recognize among those present two sturdy old Maine "Advents," Brother Fitch and Brother Stockman.

There was a throne of jasper and He who sat upon it held a book sealed with seven seals. A rainbow framed the throne, and the throne stood upon a sea of glass. Four and twenty elders, clothed in white robes, were seated about the throne. Four quite repulsive beasts joined in saying "Holy, holy, holy." The dream was about what one would expect of a disturbed Maine farm girl in the early nineteenth century, steeped in the typology of Revelation.

Ellen Harmon was no longer nervous and underweight. She

became a fundamentalist exhorter. Her vocal cords acquired such power that when she spoke at an open-air meeting she could be heard for a mile. Ellen Harmon and James White were married in 1846. He, also, was Maine-bred, and he, too, anticipated the early return of Christ to this earth. The Elder was equipped with the social gifts of the good mixer, the ability to adapt to men and situations. He had a power to sway the pentecostal people which was almost as extraordinary as that of his wife. As an instance of his acumen, it is recalled how, when some of the Whites' old books had gone to seed and were ready to be remaindered, the Elder hit on a plan whereby the church launched a Book Fund. The Fund underwrote the distribution of a package consisting of four books from the Whites' backlist and two prophetic charts for four dollars. Mother White obliged with an inspired "Testimony" urging the flock to buy the books. Elder White would have made his mark in secular politics, but he gave his life to, one might say *for*, Adventist proselytism. At one time the acknowledged head of the church, President of the Health Reform Institute and of Battle Creek College, and editor of the *Advent Review and Sabbath Herald*, White's labors were prodigious. The influence of Mrs. White was ever to spur the tired elder on. She literally wore him out.

The Whites agreed that the Fourth Commandment of the Decalogue meant keeping Saturday—the seventh day—as the Sabbath. Thus the Adventists became Seventh-Day men. The denominational name was adopted in Battle Creek in 1860. The Adventist churches followed no written creed. The Bible was their rule of faith, regarded as a sort of almanac, but more reliable than Colonel Hostetter's which was as necessary in millions of American homes as the "Celebrated Stomach Bitters" which the almanac advertised.

Millennial hopes have had a long history but never a more exciting one than when William Miller, a simple farmer living in Hampton, New York, discovered in chapters eight and nine of the Book of Daniel evidence which satisfied him that Christ would return to earth in 1843. Miller's ingenious interpretations of the time periods mentioned in Daniel and Revelation stirred deeply the theological and mathematical souls of a host of Yankee calculators. Even the Universalists got shaken up and cried, "What shall I do to be saved?" Roadside boulders were chalked with the imperative "Prepare To Meet Your God." Stores were neglected, apples rotted unpicked, children and cattle went unfed, socks undarned, bread unbaked. Devout Millerites either busily sewed on their white cambric ascension robes—or didn't—according to which of two sharply differing schools of historiography one accepts on this point. On one occasion John B. Gough, the first tosspot to make a profession out of describing publicly his interesting lapses, wandered into a Millerite meeting in Worcester, Massachusetts, and passed a spittoon as a collection plate, shouting, "We will now proceed to take up a contribution for the purchase of ascension robes."

When Ascension Day came, the followers of Miller climbed nearby hills, took up their watch in graveyards, ready for the harvesting of the saints. Some simulated the entry of the Saviour into Jerusalem, crawling around on hands and knees, carrying others piggyback. There was a holy dance, a holy laugh, foot washing in commemoration of the ceremony at the Last Supper. Some spoke in strange tongues. Others clapped their hands, shouting "Hallelujah" for nine hundred and ninety-nine counted times. Some turned out with laundry baskets to ride in when they were translated.

Mrs. Lizzie Davis made a darling nightie for the little daughter of Aaron Mason, of Groton, Connecticut. It was of white cotton cloth that had a little black sprig scattered over it, since all the plain white cloth had been sold out.

"But," she said, "you couldn't see the sprigs from a little distance, so it made no odds."

"Aunt Betsy" Farnsworth got a new set of false teeth for the great day and carried a green silk umbrella. David Parsons of Worcester painted and varnished his shay so the Lord could ride in it. With this kind of literalism as their heritage, followed by the ridicule of the world after the Great Disappointment—humor mingled with apprehension and resentment—the Second Coming people became withdrawn, suspicious, a tight we-group.

A new date for the going up was set, October 22, 1844. Again homes were abandoned, cows left unmilked, stores unattended. Some folk lost their reason. Again came bitter disappointment. Angry mobs stormed the meeting places at Ithaca, Dansville and Rochester, New York. Tar and feathers were applied at Toronto, Canada. At Collins, New York, the ex-Adventists fell to kissing and embracing and "promiscuous lodging." Says Whitney R. Cross, in *The Burned-over District*, a history of enthusiastic religion in western New York, "Extreme fervor, whatever its exact nature, had periodically run over into experiments in sex relations. This had happened with revivalism, perfectionism, and Adventism."

Oddly enough, the letdown did not extinguish the millennial faith. Out of the Millerite excitement, with new emphasis upon the Saturday Sabbath, came modern Adventism. Proud, stiff, bold, aggressive, quick to cry "Apostasy!," the sharp-tongued Adventist ministers were perfect timber for martyrdom. But the glories of that translation were denied them. They appeared too late in history for the bastinado, the iron virgin, the Inquisition's rack; too late to be tested by the ingenious Spanish donkey or the diabolical wheel.

By stage, by train, sleeping on the boiler deck of a steamboat, James and Ellen White crisscrossed the country. Mother White was able to say with increasing frequency, "During the past night things have been opened to me." Her messages for individuals and churches, her reproofs, her caveats and *ipse dixits*, her plans for the governance of the sect, were accepted by the majority as of divine origin. The messages covered a wide range of subjects—the printing and publishing work, food and diet, foreign missions, sexual mischief among the elders and sisters.

There was one spirited description of the battle of Bull Run which backfired, spoiled as a prophecy by the fact that the battle had already taken place. From that experience, Sister White learned a lesson, useful to all oracles. She became more general. If she knew through her spiritual connections about the stillness which was to come at Appomattox or the assassination of President Lincoln, she did not mention these events; and later, at the time of the San Francisco earthquake, many of the California Adventists took it hardly that their prophetess did not let them know what was on the docket for them. But Sister White had become wary. She was more in her element in describing the Ten-Horned Beast of Revelation XIII and in issuing instructions for the management of camp grounds.

The Whites were pretty stiff-necked. "Rebellion in Iowa," Elder White once docketed a paper reporting a murmuring among the Adventists of that state.

If the Adventist sensitive was harsh to her adversaries, it was because she had been trained in a rough school. Like any dictator, she could not compromise: "If the word of a prophet fail in a single instance, he is not of God." The flexibility of her position developed from the fact that she held no church office or title and insisted that she was only a worm, the feeble instrument, the messenger of God. It seems in retrospect to have been a far from humble station. "God saw that . . ." she would report; "God knew that . . ." "I present," she said explicitly, "the Word of the Lord God of Israel."

When the Adventist mystic arose in the desk at the Battle Creek tabernacle to rebuke sin in high places, to mingle comfort and censure, to issue new instructions, it became quite a sticking point with some of the congregation that they could not tell what was God's will and what was Sister White's.

When other would-be lady preachers felt the call to lead, they came down the pole fast enough as Mother White rose, almost floating by a kind of levitation, eyes wide open, staring, her lips forming the familiar "Glory, glory." Before she was through, the inspired preacheress was apt to throw a charge of "spiritual wifery." Or, to say plainly in the King James idiom which she handled so cleanly, "That woman who sat down a short time since near the door claims that God has called upon her to preach. She is travelling with a young man who just sat down in front of the desk. God has shown me that she and this young man are guilty of violating the Seventh Commandment." The Maine farm girl knew the shortest way with dissenters.

Young elders, ambitious to rise in the work, found in their association with Mrs. White a new application of an old American proverb, "You can't fight City Hall." It was the course of prudence to accept the nocturnal reports as bearing the signature of Heaven. The Church has never recognized any other individual as possessing the prophetic gift since the passing of Mrs. White, and all of its hagiographical talent has been lavished upon her memory.

The Whites had worked their way westward, passing through

that region of New York State which Carl Carmer has called a
"psychic highway," to the new state of Michigan. When the grove
meeting lay beyond the railhead, Sister White and the Elder piled
into an old democrat wagon, with straw ticks for bedding, a box
of graham crackers and bait for the horses, and carried their preaching to the Seventh Day folk wherever they were, unrolling the
weird muslin-backed lithographs which were standard equipment of
Adventist ministers: primitive pictures of the Beast with seven
heads and ten horns and the rest of the Adventist menagerie. What
an effective scene it was, Nebuchadnezzar's Dream limned on the
canvas, or the scarlet woman seen by the seer of Patmos, Oriental
beasts and dragons translated by crude paint and canvas into harsh
Yankee realities. Against a background of dark trees, under the
drifting smoke of the cooking fires, the congregation scattered
about on rye straw, turned earnest faces toward the thundering
voice of the preacher echoing down forest aisles: "Get ready, get
ready . . . it's court week in heaven."

Adventism's Western Reform Health Institute opened for business in Battle Creek in September, 1866, Dr. Lay in charge, without the blessing of the American Medical Association, under Act
242 of the Public Acts of Michigan, 1863, which provided for the
incorporation of charitable and eleemosynary institutions. The
property consisted of a simple farmhouse and about seven acres of
land situated on a gentle rise just west of town. A windmill and a
water tank were installed, capable, in a spanking breeze, of keeping
three hundred barrels of cold water poised over the heads of the
patients in the bath department. There was no checker playing or
levity at the Western Reform Health Institute, but plenty of old-
time religion, oatmeal pudding, and Mrs. White's pudic version of
the bloomer and sacque separate. A vigorous course of water treatment was applied to the patients and some were benefited.

The cure was floundering in the 1870's. A Dr. J. H. Ginley
succeeded Lay and then departed. Other superintendents came and
went. As a showcase for Adventist teachings the Institute was a
failure. Patients with money were disappointed in the doctors. The
health hunters who stayed always seemed to be the ones who came
at a cut rate. The Whites saw that educated doctors were necessary.

Naturopathy and Indian-club drills would do for the plain folks, but the Institute would never catch on unless it replaced its amateur shaman with a leader the well-healed patient could respect. They wanted a man who knew chemistry, physiology, anatomy and materia medica. That meant something more in the way of preparation than a short course at Dr. Trall's Hygieo-Therapeutic College, which gave a degree for twenty-five dollars and a reference.

White's eye fell speculatively upon a son of John P. Kellogg. J.P. was a quiet, devout Adventist, a broommaker, who sat in the third pew in the Battle Creek Tabernacle right beside the Whites. His young son, John Harvey, was small, the runt of the family, but bright as a new penny. Young Kellogg combined brains, idealism and the faith of the "remnant" church.

Johnny's oldest half brother, Dr. Merritt G. Kellogg, had been launched by the Whites as a medical lecturer. But Merritt had not been effective. He was clearly not the leader needed to shake the people. A good man, although a dull one, Dr. Merritt Kellogg retired from the Battle Creek scene to California, sailed to Pitcairn Island as a medical missionary with fomentation flannels, a fever thermometer and a syringe. He was useful later in Australia, when the Whites were there in the 1890's, and finally settled down at Tongo.

While the issue was still unresolved, whether or not young John Harvey should receive a first-class medical education, Merritt added his timely persuasion; and the thing was done. John Harvey entered upon his studies at State Normal at Ypsilanti, continued at the University of Michigan Medical School, and finally, with a thousand-dollar loan from Elder White, transferred to Bellevue Hospital Medical College in New York City.

Never was the sound judgment of James and Ellen White more clearly demonstrated than in their perception that young Kellogg would hatch out into a dynamic medical evangelist. "God established the Battle Creek Sanitarium," Sister White was wont to declare. But it was uncharitable as well as inaccurate to omit saying that Dr. John Harvey Kellogg established something, too—its success.

The Cornflake Kelloggs Found a Home in the West

JOHN PRESTON KELLOGG was a broommaker and the progenitor of sixteen children of the cornflake tribe. The family arrived in Battle Creek from Hadley, Massachusetts, by a circuitous route. There had been Kelloggs from Essex County, England, in Hadley since 1661. They were surveyors, tobacco farmers. Several had worked as ferrymen on the Connecticut River and served in various local civic capacities.

The first Kellogg in Hadley, Joseph, a weaver, rose to be selectman and lieutenant of the Hadley militia company. A great-grandfather took part in the Crown Point expedition in the French and Indian War. John P., himself, born on St. Valentine's Day, 1807, had worn the blue coat of the Hadley militia before he started on his long journey to Michigan Territory with his wife, Mary Ann, and two small sons, Smith and Merritt.

The Kellogg family left Hadley in July, 1834, by horse and wagon to Albany. They crossed New York State on the Erie Canal and took the steamboat up lake from Buffalo to Detroit. There, J.P. bought another team of horses, a wagon and supplies, a few tools and implements, and teamed it over the wagon trail through wild forests and burr-oak openings, through black swamp and over logway, through patches of wheat, girdled trees and "wet prairies," undoubtedly with "old crumpled horn" tied on behind. The going was bad. It was a saying of the lower peninsula in the 1830's that the emigrant spent two nights at each stage-tavern, the first when he got there, the second because he hadn't got far enough the next day to reach another one.

The trail led to Dickinson Settlement, sixty miles northwest of Detroit, named after Lansing Dickinson, an old Hadley friend. The Settlement lay two miles north of the hamlet of Flint. There J. P. Kellogg took up a half section, 320 acres, of government land. But John Preston hadn't settled himself yet. In 1839 he moved to another farm in the same vicinity. And there his wife, Mary, sickened and died, leaving her husband with five children under twelve.

A young schoolteacher, Ann Janette Stanley, daughter of a classically named blacksmith, Flavius Josephus Stanley, had taken full responsibility for the household during Mrs. Kellogg's illness. Even at eighteen, Ann Stanley was a remarkable woman. She rode horseback from her home to teach school in Shiawasse, alone through the forest, with only blaze marks on the trees to guide her, far from the sound of the settler's wedge and beetle. Those were times when a wandering Indian might turn up anywhere with his fractured French, his *boo shoo* and *marchee*. Wildcats were plentiful, an occasional lynx was heard. Bears still sniffed around the "betterments" for a pig. But most of the Pottawattomies were removed to Kansas between 1837 and 1840. Tuberculosis, helped along by trader whiskey, was rapidly rendering them harmless.

One day, in the spring following Mary Ann Kellogg's death, J.P. hitched up the team and told his children he'd be gone for the day. Toward evening came the creak of wagon wheels at the gate. Smith, the second oldest child, looked out.

"Father has come, and he has a woman in the wagon with him." And then the children recognized her and crowded around —"Miss Ann, Ann, it's Ann Stanley!"

"I am glad to see you, Merritt, and you, Smith, and you, Albert, and you, Julia," she said, and took little Martha up in her arms.

"You mustn't call her Ann," said the father. "Call her *mother* now," and "Miss Ann" gave them each a kiss and said, "I have come to be a mother to you all."

The second Mrs. Kellogg took off her bonnet and prepared the wedding supper. They had corn-meal mush and milk, and read a chapter from the Bible. Thus began another woman's life in pioneer Michigan—the hanging of the almanac from the clock shelf, the childbearing, the round of baking, sewing, washing, canning, threading dried apples on strings, the interminable making of carpet rags; quilts and comforters; filling bed ticks with oat straw; of ironing, patching and mending.

Ann Janette Kellogg became adept at the spinning wheel, pressed and hooped cheese, sold butter (12½¢ a pound), set up a loom in the parlor to weave woolens from the fine merinos she insisted that they raise. The boys wore sack coats, trousers and a "warmus," a sort of belted shirt. Pants were cut out of "hard-times cloth," with a woof of coarse black cotton, a warp of white cotton, hard spun. Ann plaited straw, sewed and shaped it into hats for summer wear. She was an executive, the planning brain, the partner with judgment and imagination, in many ways, one suspects, the driving power in the family.

In December, 1842, J. P. Kellogg moved again and located in Tyrone township, Livingston County, about thirty-two miles from his former home and fifty miles from Detroit. Here the Kelloggs stayed for twelve years until J.P. gave up farming for good. At Tyrone, Ann saw to it that "land plaster"—lime—was put on the fields, added sheep, as she had done before, put the meadows into clover instead of the conventional redtop and timothy. At Tyrone, there came a measure of prosperity. Then again grinding poverty because John P. had gone on notes for friends and speculated in bank stocks. And every other year there was a new baby until Ann Kellogg had become the mother of eleven.

A family ideology took shape. J.P. had been a Whig up to 1840, then got disgusted with Harrison's log-cabin and hard-cider campaign. After the Fugitive Slave Law of 1850, he was an active agent on the Underground Railroad. About this time the Kelloggs became interested in Second Advent doctrines. It is worth noting that the Whites held a camp meeting in Tyrone in 1853.

The medical views of the early Adventist ministers held a special appeal for the two Kelloggs, and for reasons that were keenly felt. The first Mrs. Kellogg had been bled in her last illness by a doctor from Flint, when she was already losing blood from a wasting cough and sudden hemorrhages. The phlebotomy without doubt hastened her death. Again, when the father sustained a nasty axe wound in the timber, another doctor maltreated the cut so thoroughly that it seemed a miracle that it ever healed at all. It has already been mentioned in an earlier chapter (III) how a doctor salivated J.P. with mercury until his poor tongue stuck out of his mouth for days. And then the couple lost a child, a little girl, under the care of a "regular" doctor, who treated her for worms when there were no worms. Thereafter, J.P. subscribed to *The Water Cure Journal* and adopted its views on drugs and doctors.

Ann Kellogg contributed powerfully to the endowments of the Kellogg line. Out of her brood came expansive John Harvey, who was born at the Tyrone farm, February 26, 1852, and Will Keith, born in Battle Creek, eight years later than Johnny. Will Kellogg knew to the bitter extreme the problems of the younger brother. He was battered and badgered by his nimble brother, got the scrag end of it for more than forty years. Johnny, though himself small in physique, was, after all, eight years older than Will. He could whup him any day he wanted to, and he wanted to 'most any day. John compelled Will to shine his shoes, saw to it that he made his manners. It was a pattern which extended into later life when the busy doctor dictated while seated in his *cabinet de necessité* with humble Will taking notes and instructions; or when The Doctor would sometimes ride his bicycle in wide circles in front of the "San" while Will trotted beside him with a notebook. It was a neat combination of exercise, business conference and brotherly hazing. No wonder, then, that when *his* turn finally came at the wheel of fortune, W.K. was as short as a butter cake with his older brother.

Emma Kellogg, sister of the two loving brothers, was wont to say, "The Kellogg women are amenable, but the Kellogg men can be *mean*."

A time came when John P. Kellogg had had enough of scrabbling on a pioneer farm. At Jackson City he started a broom factory in 1854. Two years later he made his final remove, to Battle Creek. There he set up shop again and lived out the remainder of a quiet and moderately prosperous life.

J.P. saw to it that the young Kelloggs did not eat the bread of idleness. At a tender age they learned to make and sell corn brooms. *Circa* 1798, corn brooms were first made for sale, either by the Shakers at Watervliet, New York, according to one authority or, as another asserts, it was at Hadley, Massachusetts, in Hampshire County, that corn-broom manufacture got its commercial start. Here, Levi Dickinson planted a few hills in his garden in 1798 and harvested enough material the first year to make twenty brooms. The next year he was able to start a peddling route. Dickinson turned part of his barn into a shop for broommaking, a good rainy-day job for farm boys. The trade spread throughout the neighborhood. By 1810, when J. P. Kellogg was three years old, Hampshire County was turning out seventy thousand brooms annually, and brooms were a regular part of the tinware peddler's stock, "stacked in bundles on the back of his wagon," says Richardson Wright in his *Hawkers & Walkers in Early America,* "like great aigrettes." From Hadley, then, J. P. Kellogg and other Massachusetts men brought the broom-making craft to Michigan.

John Harvey was kept at home without schooling until he was nine years old. He was a delicate boy and had a bout with tuberculosis at an early age. The neighbors predicted the Kelloggs would never raise him. At this time the parents had become convinced that the Second Appearing was just around the corner. With the prospect that they all would soon be called to "greet the Lord in the air," J.P. thought it hardly worth while to teach Johnny to read, write and figure. A local elder, however, suggested that John be educated, for he was sure the Lord would be pleased when He came to Battle Creek to see the children at their books. The incident suggests the suavity of James White, though the name of the elder has not been preserved.

Like a good Adventist, John Harvey had a dream or vision when he was ten years old. His mother had asked him what he wanted to make of himself in life.

"Anything but a doctor," he answered.

The sight of blood made him ill. His call was to teach.

"One day, shortly after my mother asked me that question," he said, "I saw in a twinkling the vision of my life. I was sitting on the back steps of my parents' little home here in Battle Creek, with my face buried in my hands. . . . Suddenly I saw a brilliant picture—I suppose you would call it a daydream. The barn, the wood pile and other familiar objects disappeared, and I seemed to see a wild place in the country, with a long road, down which dirty children were pouring. They were pointing toward a school-house, where I could see myself clearly, standing in the doorway, beckoning for them to come in.

"That picture always lived with me. It gave me the idea of my life work. I must prepare myself to help children who had no chance. This has been the passion and ambition of my life. The Sanitarium and our College here and our Race Betterment Foundation all have behind them that one great ideal."

John Harvey learned the broommaker's trade when he was eleven. From that time on he earned his way in the world. After putting in ten hours in the broom factory, he went home to milk the cow, bed down the horses and help with miscellaneous chores.

John Harvey's movements were rapid in talking and walking; and he was fast on his feet mentally, too. He was taken into the Seventh Day Adventist printing plant as a likely lad to learn the printer's trade, and caught so many errors that he was soon moved up to the editorial department and set to reading proof. By the time he was sixteen he was editing the entire paper.

Will Kellogg, too, was making brooms before he was old enough to carry matches. He worked part time from the age of seven, and recalled that he paid for most of his clothing from the time he was ten. He was fully self-supporting at fourteen. When the thrifty father planted onions in vacant lots around town, Will was expected to harvest them. As a boy of nine, he pulled and topped three hundred and fifty bushels of Bermudas. He learned to sell brooms as well as make them.

"When I was between fourteen and fifteen years of age," he related, "I was put on the road. I travelled by horse and buggy or cutter throughout this portion of the state and as far away as Saginaw and Bay City. I was paid a dollar a day in addition to my board and clothing."

At this time, Elder White was partner with one George H. King in a Texas venture, a broom factory at Dallas. It was not doing well.

"Hire one of the Kellogg boys to show you how to make brooms," the Elder suggested.

So, for a year, in 1878-79, W.K. acted as superintendent of the Texas enterprise. He put it on its feet and returned to Battle Creek

with savings of five hundred dollars, a distaste for brooms and a
liking for horses, provided they were Arabians. When Will was just
a little tad, there had been a horse in the family named Old Spot.
Old Spot was gentle and could do tricks. The children hung about
his neck, rode him bareback from his stall to the watering trough
or pasture. They grabbed his tail and dragged their feet. They
clutched the girth below, and rode upside down. Spot never fussed
or kicked. It was Will's fond supposition that Old Spot was an
Arabian of high lineage; at least part of him was. It was a tragedy for
the tight-lipped boy when his father disposed of the horse. This
episode was recalled long afterwards when W. K. Kellogg himself
acknowledged the link between his boyhood memories of Old Spot
and the establishment in 1925 of his spectacular "W. K. Kellogg
Arabian Ranch" at Pomona, California, great horse country.

W. K. Kellogg's formal education was concluded with a four-
month course in a Battle Creek business college, which certified at
the end of that time that he was a bookkeeper. Youth was over,
but Will could hardly feel the difference.

"I never learned to play," he said.

An incident which foreshadows Kellogg's administrative gifts,
his ability to take care of his own interests, occurred when he was
sixteen years old. He had moved over to Kalamazoo to work in a
small broomshop which was operated by his older half brother, Albert. W.K. knew from his work with his father how the panicles or
long, green bristles of the broomcorn came pressed into large three-
hundred-pound bales, wired up with No. 9 fence wire and a lath at
the corners. He could sort for size, straightness, color; had scraped
the seed from the brush by drawing it through a hoe with comblike
teeth, mounted on a bench. He knew how it felt to get the chaff
in his eyes, and the feel of "broomcorn itch" on sweaty skin. He
had sat for many a tedious hour, with a ball of string on the floor
between his feet as he wrapped the twine around and around the
brush, and tied each broom by hand. In the final sewing it was
necessary to press a large iron or hardwood needle through the
broom with a leather "palm," such as sailors used. Then he sharp-
ened the handle, drove it into the broom and nailed it. The bottom,
trimmed off square, made the broom complete.

With materials worth five to six cents, and ten cents' worth of a boy's time, it was possible quickly to build up a stock of brooms worth twenty-five cents each at wholesale. For the trade, the brooms were put up into bunches of a dozen, handles tied, and sewed together again through the brush.

Instead of working at a bench in Albert's shop, however, W.K. took a contract to produce brooms, trained other boys as helpers, paying them a dollar a day. This operation netted Will fifteen dollars a week without labor other than managerial. By the time he was seventeen years old he had accumulated a thousand dollars in Kalamazoo. It was genuine working capital, because Will put it out at 10 per cent interest.

Albert's factory failed. Had it not, one suspects that W.K. would soon have owned it anyway. As it was, he returned to his father's roof and business, travelling with brooms to Hastings and Lansing and Bay City for the same wages as he had paid others when he was briefly a labor contractor in Kalamazoo.

But there was a final adjustment to be made with Albert. Finding a reluctance on the part of the older half brother to square up for back wages, Will moved his trunk to the front porch of the Albert Kellogg home and announced that he would board there to work out what was due him. It is almost unnecessary to say that Albert hastily paid up.

Though the John Preston Kellogg family lived a life of toil and strict economy, that was the common lot in the Battle Creek of the 1850's and '60's. Their circumstances were, if anything, more comfortable than those of the neighbors in the West End; for in 1854, J.P. offered to lend the Adventists two hundred dollars toward the purchase of their first big preaching tent. It must have been set up on the old Fairgrounds where the families gathered from the outlying farms, the men in long linen dusters and high No. 12 boots, greeting brethren and "cousins" and asking Maria what victuals she had in "that 'ere box."

After Mrs. White's revelation that the Seventh Day Adventists should have their own water-cure establishment in Battle Creek, Elder John N. Loughborough took a stock subscription paper and went first to J. P. Kellogg. Brother Kellogg took the paper and wrote his name in a bold hand, and opposite it the figure $500; "a seed to start the institution," he said, "sink or swim." It was the largest single item in Battle Creek's contribution of $1,825 toward the new health evangelism.

At the same time the Whites saw John Harvey started on his medical studies, it was also evident that the denomination could not advance without an educated ministry; and so a college came into being in 1875, across the street from the medical boarding-house, on the west side of Washington Street. Here, on a thirteen-acre estate had lived Erastus Hussey, Quaker, merchant, a noted Abolitionist, the chief "conductor" on Battle Creek's busy Underground Railroad.

On the site of Hussey's residence was erected a red brick college, in the favored form of a Greek cross, with a cupola on top. Goodloe H. Bell, a patient-gardener around the Sanitarium, who had been a kindly friend to the White sons, Willie and Edson, as they swung on the family gate, was installed as head of the new college. It was his duty to attract students off the farms, give them an education and "to train them in the fear of God." The graduates were expected to go out into some sphere of Adventist usefulness, as missionaries, house-to-house canvassers or lady Bible workers. They served the medical movement as nurses, bakers, orderlies, hydropathic scrubbers, morticians, keepers of the stores.

Young Adventist doctors could now begin their education at Battle Creek College, in the midst of wholesome influences, instead of going as formerly to the Homeopathic College where they would be exposed to the worldly and sybaritic atmosphere of Ann Arbor. The new college was equipped to give them their languages, German and the Scandinavian tongues, so necessary for work in the primary foreign fields. Doctrinally, they would be safe with Uriah Smith as Professor of Bible.

Mrs. White did not want the college in Battle Creek. She had always visualized it in a country setting, and she wept with vexation when the final decision was made to establish it in Battle Creek. She did not give up. "God," she said flatly, "wants the school to be taken out of Battle Creek."

His will was finally done in 1901 when the General Conference heeded Mother White's "instructions" and shifted the student body and all movables to Berrien Springs, Michigan, under the name Emmanuel Missionary College.

At Bellevue Hospital Medical College, John H. Kellogg attended lectures on auscultation and percussion, ovarian tumors, nonpharmacological therapeutics. He learned diagnosis and "chemical manipulation," followed the dressers into the surgical amphitheatre, studied the museum of specimens. He put his "dissecting ticket" (ten dollars) to good use. There was no expense for subjects. Due to the exigencies of life in a great metropolitan center and the efficiency of the coroner's office, there was an abundant daily supply of fresh specimens. And so, with lectures and evening recitations, the time of John Harvey's "pupilage" passed rapidly and fruitfully. He took diligent notes on the asthmatic who survived his wounds at Chancellorsville only to succumb to "pulmonary phthisis." For the observation of typhus, smallpox and syphilis, J.H. travelled up to the Fever Hospital at Blackwell's Island. And so, having presented a thesis in his own handwriting, Dr. Kellogg graduated in the class of 1875.

While he lived in New York, young Kellogg breakfasted on seven graham crackers and an apple, one coconut a week and an occasional side dish of potatoes or oatmeal.

"The breakfast food idea, so far as my knowledge goes," said The Doctor, "first made its appearance in a little third-story room on the corner of 28th Street and Third Avenue, New York City. . . . I was boarding myself while attending medical college, partly as a measure of economy and partly because I was making experiments in diet, and no boarding house in New York would have provided such a diet as I wanted. My cooking conveniences were very limited. It was very difficult to prepare cereals. It often occurred to me that it should be possible to purchase cereals at groceries already cooked and ready to eat, and I considered different ways in which this might be done.

"Two years later, after I had returned to Battle Creek and reorganized the little health institute into the Battle Creek Sanitarium . . . I took the matter up and prepared the first Battle Creek health food which I called Granola. This food consisted of a combination of grains which were partially digested by exposure to heat for several hours."

What Dr. Kellogg had done was to add to wheat a mixture of oatmeal and corn meal out of which he made biscuits about one-half inch thick, baked in a slow oven until slightly browned. He ground them up coarsely and found the bits tastier than zwieback. When The Doctor gave the account quoted in the previous paragraph, he had forgotten that originally he called the product Granula, the same name as was used for the whole-wheat food of the zwieback type manufactured at Dansville. He was sued by the Granula folks, and in 1881 changed the name of his article to Granola. Granula or Granola. Either way it closely resembled toasted bread crumbs, and sold at twelve cents per pound in one-, two- and five-pound packages, which was well above the going market on bread crumbs.

Even before his return to Battle Creek, Kellogg was already adept at popular medical journalism. Starting in 1874 with *The Proper Diet for Man*, and followed in 1876 with *The Use of Water in Health and Disease*, the first published before he was an M.D., the second soon after, Kellogg issued a stream of books from various presses, especially his own, for some sixty years. Most of his writings were at one time required reading for all good Adventists, advertised in church publications and sold by the church sales force of colporteurs. The Doctor was well repaid for his literary labors. From them alone he could, had he wished, have died a wealthy man.

As soon as Dr. Kellogg had his medical degree, Elder James White importuned him to return to Battle Creek and take over the languishing health institute. But The Doctor wasn't ready. Instead, he went to Wilmington, Delaware, to work on a book, perhaps lodging at the "Hygeian Home" operated by the husband-and-wife combination, Doctors Pusey and Mary H. Heald. The Heald water cure was headquarters at the time for sanitarians visiting the great Centennial Exposition at Philadelphia. Dr. Kellogg went up to Philadelphia to arrange a health exhibit for the Centennial; and while there must have inspected the great Corliss engine, noted the unappetizing smell of the Philadelphia slaughterhouses in the August heat, approved the removal of the voluptuous art from public view. We can imagine his careful study of the fifty machines from the Mechanko-Therapeutical Institution at Stockholm. One had a saddle and moved like a knock-kneed horse, early prototype of Dr. Kellogg's own invention, the mechanical horse, which a generation later gave Calvin Coolidge the daily shaking up that he so greatly needed.

Kellogg must, too, have studied the anatomical models of Dr. Auzoa, famous French anatomist; and admired the natural-science exhibit of Henry A. Ward. Ward was the first man to bring a stuffed gorilla to Rochester. He had equipped Vassar College with a science cabinet, and his osteological work—skeletons of a horse, and ape and orangutan—carried the new story of science to thousands who got to Philadelphia on a shoe-box lunch and an excursion ticket.

However, the tie with Battle Creek grew stronger. Kellogg's name appeared at the masthead of *The Health Reformer* as editor. And in the autumn of 1876 he finally agreed to assume the post of medical superintendent at the Western Health Reform Institute where he proceeded to take what he described as "those natural curative agencies . . . chiefly originated with the laity" and added to them the precision of scientific method. The young superintendent was versatile, intellectually alive. He knew something of astronomy, read French and German, though he was never able to speak a foreign language with facility. He drew rather well and was an excellent mechanic, which served him well when he was engaged in his flaked-food experiments. His surgery left a small scar.

A former "San" patient remembers: "Once when I was at the 'San' the head of Johns Hopkins came out to see Doctor Kellogg operate, and wrote afterward, 'I have never seen such beautiful human needlework. . . .' Doctor Kellogg replied that he had been a very delicate child. To keep him quiet his mother had taught him to sew."

Dr. Charles Mayo was examining a woman.

"I see you have a Kellogg scar," he remarked.

"How did you know?"

"Small and neat, like a signature."

Through Dr. J. H. Kellogg, more than any other instrumentality, the Seventh Day Adventists were an important civilizing influence upon the eating habits of a rough society which in the 1870's and '80's cooled its coffee in its saucer, chawed and spat, drank to the point of insensibility and bolted its heavy rations in silence. The water treatment was a specific for constipation if applied internally; for "the Michigan rash," a dirt disease, if applied on the outside. The Doctor lived long enough, either because of the validity of his health teachings, or because of a superb somatic inheritance, to be a power in a different kind of America, the world of railroad presidents, leaders in commerce and industry, politics and the arts. He retreaded tired advertising men, popular lecturers, corporation executives suffering from "managerial fatigue." For these services The Doctor has scarcely had his due, since the primary source of information, the Adventist writers of 1900 and later, has minimized his career and accomplishments for quite understandable reasons—from a sectarian point of view.

The return of Dr. Kellogg to Battle Creek was recorded quietly. On October 11, 1876, a newspaper printed this modest item:

"Dr. William Russell, at the water cure for seven or eight years, is to take charge of the water cure at Ann Arbor. We understand that Dr. J. H. Kellogg will take his place, an arrangement which no doubt will prove satisfactory."

At this time, it was the private intention of Dr. Kellogg to leave the job after a year. He was late in getting away by sixty-six years. But then The Doctor was always surprised at the way time slipped by.

VIII

The Cable Address Was "Health"

WITH the possible exception of John Alexander Dowie's Zion City, where steam whistles blew for public prayers, the lacto-ovo-vegetarian Battle Creek Sanitarium under Dr. John Harvey Kellogg was perhaps the most extraordinary United States social organism developed by a religious cult and still extant around 1900. The "San" was the result of a fortunate conjunction of the time-spirit and the man. Water cures were everywhere in the mid-nineteenth century, associated in a general way with a nostalgia for the life lived by stone-age man, and a boundless enthusiasm for Wordsworth's poetry; "the world is too much with us," and so on. The cures did much good. It was better to bathe than to itch. The internal water regimen restored to normalcy many a gut long tied up by a monotonous diet, or made costive by the rigors of wintry visits to the little sentry box which once stood discreetly at the rear of every American home.

These Battle Creek hydrotherapists had their own apotheca of herbs, vegetable teas, tinctures, powders, stomachics. They brought out acorn coffees, hygienic sandals, and created a new market for tubs and rubber hose. To those who had not embraced their faith, the practice of switching through the dew-drenched grass early in the morning, the cold hip bath, the douche, the wet girdle and cold mitten, the odd appearance of white-capped lady patients in bloomer costume, the noisy, unlettered physicians, all suggested ultraism. The popular vogue for the *umschlag*, the *leintuch*, so solemn, so ludicrous in appearance, made water hygiene fair game for satire. *The Knickerbocker Magazine* poetized:

It's water, water everywhere,
And quarts to drink, if you can bear;
'Tis well that we are made of clay
For common dust would wash away!

In 1851 there were some fifty water-cure resorts advertised or mentioned editorially in a single issue of *The Water Cure Journal and Health Reform*, and twenty thousand subscribers supported the magazine. By 1867 the tough old radicals, who warred with orthodox medicine, had softened and become eclectic. Most of the establishments which endured came to handle water as simply one of a number of remedial agencies.

Fully abreast of these developments, Dr. Kellogg went to work swiftly to repair the reputation and amend the doctrine of the Institute. He narrowed down the use of water, eliminated the heroic treatments and added new procedures. Hydropathic methods became "rational"; that is, they became the subject of experimental study and clinical observation, used only on prescription, no longer a "course," but graduated, a sort of "hydriatic ladder." Electricity, massage, medical gymnastics, classes in Delsarte were added. The Doctor introduced surgery, made his peace with the medical regulars, became something of a joiner—the American Public Health Association, the American Society of Microscopists, the Association for the Advancement of Science, and so forth.

A good judge of medical competence, Dr. Kellogg restaffed the Institute with men and women whose training had been thorough and orthodox. An ethical doctor could not advertise. But a sanitarium could, though The Doctor preferred to call his advertising division the Extension Department. In the early days testimonials were gathered in from Wendell Phillips, Mrs. Mary Livermore, Bronson and Louisa M. Alcott. Dress reform remained firmly fixed among Dr. Kellogg's concepts. But there were no more whimsicalities, such as Sister White's ill-fated Advent uniform.

The subject of mineral springs was a touchy one. People wanted to know: Did the Kellogg Sanitarium have one? According to a slashing article in the Adventist *Family Health Almanac*, a good working spa could be duplicated very easily. The polemic style gives every indication that the piece was written by The Doctor himself: ". . . take a run of hard water, connect by sewer with barnyard for 'sulphurated hydrogen,' add old boots for flavor, then throw in a bag of salt per week, a bushel of lime, one-half peck Glauber's salts, five pounds of copperas. It will cure as well as the others, and the strong waters will go far to make a fashionable resort."

As soon as he could get around to it, The Doctor renamed the institution "The Medical and Surgical Sanitarium," explaining that the conventional word "sanatorium" meant a hospital for invalided soldiers. As the nineteenth century wore on, "sanatorium" came to refer to an establishment for treating tuberculosis rather than the rest-air-exercise-diet regimen for a general group of nervous and metabolic ailments. The common name for the Medical and Surgical Sanitarium was the "Battle Creek" or sometimes simply the "Kellogg Sanitarium." In 1897 the corporation's charter expired and it was reincorporated as the "Michigan Sanitarium and Benevolent Association," but it was still the same old "San." Whether it was, in fact, benevolent, as its corporate name asserted, was a question argued with great vivacity by local, state and federal tax authorities at various times, and by Charley Post and others among Dr. Kellogg's ill-wishers.

On one occasion when Battle Creek began to talk of building a new water works and a city hall, Post thought his fellow citizens were getting too big for their britches and, in saying so, "C.W." took a neat cut at Dr. Kellogg.

"You will also remember," he admonished Battle Creek through the local press, "that, in addition to the other heavy loads the Battle Creek citizens must carry is the heavy debt put upon us by the Kellogg Sanitarium in shifting all of its taxes to the people to pay."

There were several battles over the Sanitarium's tax-exempt status, fought in the newspapers and in the courts. The diminutive Doctor won them all.

The word "sanitarian" was in common use at the time Dr. Kellogg assumed the superintendency of the "San," describing one who worked professionally in the field of public health or favored sanitary reforms. Kellogg was undoubtedly a regular reader of *The Sanitarian* magazine which covered this field. So it was not a difficult leap for The Doctor, who knew the fundamentals of medical etymology and prescription Latin, and had a happy way with words, to come forth with "sanitarium." Kellogg often called attention to this neologism, along with some of his sloganeering, like "Biologic Living," "The Battle Creek Idea" and "The University of Health" —his pet name for the "San." He presumably did not know that the word "sanitarium" had already been thought of in 1851, the year before he was born.

Hydropathy left behind it the Turkish bath and the memory of some picturesque leaders. Among its more enduring effects were new emphasis upon physical exercise, and new attitudes toward the care of the body. Over two thousand "Sanitary Resorts" existed in 1875, attended by more than a half-million people annually. They represented all ages but only one economic group, "the wealthier class." These resorts, supplementing the hospitals, were devoted to the restoration of the well-to-do who had intestinal and gastric disorders, or suffered from "Americanitis." About half of the guests who went to sanatoria, spas or mineral springs went for pleasure or prevention. Included in their numbers would be the fathers of daughters over twenty-two who hoped that interesting contacts might develop at a watering place; and the lady who said, "Doctor, what disease must I have to go to Saratoga"?

The atmosphere of most such places was that of a vast summer hotel, with easy chairs and scads of people scattered around the lobby, many looking perfectly well, so well that Julian Street, then a young journalist, visiting Battle Creek professionally, quipped, "I saw one young woman who looked so well that I couldn't take my eyes off her."

The Sanitarian approved of the attendance of those in the pink of health "for, whilst amusing themselves they add delightfully to the general gaiety and contribute . . . to the recreation and restoration of the real invalids." They served a useful purpose, too, in breaking up the prosy tale of old operations and the ritual of counting symptoms each morning to see if one was missing. Among those sanitarium guests who really needed medical treatment, The Sanitarian estimated that the ranking diseases of the summer season were rheumatism and gout, malaria, "neurasthenia" (a catchall term for psychosomatic disturbances) and dyspepsia. In the winter time, diseases of the lungs headed the list.

These generalizations seem entirely applicable to the Battle Creek resort. Most Battle Creek patients were on a diet. Women who were reducing were so filled with zeal that they would even take the side combs out of their hair when they stepped on the scales. Those wishing to gain were not so careful. The insane, the epileptic, shutter cases, patients with communicable diseases were refused admittance. The overweight woman and the overworked man were the ideal guests. They usually caught the Sanitarium habit, became repeaters or old "San" hands, and remembered the "San" in their wills. To such patients, Kellogg gave generously of his time and seemed able to exercise an almost mesmeric charm upon them.

The Simple Life might be had at home, too; but health hunters like to flock together. What private home, after all, could offer room service, a "wheel chair social" on the front lawn, a Grand March in the gym and a string orchestra in the dining room? And so people travelled in increasing numbers to the great Sanitarium which grew up around the little Advent Doctor. The good results did not necessarily validate all of the Battle Creek theories. When people for any reason improve their general habits, an effect will be noticed. Hence widely differing and even contradictory cults may give a good account of themselves, so long as they advocate sleep, exercise, and plain, wholesome food under a leader capable of inducing a positive outlook.

As patronage grew, Dr. Kellogg acquired more real estate, leased cottages, added a truck farm, raised a new four-story building. Like a building bishop of the Middle Ages, The Doctor lifted a roof and inserted another story underneath it, pushed out a wing, and before it was occupied found that he needed still more space. There was nearly a half mile of glassed-in halls and wide verandas, in a well-manicured setting of lawns, shrubs and landscaping, curving walks, fountains and gravelled drives. A tame bear, black squirrels and marmosets, a deer from Indian Territory helped to divert the guests.

By the mid-eighties, the buildings were a congeries of "Old Main" and "New Main," of mansard roof and crested towers. Since there were standpipes and fire hose and a stern Adventist ban on smoking, the hazard of fire seemed almost nonexistent.

The structures were described as of brick. Actually, they were brick veneer on frame construction.

The expanding administrative details of the "San" called for a financial man, a watch dog and expediter. In 1880, The Doctor recognized the need and hired his brother, W. K. at six dollars a week plus board and room to be a kind of steward. The younger Kellogg's duties immediately became richly varied. He kept the books, bought the lumber and made the crates for shipping The Doctor's books. He purchased the paper and supervised the printing of the books, and was sometimes pressed into service as a hospital orderly.

"Apparently The Doctor was afraid he was not getting full value for the salary he paid me," said W.K. later, "for he soon asked me to run the little printing press he was operating . . . then he made me manager of subscriptions and advertising of *Good Health*."

The philosophy held at the "San" that good health promoted good morals and sound religion was sufficient to recommend the health movement to the Battle Creek of 1880, even though the Advents were generally regarded as being pretty queer sticks. Evidence accumulated that the Sanitarium was making the world sit up and take notice of Battle Creek. New money and new citizens came to the town because the "San" was there. Dr. Kellogg was ever the gracious host to any medical brother who might stop in for a look at his procedures. The visitor got the grand tour and the professional discount. His remarks, if favorable, appeared in the Battle Creek newspapers, and were reprinted back where he came from.

The "San" frequently entertained organizations—the state teachers, the Y.M.C.A., and the Horticultural Society, a congenial group because of a common interest in the apple. Sometimes it almost seemed the "San" was in the convention business, every delegate getting a look at the Gents' Treatment Rooms and a free lecture on natural breathing. Because of the conventions, because of the coming and going of doctors and patients, all reflections of Kellogg's inspired salesmanship, so much passenger traffic developed at Battle Creek that all through tickets on the two railroads which served the city were good for a stopover. Detroit was the only other city in the state which had a similar arrangement. The old red brick "San," the largest building in Battle Creek, was, as the *Battle Creek Daily Journal* said appreciatively, "a goodly temple upon a hill."

Kellogg was wary in the early years about pushing the meatless fare; and until Sister White came forth with a fiat that meat was to be completely eliminated, the "San" dining room offered three kinds of food service. The conservative table included meat and permitted white bread, tea and coffee. The liberal table, as the polite waitress (no tipping) would explain, allowed meat but no narcotic beverages. The radical menu eliminated *all* poisons and ptomaines. Patients who got converted moved up, table by table, to the radical. There they were welcomed as members of "the food protest."

It was around 1900 that Mrs. White advanced to the point where she saw that meat must go.

"My brother," she announced to Kellogg, "there is no longer to be a meat table."

Two meals were served, breakfast and dinner. Those who had to have another got it alone, on a tray. But the trend was toward lenity. In the present century three meals were customarily provided.

The Sanitarium was not a comfortable place for infidels. There were two daily religious services. Between the devotions and seasons of prayer, Elder Tenney and Sister Phoebe Lamson watched over the spiritual life of the inmates, and Dr. Kellogg passed on a "flash" to the bath hands whenever Mrs. White was "taken off in vision."

The schedule for a Sanitarium Sabbath went something like this:

7:20 A.M., morning worship in the parlor.
7:40-8:40 A.M., breakfast.
9:45 A.M., Sabbath School in the Chapel.
11:00 A.M., preaching in the Chapel.
12:30-2:00 P.M., dinner.
3:30 P.M., missionary talk.
5:30-6:00 P.M., cashier's office open.
6:00-6:45 P.M., supper.

6:45 P.M., Grand March for Guests and Patients only.
8:00 P.M., Basketball game in gym, 25¢.

In the *Rules for Helpers*, issued in the 1880's, there were some thirty-three caveats. All workers were required to observe the Saturday Sabbath and attend religious meetings, whenever the elders chose to sit them down to hear a returned missionary from Natal or somewhere. The workers were at all times to tend to business and avoid "a domineering spirit." They were not to argue theology with the customers, but "to conduct themselves in a manner becoming to Christian ladies and gentlemen," and take a bath once a week. Flirting or evidence "of a willful character" meant discharge.

Many of the helpers at the "San" were paid-up members of the Michigan Sanitarium and Benevolent Association. Equivalent to stock ownership, their membership carried the right to vote at annual meetings, to elect a Board of Directors who in turn appointed the Superintendent. Thus, the help were, in a remote sense, the employers of the imperious Kellogg. But in a very immediate sense, Dr. Kellogg had the whip hand. He could fire any one of them out of hand, and jobs were not too plentiful in the era of the six-day week for the Seventh Day people who refused to work on Saturday and couldn't get work to do on Sunday. On the whole, the Adventists labored long hours with good heart, and occupied with resignation the humble station to which they had been called. The Doctor was perfectly willing for them to have authority so long as they did not exercise it. And so, due to the economic disabilities of being an Adventist and to the sacred character of the medical work, the "San" enjoyed an abundant supply of docile helpers.

Many kinds of workers were needed: hackmen for the livery, waitresses, day and night greeters, bellboys, kitchen maids, hostesses and orderlies, night watchmen, maintenance men and bath rubbers, bakers and hourly workers in the Sanitarium Food Company. Adventists made good clerks, stenographers and accountants for the business department, and excellent salesmen for pushing The Doctor's books. It was the golden age of the subscription book, when rural America was able for the first time to think about

The Finer Things of Life, which turned out to mean town and county histories, lives of Civil War generals, devotional and pietistic works. The goggle-eyed farmer or wagonmaker saw the prospectus of the subscription book embossed in gold and jet, with half buffing and marbled edges, heard the bewitching sales talk, and signed on the dotted line, unaware that oral statements made by the agent were not a part of the purchase contract. Popular health works, such as Kellogg's *Man, the Masterpiece,* shared in the bonanza, along with *The Liquor Problem in All Ages* and the *Personal Memoirs of U. S. Grant.*

Many Adventists went out from Battle Creek as teachers or nurses; others aspired to the life of the Advent elite, that of the medical missionary assigned to some foreign station. Few wished to be lawyers, because of the church's teaching that an Adventist should follow a calling which springs from a love of his fellow man and is of unquestionable benefit to society. By the same token, an Advent could hardly be a hotel detective, nor, because of the Decalogue—"Thou shalt not kill"—could he join the Force. He could not distill whiskey, peddle narcotics, roll cigars, tend bar, sell electric belts, run a floating dice game or operate a horse room. The reason, in each case: the content of humanitarian service was too low.

It must be acknowledged that the pay at the "San" was frugal. A first-year nurse, for instance, received her board, room and uniform: no cash. When it came to The Doctor's ear that the help was murmuring, he would pop into the cashier's office, gongs would ring, and he would assemble the workers for a pep talk. Movingly, he sketched the history and importance of "the work," mentioned rapidly that he took no salary himself, rising and teetering on his toes to emphasize the point, extolling the advantages of working at the Sanitarium. The privilege of serving was real and earnest to that devout people. And The Doctor was at his best when the chips were down. The better instincts of the helpers always prevailed, and all hands joined in singing "Onward Christian Soldiers," breathing deeply from the diaphragm. They returned to their posts with a renewed sense of mission, their belief confirmed that they were making, as Kellogg so truly said, "a partial contribution of their services." The "San" workers lived quietly. Their diet was ascetic, their expectations of life no more than listening to the gramophone, or gathering at the home of a *Review and Herald* pressman to hear a talk on the propagation of the faith in Tahiti.

Dr. Kellogg made many trips abroad to study surgical techniques and invented a number of stitches used in abdominal surgery. He was as fast as Sir Arbuthnot Lane and, like Lane, he had a specialty, the colon. Each performed a particular operation which became a classic. Both required abdominal section, and both were concerned with the pyloric sphincter or ileocecal valve, the check valve between the fore-gut and the mid-gut, where adhesions of the terminal ileum were a frequent cause of stasis. Sir Arbuthnot believed in "short circuiting" the colon. The British surgeon's genius is recalled in the name of the operation, "Lane's Kink," and in the jest of an American colleague who commented, "It's a long lane that has no kink." The more conservative Kellogg concentrated on the repair of the balky sphincter. His work on obstructions was widely hailed as original, and came in time to be more highly regarded than Lane's.

During his foreign travels, Dr. Kellogg levied upon each country to serve the Battle Creek Sanitarium in one way or another. He walked in the morning dew with German naturopaths and, like Dr. Trall before him, made a pilgrimage to Preissenitz's Graefenberg in Silesia. He brought home as curios the tiny shoes of the Chinese foot binders, and made comparisons with American stays and the wedding-ring waist. He collected grains of corn in Peru which were a thousand years old, and acquired an enthusiasm for the edible soybean which his fellow countrymen stubbornly refused to share.

If there was a hygiene exhibit in Dresden, Dr. Kellogg was there to inspect it. As radium came into medical use, The Doctor arrived in Paris to keep in step with the new discoveries, to ransack the bookstalls for out-of-print monographs and to join the Société Française D'Hygiène. German scholarship was plowing deeply into physiology and food chemistry, bringing to bear on nutrition the new disciplines which had already been applied to Biblical criticism and the science of war. The Germans developed daily dietary standards. They were pushing chemical research, refining their methods, as biological science threw new light on enzymes, micro-organisms and ferments. Few in North America at the time were more conversant with the work done on the processes of metabolism by von Liebig, Moleschott, Wolff and Voigt, and Bernard in France, than the kinetic Battle Creek doctor.

Kellogg worked while he travelled, dashing off a medical lecture for the laity, preparing a long-promised technical article on "Surgery of the Ileocecal Valve," dictating a popular paper, "Nuts May Save the Race." He edited *Good Health* in his odd moments, on trains, while the steamboat loaded at the levee. On one not atypical occasion, while at an oasis in the Sahara Desert, Dr. Kellogg took off his white suit, donned a loin cloth, and dictated an entire issue of *Good Health* to his expert secretary, A. F. Bloese. On his holidays Mrs. Kellogg worked up the tourist points of interest, while The Doctor bustled off to hobnob with Dr. Wilhelm W. Winternitz, Professor of Nervous Diseases in the Royal and Imperial University of Vienna. But Ella Kellogg saw to it that somehow he got to see the *schloss* and the *grossplatz.*

Home again with new ideas about Kaffir tea and psyllium seed, new methods, new vigor, The Doctor plunged into the task of keeping the "San" filled with some twelve hundred paying guests. Kellogg went through a number of dietetic enthusiasms. He had his Bulgarian yogurt phase, his nut-butter period, during which he invented peanut butter and "Malted Nuts," a milk substitute which may not sound like goobers but was, nevertheless, the elixir of No. 1 Spanish peanuts.

From the first days of Dr. Kellogg's connection with the Sanitarium there was a bakery on the premises. It baked "dyspeptic crackers" for the dining room; a fragrant place where a West End boy who made friends with the baker could get free crackers for his supper. Former patients wrote back for the Sanitarium foods and created a modest demand, filled by mail. Some grocery jobbers stocked the Sanitarium staples—gluten waters, Avenola and Granola, which one grateful and no-longer flatulent invalid called "the wonder of the nineteenth century." There was some sale abroad. The Adventist missionaries carried the flag for the Sanitarium, and the "San" performed the same service for the Kellogg health foods. And so the goods went to Canada, Australia, New Zealand, India and Persia.

The Sanitarium bakery was known under various styles at various times. At one time it was the Sanitarium Health Food Company, but the "Health" was knocked out of the name by a trademark infringement suit. And so the bakery became the Battle Creek Sanitarium Food Company. A new name was never a problem for Dr. Kellogg. Nor was the introduction of new products difficult. It was compulsory in "San" circles to eat what The Doctor commanded to be eaten.

A time came when the Board of Directors of the Sanitarium balked at the cost of further experimental work. Kellogg began to develop new foods on his own account. The old lines continued, the zwieback, crackers, Caramel Cereal Coffee and Granola. But The Doctor set up a new company to develop his food inventions, the Sanitas Food Company. He was sole owner. There was soon also a Sanitas Nut Food Company, corresponding, in 1890-91, to his "vegetable meat" phase. This was the era of Savita Gravy, of Protose (like beefsteak) and Nuttose (like veal). The two companies were merged into a limited copartnership called Sanitas Nut Food Co., Ltd., in 1899. That lasted until 1908 when The Doctor changed the firm name once more, that time to annoy his brother, which was a mistake. Eventually, through a series of manipulations which baffled a whole corps of lawyers, Kellogg ended up owning *both* the Battle Creek Sanitarium Food Co. and the Sanitas Co.

Dr. Kellogg was also financially interested in a flesh brush, surgical appliances, an exercise machine, a muscle beater, all sold through his Sanitarium Equipment Company. This concern advised gym operators to install a Swedish mechanical department. "There are few kinds of appliances," it was pointed out, "that make as impressive an appearance." There was also an electrical supply company which sold a bath cabinet heated with a light bulb. The firms which marketed the products of The Doctor's fertile brain made quite a miscellany. They were not corporations but operated under "assumed" names, their complicated interrelationships constantly shifting.

Something new was always coming up. On a European jaunt,

Kellogg would call on Elie Metchnikoff at the Pasteur Institute, get an idea about changing the intestinal flora, and return home to try to popularize the idea. And so an associate, such as brisk, young Roy Eastman, then an editorial assistant on *Good Health*, would come to work on some fine morning and find that he was head of a new company, say the Colax Company. Colax was going to manufacture agar-agar, colored with butter dye.

To meet the problem of personal contact with the crowds that surged through the "San," The Doctor devised his Monday evening Question Box lecture, where he could be seen and heard on the subject uppermost on his mind at the time, the Oyster or Uric Acid. He rather relished scaring his auditors, and could be genuinely disgusting for the cause of health as he described the tiny white speck to be found in one's pork chop, the muscleworm parasite.

In the early days of his connection with the Battle Creek Sanitarium, Dr. Kellogg had some sort of official status in the Adventist church as "Physician to the Faithful," wore a special silk robe at camp meetings and was something of an exhibit himself. Once he even arranged a microscope with a piece of diseased meat on a slide in the lobby of the state capitol at Lansing. He made the lazy colon almost fashionable as a topic of polite conversation, feeling, no doubt, as did the Professor in "Back to Methuselah," who remarked to the housemaid, "My good girl, all biological necessities have to be made respectable whether we like it or not."

It was a curious contradiction in Dr. Kellogg's personality and professional life, that he could be the skilled surgeon, the administrator and publicist, the follower of scientific truth, in good repute with the American Medical Association and his foreign colleagues, yet hew so closely to the Sylvester Graham-Adventist line. In Kellogg we meet again the tabus on tea and coffee, the compatible-foods theory of digestion. Milk and fresh fruit are not to be eaten together. Ice cream is injurious because it is an "unnatural" preparation. Fruits and vegetables don't sit well together because vegetables digest slowly, fruits quickly. Legends persist that there was actual malnutrition at the Sanitarium in the gaslight days. The Doctor *was* quirky. Pieplant, for example, that welcome harbinger of spring, didn't make the grade at the "San" until 1907.

There were sound enough reasons for avoiding meat, at least some meat, in the days of the small local abattoir, before refrigeration and federal inspection. But Kellogg's case rested upon sentiment and aversion: a right answer for the wrong reason.

Kellogg glossed over the fact that the herbivorous animals have capacious intestines ten to twenty times their body length, and a large caecum where grass can be digested by bacteria; that the carnivorous animals have a short digestive tract only five times their body length. Their caecum is small. They cannot digest cellulose. Man is in between, but barely distinguishable from the great cats of somewhere near his weight, while separated a vast biological distance from the cow with her four stomachs. Able to digest *both* the meats and the starchy cereals, man does best on a mixed diet.

Nutritionists acknowledge that humans can obtain satisfactory nutriments from a vegetable diet, incomplete though the vegetable proteins are in the essential amino acids. So too can a carnivore. To prove it, Kellogg maintained many a glossy-coated vegetarian dog, and once even tried to convert a wolf to his progressive views. He proved that a dog could be kept healthy on a cereal diet by a dietetics expert willing to go to a great deal of trouble. It was a stunt, but hardly convincing evidence that man's best friend is a hay burner.

Kellogg never tired of emphasizing the antisocial behavior of the meat eaters, red in tooth and claw, in contrast to the pacific ruminants and browsers, although to do so, he had to overlook the grass-eating bull and the morose gorilla. The Doctor's spiritual vegetarianism was a heritage which he could not slough off. It brought him into relation with a strange crew: antifur wearers, Rosicrucians and Indian swamis, Buddhists and antivivisection, alfalfa-tea men, nudists, raw fooders, assorted bird lovers and New Thoughters.

A nimble brain and pen was added to the food protest when Dr. Kellogg married Ella E. Eaton of Alfred Center, New York, on February 22, 1879. A graduate of Alfred University, Ella delivered at her own commencement an address, which was greatly admired, on the subject of "Whither?" For her personally the answer was—Battle Creek. She came to study hygiene and nursing.

Ella Eaton Kellogg was a spry little wisp of a woman, hair

wavy and parted in the middle. She wore rimless gold-bowed glasses and a slightly quizzical expression. It was the face of an old maid of superior endowments. For Ella Eaton became a wife yet remained a maid. It was well understood among Dr. Kellogg's associates that the couple occupied separate apartments. Kellogg often alluded to the reason. In the days of his youth, he said, a young buck was almost expected to contract a venereal infection as proof of his manhood. Dr. Kellogg proposed to live without sexual activity to prove that it was not necessary to health. But there were always some skeptics around the West End who said the real reason was mumps. The marriage was a partnership of work and intellectual companionship, although Dr. Kellogg collected forty-two children "in Providential ways," he said, who were reared in the Kellogg home, sometimes as many as twenty at a time. Some of the brood were legally adopted. Most were waifs from substandard homes upon whom Kellogg exercised his environmentalist theories.

Mrs. Kellogg was the very ideal of the Victorian helpmeet, occupying the second role gracefully, busy with her flowers, running a complicated household smoothly, getting off a social note to Frances Willard, seeing to the children's schooling while she read Margaret Fuller, Herbert Spencer, Rosseau and Froebel. And she did more. For forty-three years she contributed to *Good Health*, believed in Dr. Kellogg and progress, and, herself, turned out books and pamphlets almost as facilely as did The Doctor. Especially useful were her cookbook compilations which loyally extolled the Sanitarium food inventions. For a superior apple-pie crust, use "the prepared Granola manufactured by the Sanitarium Food Company." She also recommended Fruit Granola, Peach Granola, Raspberry Granola, Grape Granola, and good old plain Granola.

The Doctor's wife saw clearly that there was a serious problem in the dining room at the University of Health. When Dr. Kellogg said "eat" to the denizens of Advent Town, they ate. When he said "don't eat," they stopped. But it was always possible that the full-price guests up on the Hill might rebel at the bland fare and take off for Saratoga or White Sulphur Springs.

"The repast," said Mrs. Kellogg, "must suggest not the handing out of food medicine or medicinal foods, but . . . a good share of life's joys." And so she cooked and experimented and played an important part in the development of the greatest of the Kellogg food creations, the ready-to-eat breakfast foods. The Doctor said in tribute to her:

"Without the help derived from this fertile incubator of ideas, the great food industries of Battle Creek would never have existed. They are all direct or indirect outgrowths of Mrs. Kellogg's experimental kitchen, established in the fall of 1883."

The J. H. Kelloggs built a twenty-room mansion in the 1890's on part of the site of the old Fairgrounds where Mrs. Ellen White once instructed the Adventists in the use of graham flour and straight-sided gem pans. The house was a monumental pile in the Queen Anne style, with turrets, sharp gables, angles and bewildering changes in material and texture. It might have been a medieval castle except that it was located in Michigan, was built of wood and had indoor plumbing. Set in spacious grounds, with a deer park, swimming pool, greenhouses, orchards and truck gardens, the Kellogg home was known in the days of its glory as The Residence. Under its *porte-cochère* there was a busy coming and going of hacks, hauling Very Important People to and fro. Seated under the great mantel copied from Ann Hathaway's cottage in Stratford on Avon, Ella Kellogg was the accomplished hostess, nodding and becking, watching the lips of the guests closely as deafness grew upon her, smiling somewhat uncertainly, resting her hand on the edge of the piano to "feel" the music when Dr. Kellogg played "Dixie."

It was at The Residence that Mrs. Kellogg died in 1920, and here that The Doctor lived on alone for almost another generation. Mrs. Kellogg's work had been to make the "San" diet more attractive, and keep the weaker sisters enthusiastic about the Simple Life. Her home was order itself.

And it was sanitary.

Like heavy swells that warn of a coming hurricane, there were signs long before Ella's death that a storm was blowing up between Sister White and The Doctor. As the "San" grew in fame and influence, Dr. Kellogg showed a disposition to minimize the church connection. All the prayer meetings and missionary talks in the "San" parlor could not conceal the fact that Kellogg's medical training, his strong belief in organic evolution, his growing character as a cosmopolite, tended to weaken the hold on him of the fundamentalist faith. And what could exacerbate smooth relations with a testy old prophetess more than to have her own man agree with Dr. Jackson that her trances were simple hysteria? Even the good Adventist, Dr. John Harvey's half brother, M. G. Kellogg, who observed Mrs. White closely in Australia, wrote to John Harvey predicting that the visions would cease when Mrs. White arrived at the menopause. And so they did.

Circumstances postponed the showdown for many years. The Doctor was positively diabolical in his suave ability to maneuver beyond Mrs. White's authority, and world-wide responsibilities kept Sister White away from Battle Creek for long intervals in California, in Europe and Australia. Meanwhile the Adventists, as did also the world of fashion, entrained for the Jerusalem of fundamentalism to get refitted.

"I stood on a stool," one worn pastor remembered, "and took hold, with my hands, of iron hooks in the wall above my head, while my attendant took handfuls of salt, mixed with water until it was like mush, and rubbed me with it from head to foot, until there was a redness all over me." This was followed by a spray, warm to cold, then massage and body oil.

Each experience was a new wonder. It was a grand and glorious feeling to take the electric bath, co-operate with the machine that passed fifteen gallons of water through the intestines, and then rise in the elevator to the festive dining room and sit healthfully erect, radiating literally a salt glow, in the Kellogg physiologic chair. It was required of all that they munch a bit of zwieback before sampling the Nuttose croquettes or quaffing the Health Koko. Dr. Kellogg liked thorough mouth work. It started the flow from the sublingual, submaxillary and parotid glands, a necessary preliminary to good digestion. Later, in the parlor, there would be a pleasant buzz of conversation—the stimulating prospect of striking up an acquaintance with a congressman or the president of a railroad.

A social evening at the "San" was something that could only have happened sometime between the completion of the U.S. rail network and the great days of chautauqua. It was jolly, instructive, morally improving; a group of Jubilee singers appeared, or the Reverend George W. Leitch, twenty years a missionary in India and Ceylon, who gave a stereopticon lecture, sang a song in native dialect and took up a collection.

Another night, in lighter vein, came "Professor" Samuel Siegel, mandolinist. Siegel was a real Sanitarium booster, the composer of the "San's" official song, "The Battle Creek Sanitarium March," a lively two-step dedicated to Dr. Kellogg. And on Monday nights The Doctor himself packed them in to take "A Peep Into a Packing House."

By 1900 the vogue of the Battle Creek Sanitarium was worldwide, fully justifying its cable address: "Health." "Going to Battle Creek" had a certain cachet. The prices being what they were, the visit was an impressive indication of sheer fiscal capacity to return to nature expensively. Elbert Hubbard, the Roycroft Sage, called The Doctor "the Battle Creek Dynamo," and saw back of him "the Sanitarium and a great religious denomination, preaching a doctrine of fear and making invalids faster than Kellogg can cure them. Orthodoxy supplies the raw stock—Kellogg does the rest."

Out of his popular health writings Kellogg made a fortune, yet he handled little money himself. His earnings went to support his philanthropic interests. On the professional level, The Doctor published a technical journal, *Modern Medicine and Bacteriological World* which contained abstracts of current scientific literature, a paper on "The Treatment of Hepatic Colic," a translation of Dujardin-Beaumetz's most recent work on the liver. Kellogg pressed his younger associates to publish. In general, *Modern Medicine* reflected Kellogg's special fields of interest, *bacillus coli*, anthropometry, feminine waists (natural) and the sad end of John L. Sullivan (liquor). Kellogg turned out professional papers with the same fecundity he showed in his propagandistic writings. The Catalogue of the Armed Forces Medical Library lists approximately seventy Kellogg titles. The Catalogue of Books Represented by Library of Congress Printed Cards has eighty-one author entries. And the Kellogg entries in the *Index Medicus* and successor publications add up to a hefty two hundred and twenty-eight.

When in Battle Creek, The Doctor had a heavy operating schedule, some public affair like a Health Congress always coming up, delicate problems of church politics. Each day he raced through a voluminous correspondence with the help of a whole battery of stenographers, who transcribed and signed the outgoing mail. And he had to fend off clamorous patients who wanted only *The* Doctor and no other to relieve them of their peristaltic woes.

No aspect of sanitarium operation received greater consideration at Battle Creek than public relations. A newsman from the *Detroit Tribune* once lamented that Dr. Kellogg didn't seem to like newspapermen. This sounds like a pure fabrication. It goes against the whole, open record of a long and very public life. In his later years Dr. Kellogg would strip to his waist and pound his chest at the mere sight of a man with a Graflex camera. His patience with reporters has been recorded by many grateful Sunday-feature writers. Whether his readiness with a quip or a quote was due to a sincere desire to advance the Cause, or to a taste for the limelight, is a question which different people answer in different ways. "He was all for Doctor Kellogg," one remembers; while another insists that the Kellogg faculty for being in the news was merely an illustration of his practical idealism.

Dr. Kellogg believed implicitly in his Nuttolene and his ingenious manipulations of the small grains. He also understood the economics of sanitarium management. Meat was expensive, cereals cheap. So when The Doctor invented more than a hundred vegetable foods that would make the inexpensive nuts and grains more palatable, he served two good purposes. The appetizing creations would keep the guests' health up—and the "San's" costs down. It was in the further pursuit of this double objective that Dr. Kellogg hit upon the crinkly food which best symbolizes the whole health crusade—corn flakes.

Ella Kellogg's Dough Board

In the Centennial year of '76, or any other year thereabouts, the basic breakfast of most American homes was built around fried potatoes and salted meats. The meal was objectionable from the Battle Creek point of view because the meat was meat and the salt was salty. A man with a thirst developed at his own breakfast table, Mrs. J. H. Kellogg observed, became "almost frantic before he could get to the first saloon" while some good woman stood in the doorway and prayed silently that he might be kept away from tosspots for one more day.

Meanwhile, for convinced vegetarians, the day's first meal was a bleak one: Monday, boiled rice with syrup, or milk and sugar, some fruit, light brown bread, cocoa; Tuesday, wheat-meal porridge, and the same accompaniments; Wednesday, milk toast, gruel and cocoa; Thursday, oatmeal porridge, and the regular fixings; Friday—"as on Monday," and Saturday—"as on Tuesday." At the boarding hall of Oberlin College the students started the day on graham bread and thin gravy, until the founder, P. P. Stewart, filled with benevolence for the less fortunate, rose after prayers and said:

"Brethren, I have been thinking of a way in which we can bless others . . . can we not substitute parched corn for our graham diet, and thus save something with which to feed God's lambs?"

At the Health Reform Institute in Battle Creek, the first meal of the day consisted of what was left after all meats, butter, sugar, condiments, pies, tea and coffee were excluded. That meant porridge or mush, graham gems, parsnips, tomato toast, "some kind of sauce" and a little milk.

"Those after eating in this kind of a way for months," said worried Ellen G. White, "knowing what will appear before them at every meal, come to dread the hour."

The porridges, gruels and puddings referred to in pre-1890 cookery literature were pearl barley and cracked wheat, which called for several hours of steaming in a double boiler, first a hard fifteen minutes of boiling, and then several hours of slow simmering; usually an overnight operation. But increasingly the hot breakfast dish was oatmeal. The reliance upon oatmeal among the Irish and Scotch in the old countries was traditional. At Fetter Angus, a Margaret McDowal, who lived to be one hundred and seven years old, kept score on the oatmeal she had eaten in her lifetime—219,760 quarts. In England, on the other hand, oatmeal was considered fit food only for criminals. A man under a criminal charge, tried at Old Bailey and convicted, had his head cropped. He was delivered into servitude on the treadmill, and put on an oatmeal diet.

Although known in the United States from colonial times, oatmeal was considered up to the middle of the nineteenth century a suitable food only for children and invalids and foreign groups who clung to old-country tastes. Oats were dispensed by the ounce, not at the grocer's but by the apothecary, usually upon a doctor's prescription. Most North American travellers of a hundred years ago, excluding Canadians, would not have known what the dish was if offered oatmeal at a public table.

Oatmeal is not mentioned in *The Orphan's Friend* (Boston, 1845), *The Kitchen Directory* (New York, 1846), or *The Lady's Receipt Book* (Philadelphia, 1847). Gruel for the sickroom was commended by *The Modern Housekeeper* (New York, 1850), and the anonymous author of *Cookery As It Should Be* (Philadelphia, 1859) recommended the addition to oatmeal of a large spoonful of the best brandy, "if the patient can bear it."

Oats as a breakfast dish was first popularized in the United States by a Hanovarian German immigrant, Ferdinand Schumacher, who started a ten-barrel-a-day mill near Akron, Ohio, in 1856. He published in 1870 in the *Akron Beacon* what is believed to be the first cereal advertisement, and so loosed upon us the vast Niagara of breakfast-food advertising.

The consumption of oatmeal quickened in the 1870-80 decade. Oatmeal cookery was given space in *Miss Beecher's Housekeeping* (New York, 1873), and *Anna Maria's Housekeeping* (1884). A modern historian of the "proper" Bostonians, Mr. Cleveland Amory, describes the oatmeal breakfast as a Boston ceremonial. It is pleasant to think of the Lowells, Cabots and Higginsons spooning down their webby porridge knowing that they "do so, of course, without considering the irrelevant question of whether they like it or not."

Through experiments with his first granular foods, Dr. Kellogg became interested in the application of dry heat to the cereal grains. As the conviction grew upon him that the conventional hot breakfast cereals required high temperatures to become thoroughly cooked, he turned his guns upon the products of "kettle cookery."

"The original purpose in making the toasted flaked cereal," he said, "was to displace the half-cooked, pasty, dyspepsia-producing breakfast mush."

There must be something beyond Granola, he reasoned, some other and even better way of making food factories a sort of stomach outside the body so as to ease the strain on the abused organ. Ever since Kellogg had been a young interne at Bellevue Hospital, with his oatmeal gruel, his crackers and apples, on which he gained seventeen pounds at a total cost of sixteen cents per day, the criteria had existed in his mind for a good breakfast dish. He visualized a cereal in a form that would have good keeping qualities, require little or no preparation, would be attractive in flavor, light and easy on the digestion.

It would be "the very best capital," Mrs. Kellogg contributed to the thought, "upon which people who have real work to do in the world can begin the day." The idea must have been in the air. Dr. Alexander Milton Ross, a reforming colleague in Toronto, President of the Food Reform Society of Canada, the Anti-Compulsory Vaccination League and Canadian legate to the U.S. vegetarian movement, also sensed the same need. Writing of "What I Hope To Live To See," Dr. Ross opened his list with a United States of Europe, closed it with the hope of finding an honest man, tucked in the middle a declaration calling for a "Food prepared in a condensed form, exactly suited to the wants of the human system."

One answer to the need made an obscure and local appearance in the very year, 1893, when Dr. Alexander Ross expressed the hope of living to eat a condensed cereal food. It was shredded wheat and appeared, not at the Battle Creek Sanitarium, but in Denver, where the pangs of dyspepsia had pushed a picturesque genius into creative endeavor. Henry D. Perky was an Ohio farm boy who had knocked around the West as schoolteacher and storekeeper, had studied law in Nebraska, was admitted to the bar and sat for a term in the State Senate. In pursuing an absconding debtor to Colorado, he was so impressed with the atmosphere of enterprise in Denver that he settled there in 1880. Perky was dogged with stomach trouble. An expansive, promotive type, he tackled "the food problem" for the same deeply personal reasons which had moved a long line of his predecessors. He studied the dietetics of his day, became an apostle of the wheat berry as the perfect food. While living temporarily in Boston, he hit upon the idea of shredding wheat.

Returning to Denver, Perky experimented with boiling and steaming wheat to get the grain in a pliable condition. While still soft, the whole wheat was drawn through short rollers, one grooved, the other smooth. Out came a continuous, fine, porous, thread or rope, which dropped on a belt to form the sixteen layers that made one biscuit, exactly. There was enough heat to raise the biscuit without baking powder. The product was fresh, like bread, not dried through and through as we know it now. The biscuits had a high moisture content and would keep in a salable condition for only a brief time. Perky peddled his novelty from house to house in a large basket, sold them in a salesroom connected with a vegetarian café. Some retail grocers stocked the item, but there was a heavy return of unsold goods. It was hard going. No one had ever heard of such an article before.

Perky obtained the first of a large number of patents in 1892 and in '93. He leased out machines made by his Cereal Machine Co. to wholesale bakers in Denver and Colorado Springs. The high cost of distributing an unknown food product which, in addition, quickly became mouldy, suggested another tack. Perky decided that the key to success was to sell shredders for home use. The early advertisements of the Cereal Machine Co. contain lists of the strange stuff the machines would produce, including "Shredded Whole Wheat Bread" and "Shredded Cereal Coffee." Ceres was the trade-mark, but the corn goddess of the ancient Romans was not doing very well.

So far, promoter Perky had not visualized his new enterprise as a processed-food manufacturing business. The idea of selling whole wheat at fifteen cents a pound, mechanically shredded and thoroughly cooked, distinctive in form, texture and flavor, without sweetening, long on keeping qualities, had not yet hatched out. The *deus ex machina* which changed the product and the thinking about it was John Harvey Kellogg.

The Doctor had a Sanitarium patient in 1893-94, a lady with digestive troubles, who received from a Denver friend some of the little whole-wheat mattresses which Henry Perky was peddling around the neighborhood. She showed them to The Doctor. Obtaining a sufficient quantity for experimenting, The Doctor tried the biscuits out on his ready-made panel of experts, the Sanitarium's own gastric cases. The patients handed down an adverse report. The wheaty filaments were tasteless, difficult to chew, they said; "like eating a whisk broom."

On his way to the West Coast in the spring of 1894, Dr. Kellogg dropped off at Denver, saw Perky at his restaurant and again at his office.

"He showed me his device and explained his process," Dr. Kellogg said.

Perky agreed to send Kellogg a machine and to stop off at Battle Creek himself on his way to Boston where he intended soon to establish his plant. But the Denver inventor had some second thoughts, decided that it was dangerous to let the ingenious Battle Creek doctor have the machine. Dr. Kellogg never saw the machine again, or Perky.

Just what exchange of idea or inspiration occurred between the two inventors at the Denver meeting, we are not likely ever to know. Dr. Kellogg was already an advocate of dry heat, high temperatures. According to his account, Perky got the idea from him, then and there, of baking his product until the starch of the wheat was thoroughly dextrinized. At any rate, after moving to Boston, Perky did shift to the completely baked, long-keeping product which is known throughout the world today. And he began to use the methods of advertising and distribution necessary to the profitable operation of a modern food-processing plant.

First from Boston, then Worcester and finally from Niagara Falls, came the increasingly familiar little pillow-shaped biscuit. The Niagara Falls plant, an early example of modern factory architecture, was dramatized as the "Conservatory of Food," a "palace of light." Perky advertised the product, the process and the model plant, all of which could be seen by thousands of tourists who came to visit the Falls but stayed to see the Shredded Wheat, too. Thus, and with consummate shrewdness, the tiny filaments of wheat were inextricably entwined among the tender honeymoon memories of countless newly wedded couples who would never forget the Falls, nor "Shredded Wheat—it's in the shreds."

The little pillows of whole wheat came in a carton which proclaimed the value of the secret of shredding by listing forty-three patents on a side panel, a warning to all evil men who might be tempted to imitate it. Only one man did defy the warning and live, in a commercial sense, to tell the tale; the bulldog, W. K. Kellogg, who admired the wheaty Niagara Falls product as much as the public did and couldn't be happy until he got one like it for himself.

Information which has recently come to light suggests that when J. H. Kellogg visited Denver, Henry Perky had become discouraged and was willing to sell out. A deal was almost consummated which would have made Battle Creek the original home of Shredded Wheat.

"The greatest business mistake I ever made was in not buying Shredded Wheat when it was offered at a reasonable price," Dr. Kellogg told an old friend afterward.

Confirmation comes from Roy V. Ashley, secretary to Dr. Kellogg in the early nineteen hundreds, who was fairly close to these events.

"The price agreed upon, I remember, was one hundred thousand dollars, more money than Mr. Perky had ever seen at that time. The Doctor undoubtedly knew that—and began to hesitate and wonder if he could not do better."

In the light of Shredded Wheat's stunning success, what appeared to be a reasonable price in the 1890's looked like a gift later when Kellogg spoke regretfully of an opportunity missed. The Doctor was always determined to find the rock-bottom price on any proposition. There were other instances in his entrepreneurial life when he missed out on a good thing because of his stubborn determination to make every deal a sort of remnant sale.

Even after Shredded Wheat had evolved into the modern product, the idea that it was a breakfast food developed slowly. Perky was still trying to promote the biscuits as a food ingredient, a "pudding proposition." He advertised Shredded Wheat in strange combinations with fruits and vegetables, devised Shredded Wheat main dishes. Articles appeared in *The Chicago Vegetarian* and elsewhere suggesting Shredded Wheat as an accompaniment of soup courses in place of croutons. There was cheese-and-Shredded Wheat toast, creamed peas in "biscuit baskets," fried mushrooms on split biscuits, banana croquettes with Shredded Wheat crumbs. Perky even founded a domestic-science institute, Oread Institute, in Worcester, to train demonstrators who could educate the housewives in how to use the product. Perky advertised the whole-wheat biscuits as a "natural food" which invokes again the shade of old Sylvester Graham.

Disinclined to blame himself for the fiasco with Perky, Dr. Kellogg got his mad up over the episode. He vowed that he would find a substitute of his own that would be a better product than Shredded Wheat. It would be chewable, dextrinized bread in a new form. The first experimental work was done at The Residence. Cooked wheat was forced by a plunger through a metal plate filled with small holes, a procedure which undoubtedly reflected the influence of the Perky process. It was a failure. The bran clogged the apertures of the plate. The next experiment involved a dough board borrowed from Ella Kellogg's kitchen, with Mrs. Kellogg herself helping The Doctor roll the soft steamy wheat out on the board with a rolling pin. Dr. Kellogg was reaching for an idea. It was to make a little piece of toast out of each wheat grain. The first step was to flatten the wheat. He soaked raw wheat and it swelled up. But it wouldn't roll. He boiled the wheat, steamed it. It formed a pasty mass, and could only be removed from the board by scraping it off with a bread knife.

Later, The Doctor shifted to a pair of rollers which operated somewhat like a laundry wringer. The wheat still stuck to the rollers. According to each of several accounts the rollers were turned either by Ella Kellogg, one of the adopted Kellogg children; a young woman doctor, Dr. Josephine Knapp; Brother Will Kellogg; or Hiland G. Butler, husband of Clara Kellogg, The Doctor's younger sister. At any rate, some one of them held a spatula so as to scrape the flakes off the roller while Kellogg himself fed the soft wheat into the device. The Board of the Sanitarium, which was not interested in expanding the food business commercially, had refused to appropriate fifty dollars to buy rollers for the experiment, which suggests why the work was conducted, for a while, at The Doctor's Manchester Street home.

However, The Doctor directed W.K. to boil up a quantity of wheat on the Sanitarium range one night. Dr. Kellogg took it to another part of the Sanitarium basement where there was a set of smooth rollers used to grind up Granola. The rolls, W.K. recalled, were eight inches in diameter and twenty-four inches long. The Doctor put the whole wheat into a hopper. W.K. squatted down underneath the rolls and scraped the flakes off the roll with a chisel. Later, he went to the printing office of the *Review and Herald* and got a paper knife. W.K. weighted it down against the rolls, held the knife as the wet flakes came off the rollers. The experiments were a failure—until they used mouldy wheat. It was a case of sheer serendipity. Because of The Doctor's aversion to the use of sugar and salt a batch of the prepared wheat went rancid. Casually, he started up the donkey engine, and decided to roll the wheat anyway. To his astonishment, the flakes came out large, thin, beautiful, one to each wheat berry. When baked, they were crisp, tasty—if mouldy!

The mouldy wheat led to the discovery of the principle of "tempering" which equalized the moisture content in the flakes. It wasn't significant that the flakes were rancid, but it was important that the cooked wheat had *stood* for several hours. The world's first flaked breakfast food was christened Granose, "Gran," for grain, and "ose" as a scientific suffix which was supposed to suggest predigestion. In an account of the invention of Granose which The Doctor related many times, the solution of the problem came to him as a result of a dream. It is reasonably consistent with what has already been said, though embellished. Said The Doctor:

"I prescribed zwieback for an old lady, and she broke her false teeth on it. She demanded that I pay her ten dollars for her false teeth. I began to think that we ought to have a ready-cooked food which would not break people's teeth. I puzzled over that a good deal.

"One night about three o'clock I was awakened by a 'phone call from a patient, and as I went back to bed I remembered that I had been having a most important dream. Before I went to sleep again I gathered up the threads of my dream, and found I had been dreaming of a way to make flaked foods.

"The next morning I boiled some wheat, and, while it was soft, I ran it through a machine Mrs. Kellogg had for rolling dough out thin. This made the wheat into thin films, and I scraped it off with a case knife and baked it in the oven.

"That was the first of the modern breakfast foods."

Forgetting Shredded Wheat, of course.

Wheat flakes made their bow to the world at the General Conference of the Seventh Day Adventists at the Battle Creek Sanitarium in February or March, 1895, and the exciting new product was mentioned in *Good Health* for the first time in February of that year. The Doctor applied for a patent which he hoped would protect the product and the process.

It was only natural that the first flakes should have been made of wheat. Wheat was the king of the northern grains. Bread was wheat. Kellogg's own Granola was made out of wheat. So was Perky's pillow-shaped goods. Wheat was soft, too. The primitive equipment then available would not crush corn or rice. The Doctor tried flaking various grains, of course, at this time. But the successful manufacture of corn flakes did not come about until several years later.

Dr. Kellogg, according to his custom, was reticent on the subject of the contribution made by his younger brother during this period. But W.K. often described how The Doctor would jot down memoranda suggesting food experiments and send them to him. To carry them out, W.K. worked up to 118 and 120 hours a week.

"He took most of the glory for the work I did," said the younger Kellogg, "I have never claimed any glory—The Doctor has claimed that."

The commercial production of flaked breakfast food began in 1895 in a little barn under the hill behind the Sanitarium. Here a pair of ordinary eight-inch uncooled flour-mill rolls were set up, and a portable oven. There was no such thing as flaking machinery, no device to feed the grain into the hopper, no scraper knife to remove the flakes from the rolls. Friction heated up the rolls. They had to be cooled down by chunks of ice. Cleaning the wheat was a tedious operation, the cockle separated out by handwork. The tempering process had been discovered, but uniformity in the toasting was still to be worked out.

The first wheat flakes did not look much like the present ones. The only precedent was granules, so Kellogg reduced his filmy flakes to granules by rubbing them through a sieve or screen which made them mush up instantly in milk. It was at W.K.'s insistence that they left the flakes alone and packaged them whole just as they came from the oven.

There is a Battle Creek tradition that the first breakfast foods were flaked on rollers designed to crush tobacco stems. Frank Lauhoff of Lauhoff Bros., a Detroit machine shop, had patented rollers for crushing tobacco stems and for flaking various grains and grits before the days of Granose. But the first contact of this firm with the Battle Creek cereal industry was in 1905 when W. K. Kellogg, as manager of the Sanitas Nut Food Company, placed his first order for a Lauhoff Flaking Mill.

Soon the little barn-plant of the Sanitarium Health Food Co. was in twenty-four-hour production. In the first year 113,400 pounds of Granose flakes were sold. Production facilities were concentrated in 1900 in a new brick building. The building represented a fifty-thousand-dollar investment. The Doctor balked when he heard how much it cost. He said that he had not authorized it and that W.K. would have to pay for it. Since W.K. had never received more than fifteen hundred dollars a year in salary at that time, the proposal was a stiff one. John L. Kellogg, W.K.'s son, testified in court later about this episode, "I guess my father did not like that very well."

It was a triumph of understatement.

With only a minimum of advertising, Granose sold at a smart rate, ten ounces for fifteen cents. The word spread that wily Dr. Kellogg out at the "San" had hit upon a magic process which would turn a bushel of wheat worth sixty cents into a fascinating breakfast food with a retail value of about twelve dollars. There was a continuous-flight oven, three or four stories high, made and erected by Adolph Johnson, a Swedish machinist, and an important pioneer contributor to the development of the Battle Creek processes. The flight oven consisted of moving shelves, one below the other, with heat coming up from below. As the flakes dropped off the end of one shelf, they fell on the next, moving in the opposite direction, and finally arrived at the bottom, crisply toasted. For years, a great deal of handwork was involved in connection with filling the cartons. The Doctor was not a leader in the introduction of up-to-date machinery.

There was a strict "locked door" policy at the new plant. During the early experiments with coffee substitutes there had been no secrets, no effort to exclude the curious guest. Anyone could see how the molasses was caramelized or the bran stirred with a paddle until toasted to the proper brown color. But unscrupulous men enticed away the Kellogg bakers and cookers and pirated the Sanitarium formulas.

Meanwhile, health drinks bearing a close resemblance to the Sanitarium Cereal Coffee were busting out all over. Postum was leading the way. Six other health coffees were starting up in the fall of 1897. Employees of the Sanitarium Health Food Co. were now required to sign an affidavit promising not to reveal the processes. But it was too late to lock the barn door.

Then it developed that the Granose patent could be easily infringed. This was true of flaking patents generally. It was no trick at all to vary the machine enough to avoid the patent while the flakes turned out to be about the same. Any detectable difference was due to the flavoring used. The real key to success was good equipment, a product of uniform quality and skillful merchandising. The best chance of protecting a cereal brand lay in the law of unfair competition, not in patents.

Despite threats and promises, ethics, affidavits, door guards, employee contracts, the courts, the sheriff and the county jail, details of the process leaked out. Eventually all Battle Creek went on a flaked-food binge. Speaking broadly, the would-be cereal kings lost their money. The experience demonstrated to a generation just beginning to grasp the concepts of social Darwinism that there was such a thing as survival of the fittest in the food business as well as in biology. As W. K. Kellogg said, in a rare burst of loquacity, "We aim to be the fittest."

But all this lay in the future. In the late 1890's the attention of local capitalists and speculators was fixed upon two almost-simultaneous developments, the commercial activities of C. W. Post, and the significance of small posters which were appearing all over Battle Creek saying, "Eat Granola and Granose: Drink Caramel Cereal."

Flakes of corn, wheat, rice and oats had been manufactured before for various industrial purposes. A toasted oat flake was produced by the Beck Cereal Co. of Detroit in the 1890's. Rolled oats were made by the predecessors of the Quaker Oats Company, but they were not ready to eat. They were hot cereals requiring home cooking. Lauhoff Bros., the Detroit roller-mill people, had branched out into the manufacture of Crystal Malt Flakes. This was a very thin corn flake, uncooked, made for the brewer's trade. The Cerealine Mfg. Co. of Indianapolis, Indiana, and the United States Frumentum Company were also making uncooked brewer's corn flakes. W. K. purchased this thin, quickly soluble type of flake from Lauhoff Bros. as an ingredient in making his wort, or malt for flavoring the corn grits.

The breakfast-food pioneers learned by experience that flaked foods would retain their crispness longer if made on water-cooled rolls. Frank Lauhoff had the patent on these rolls, the only shop ready to supply them.

"Of all the fifty or sixty Sanitarium products, the wheat flakes stood up above the crowd," said Andrew Ross, a major figure in the food business for fifty years. "The other fellows walked away with wheat flakes in a commercial sense—Malta Vita, Force, which quickly followed, under the masterly promotional hand of Edward Ellsworth over in Buffalo, and John E. Linihan's Egg-O-See, which came from Quincy, Illinois, though the company was called the Battle Creek Breakfast Food Company, to capitalize on the magic of the cereal city's name."

The Doctor was bitter about the imitators of Granose. But there was nothing he could do about it. He was spread out pretty thin. All his little companies were secondary, after all, to the medical work, to the broad health teaching of which they were only a partial demonstration, to his operating schedule as a surgeon, and to the management of the great Sanitarium.

The political pot was boiling at the "San." Sister White closeted herself in long, secret sessions with the bearded elders. High church circles, it became known, were deeply unhappy about conditions at the "San," its overgrown size, its atmosphere of sophistication. The worldlings of Battle Creek's best society were looking with approval upon many of the presentable "San" doctors. Mrs. White sensed a longing around the Tabernacle for fine feathers, tobasco sauce and a Pedro Club. And Dr. Kellogg was getting harder and harder to handle. Ellen White had given fair warning. Yet Battle Creek had not listened to her soothsaying. It was soon to be impressed upon the New Jerusalem that when the Michigan visionist asserted, "The Lord means just what he says," she knew what she was talking about.

X

A Sword of Fire Hung over Battle Creek

MRS. ELLEN G. WHITE preferred a purely pastoral setting for the "untaught" people of the Advent connection, many of whom were farmers anyway. As Battle Creek became more and more an industrial center, the venerated prophetess became ever more stubbornly agrarian in her outlook.

'Way back in 1882 she remarked, "The Lord says to many at Battle Creek, 'What doest thou here?' " Again, she recounted how —it was at Cooranbony, Australia—she wrestled through a sleepless night with the problem. She was rewarded for her insomnia with a vision in which One stood in the midst of the Battle Creek Advents, saying, "Scatter."

"I have spent hours in agonizing with God over this matter," she reported. Apparently an amicable understanding was reached. For she warned, "We need to get ready. It is not God's plan for our people to crowd into Battle Creek." They were to be pilgrims, not colonists.

At the biennial General Conference of the church in 1901, Battle Creek overflowed with delegates. Many a weary elder walked the streets of the West End, carrying his cot, looking for a night's shelter, even before the sessions opened. By Monday when the ministerial excursion rate went into effect, and the Michigan Central pulled long strings of loaded day coaches into the homeland of the Adventists, the town was crawling. During the Conference it was decided to comply with the insistent Testimonies of Sister White which directed that the College should be moved to a less worldly setting, far from the sophisticated atmosphere of the "San." Battle Creek College went to Berrien Springs, Michigan.

"The College has been moved and God is pleased," Sister White reported.

But still the flock seemed to like Battle Creek better than their seeress did.

When Noah's descendants built a city on the plain of Shinar, beside the river Euphrates, they relapsed into apostasy. Mrs. White saw a parallel developing in the valley of the Kalamazoo. Ambitious men were contending for power. It was evident in the printing office where there had been too much commercial printing done for Chicago business concerns. Worse still was the way the Sanitarium threatened to wag the church. Most publicized, most prosperous of all Adventist institutions, the "San" claimed all the far-flung sanitaria of the church as its own branches—St. Helena, Los Angeles and San Diego in California; Boulder and Colorado Springs in Colorado; Spokane, Seattle, Tacoma in Washington; Lincoln, Nebraska; Chicago, Peoria and Moline in Illinois; Detroit, Jackson and Grand Rapids in Michigan, and so on. And overseas, there were branches in England, Switzerland, Denmark, Sweden, Germany; in Egypt, Palestine, India, Australia, New Zealand, South Africa and Japan.

However, the Battle Creek Sanitarium did not export money for the support of all its scattered children. In the reorganization of 1897, under auspices friendly to Dr. Kellogg, the new charter continued the tax-exempt status of the institution. At the same time certain other features were changed. It had been a requirement that the original stockholders should have these qualifications: belief in the literal Word, belief that when Dr. Kellogg operated, an angel's hand was on his, guiding the knife. They made a small payment of ten dollars per year and were saluted as "constituents."

Sister White had often addressed words of advice and reproof to Dr. Kellogg. And not infrequently she reminded The Doctor that God had given him the success which had come to him.

"I have tried constantly to keep this before him," she told her ministers.

Such impertinences were hard enough to bear. But Dr. Kellogg was not going to have Sister White leeching on his cashbox. He could tell by the look in her eye when she wanted a piano for the Philadelphia dispensary, and a new bathhouse for an Australian venture. Most opportunely, a controversy on an entirely different front provided him with a plausible excuse for putting the Sanitarium cash beyond the reach of the church's long arm.

From time to time a strong sentiment developed among the taxpayers and local officials in Battle Creek that the Sanitarium was not a philanthropic enterprise, and that it should pay taxes like any commercial concern. This was one of those times. A Citizens' Committee investigated, found the "San" was "wholly philanthropic in law and in fact," that The Doctor received no salary, and lived by "lofty motives." And so the tax issue provided the climate for inserting one of Dr. Kellogg's neatest gimmicks into the new bylaws. First, the Sanitarium was declared officially to be nonsectarian, welcoming, as Horace Fletcher, the champion masticator, said, even "honest agnostics and born Buddhists." Second, to make certain and secure the tax-exempt status of the "San," it was written into the charter that its income must, by law, be expended in the state of Michigan. Both features, The Doctor explained, were necessary to secure, and deserve, broad public support.

The operative effect of this provision was that the Adventists could not divert the money made at Battle Creek to bolster up their treatment rooms scattered here and there. As soon as he was operating under the new charter, Dr. Kellogg could feel reasonably certain that no conversion of funds by the elders would be possible. Never had the skills of the many-sided nutritionist shown to greater advantage than in his handling of the incorporation papers. The new bylaws did not require the constituents to be Seventh Day Adventists, and the further declaration was made, that the work was "undenominational and unsectarian, and purely charitable, benevolent, Christian and philanthropic." These words were often quoted later by Dr. Kellogg. At the time he smoothly explained that they were necessary to preserve the tax-free status. As a hospital, of course, the establishment had to be not for a certain class, but for all. It was not a candid explanation; for later, when the differences between the Advents and the Sanitarium became critical, The Doctor stated crisply that of course the Sanitarium was not run in the interests of the church—"as stated in the charter." The elders had been outsmarted.

Two groups were forming, each around an egocentric leader.

When the bell tolled, half the congregation went to the "Tab," half trudged up the hill to the "San" chapel. Elders G. C. Tenney and Lycurgus McCoy, the "San" chaplain, like most of those connected with the medical work, were militantly for Dr. Kellogg. His was, in general, the party which couldn't swallow Mrs. White's claims of miraculous instruction. It should also be noticed that the "San" staff was economically dependent upon The Doctor. The "Kellogg" Adventists resented the influence of Elder W. C. White who headed up the church camarilla. Willy was a kind of male nurse to his mother. He never preached, never appeared in public, but he manipulated her revelations, and quietly led the anti-Kellogg group.

"Dr. Kellogg," said one of Mrs. White's elders, A. G. Daniels, President of the General Conference in 1901, "has an imperious will which needs to be broken."

It was brought up as quite a handle against The Doctor that he not only kept the Battle Creek Sanitarium funds out of the reach of the sectarians, but rounded up all the likely young men for the Sanitarium, leaving none for the church work. And then he taught them "spurious scientific theories," i.e., evolution. Also involved was an element of economic competition. The pastors depended upon free-will offerings, but the medics had a better source of revenue because their work was income producing. In addition, the "San" received gifts from both church members and wealthy philanthropists not in the least bit interested in spreading the Seventh Day Adventist religion.

"We want one hundred thousand dollars," The Doctor would say, as head of a nondenominational benevolent Sanitarium. "We are not going to be bashful. We want one hundred thousand dollars." He could do that, The Doctor would point out, because the work was not sectarian, just Christian. He even made the division retroactive.

"Although the original incorporators were members of a peculiar sect," Kellogg said, "the institution was never owned, endowed or controlled by that body."

Fulminations and warnings came from Mrs. White. She had been shown in a vision a great sword, gleaming and flashing and turning. It was a sword of fire—poised over Battle Creek. The prediction, if that is what it was, did not make any extraordinary stir.

Adventist symbolism was always greatly preoccupied with swords and flames. The rafters rung on the Sabbath to:

> Thy God, insulted, seems
> To draw his glittering sword;
> And o'er thy guilty head it gleams,
> To vindicate his word.

And again

> We, while the stars of heaven shall fall,
> And mountains are on mountains hurled,
> Shall stand unmoved amidst them all,
> And smile to see a burning world.

On July 19, 1898, there was a fire at the Sanitarium Health Food Co. There was another fire on July 21, 1900, this time at the Sanitas Food Company plant. But these were only curtain raisers.

Early in the morning on Tuesday, February 18, 1902, fire was discovered at the Battle Creek Sanitarium. When the steamer raced up the hill and the firemen saw the red glare on the snow, they knew it wasn't a portiere fire. This was the real thing. The little department got five lines playing on the fire, but the drafty old building was made for burning. It had open elevator shafts, vasty corridors, and even a tunnel beneath, to provide an extra draft. Within a few hours, the great Sanitarium, the Sanitarium Hospital, a house nearby where hygienic corsets were manufactured, and several smaller structures had all gone up in smoke. It happened so fast that the building was doomed even before the long orderly lines of patients filed down the fire escapes, each waiting his turn with a marvellous courtesy, no panic, no pushing, the devoted nurses and male attendants efficiently clearing the building. Ira D. Sankey, the gospel singer, of the Moody and Sankey team, just barely escaped. The guests saved their lives but little else. One patient who did not believe in banks, lingered too long in Room 123 to look after his valise containing eleven hundred dollars and was not seen again, though some boys later found some osseous substance, a humerus, a thigh bone, in the ashes of the north end. They were presumed to be the remains of the man with the carpetbag. Thus, fatalities con-

nected with the unfolding of Mother White's prophecy were practically negligible. Half a million dollars in diamonds were lost, for
this was the period when every American lady had a diamond.

All equipment was lost, including oil paintings with sentimental associations, such as a portrait of Elder James White, and the
picture of old Sojourner Truth, depicting her historic visit to the
White House in 1864, when she chatted with President Lincoln and
collected his autograph. Evangelist Stucker lost two hundred sermons, "some of my best efforts," he mourned.

Dr. Kellogg, who had been on the West Coast, arrived the
next morning and announced that the "San" would be rebuilt.
Legend has it that he worked all night on the train and had a set
of rough plans in his pocket when he detrained.

On December thirtieth, that same year, the *Review and Herald*
building plant burned to the ground and on May 18, 1903, the
"San" was again visited. This time only the stables burned, with the
loss of thirteen horses and a charity patient.

The community and the press noticed the possible element of
human agency in all these conflagrations. The sheriff offered a reward for information leading to the arrest and conviction of the
torch who set "any one of the several fires in the 'West End,' " but
the reward was never claimed. People have speculated down
through the years that some addled follower of Mother White
might have been involved. One can imagine him—or her—padding
through the darkness, muttering "For behold, the day cometh, it
burneth as a furnace"—some stray, demented, Millerite in spirit,
left over from the frenzy of the 1840's, elevated by the thought that
he was the chosen instrument for carrying out the dictates.

The "San" fire was discovered in the pharmacy. Chemicals may
have been involved. The electric wiring, too, was primitive. Officially
the cause was never determined. "I can't be positive," said Dr.
Rand, discussing the cause at the coroner's inquest. When the "San"
barn went up, a call boy made a confession, but later repudiated
it.

There was some talk of moving the Sanitarium to other cities.
Offers were reported. Some fifty locations were involved. They all
got into the papers. But the Sanitarium management finally responded to the way in which the rank-and-file Adventists, the help-

ers, enthusiastic patients, admirers of Dr. Kellogg, and the city generally came forward with pledges of help and money, so that The Doctor, as President of the Board of Directors, at last promised in somewhat florid style, that "the noblest temple of health and healing that the sun ever shone upon," would be erected on the old site.

In Battle Creek, people began to see the "San" in a new perspective. The General Committee which issued a call for a city-wide mass meeting said, "The origin and location of nearly one-third of our business interests can be justly attributed to the Battle Creek Sanitarium." A speaker, Miles S. Curtis, a Battle Creek businessman, attributed to the influence of the "San" all such improvements as the Postum works, the leading hotel, theatre and office building—"the idea of all the food companies came from the Sanitarium."

Sister Ellen G. White happened to be in Battle Creek at the time of the burning of the "San." At first she called the fire "mysterious"; later described it as a punishment for a laggard church. The burning of the *Review* plant a few months later reinforced the point. She reminded her followers that she had had a vision of the sword of fire before the event. Summarizing, she said, "The Lord is not very well pleased with Battle Creek."

These statements of divine displeasure were the cause of a certain amount of sardonic mirth on the part of Dr. Kellogg, Dr. Charles E. Stewart and others of the "Sanitarium party." Among them it was a saying, almost a slogan, "Someone told Sister White," meaning that her sources of information were always human, sometimes extremely so.

In 1903, with the College already moved out of Battle Creek, the printing house burned down, Sister White got her way on relocating the General Conference. In August, the world headquarters of Adventism moved to Tacoma Park, a suburb of Washington, just outside the District, yet only seven miles from the dome of the capitol. It was a more dignified, more suitable vantage point for sending out the literature of a world movement, a strategic spot for heading off calendar reform or a National Sunday Law. A number of other locations on the Atlantic seaboard had been considered, even New York City. Mrs. White shuddered at the idea of settling down in such a Sodom and wrote to the Locating Committee that

New York was too near hell. She plumped for the rural purlieus of Washington. As she expressed it, "Let the light show forth from the very seat of government."

Thus came about the humbling of Battle Creek Adventism. The town lost the Adventist College, its distinction as the sect's world headquarters, the "San," too, in so far as it was considered an adjunct of the Adventist movement, and Mrs. White. She moved to California. Battle Creek lived through the peculiar religious experience of dropping from world leadership to a parochial level. By 1922, seven years after Mother White's death, not even the great Tabernacle remained. In that year it, too, burned down.

Many Adventists, reluctant to follow the hegira to Washington, shared the thought expressed by the *Detroit News:*

> While the idea that the fire was a fulfillment of the "flaming sword" prophecy of Mrs. Ellen White, founder of the denomination, is flouted to some extent, it is pointed out that this [the burning of the Tabernacle] was the thirteenth big fire in Battle Creek's West End and every building save one that was a part of the Adventist group at the time Mrs. White gave what was purported to be a vision, has fallen victim of the fire god.

Despite the origin of the Adventist faith in Private Judgment, despite the reluctance with which the cult became a church, it had been shaped by the Whites into a surprisingly disciplined sect. Their point of view was strictly authoritarian. Instances come to mind. When the *Review and Herald* publishing business moved to Washington, a new corporation was formed to take over the assets of the old one. Battle Creek stockholders became recalcitrant, and it was necessary for Mrs. White to remind them of their duty to assign their old stock to the new corporation.

"Just sign your name under the printed matter on the back of the stock certificate," she said, "and send it in."

To those who wanted to sell out, she spoke chidingly:

"Leave the gift on the altar. It was the Lord's money in the first place."

Older Adventists with good memories could recall a procedure adopted by Elder White when he felt frustrated. Whether he cultivated insensitiveness to the wishes of others, or simply drove ahead in the certainty that his way was the right one, it is difficult to say now. Zealotry has often given religion its sorriest hours. At any rate, when the first expansion was undertaken at the Health Reform Institute, in 1867, Elder White happened to be away. Mrs. White obligingly had a vision that the church followers should take up enough new stock to finance the construction. The money came in, and the building was up as far as the first story, when White returned. He immediately ordered it pulled down and re-erected his way at an added cost of eleven thousand dollars. Ellen had a revised vision to straighten out the record.

"It was an infamous thing," Dr. Kellogg recalled later, "a crime, tearing that building down, for no other reason than because James White was not consulted."

The language of humility could not conceal the fact that the "San's" disaster had not brought the congregation into harmony. The schism grew wider as Dr. Kellogg developed his ambitious plans for a new sanitarium building.

"The great display you are making . . ." Sister White warned, "is not after God's order."

Providence, as she saw it, did not want a six-story, 560-foot long, Italian Renaissance monolithic pile, fireproof throughout, with mosaic marble floors, just like those of the Library of Congress in Washington, with a solarium, roof garden, glass-domed palm garden with a twenty-foot banana tree, Kellogg health chairs and a closet in every room. Here was a temple of Health reborn in a more stately mansion, a great dietetic laboratory, where the experimental work of Voit, Boas, Dujardin-Beaumetz, Ewald in Berlin, Bouchard and Pavlov, was joined to that of the recently fruitful Americans, Chittenden, Mendel, Professor Atwater, the brilliant nutritional researcher down at the Department of Agriculture—and Kellogg, just down the hall.

On the top floor, was the Grand Dining Room, at its head the imperative "Fletcherize," posted prominently to remind the guests of a pleasant and wholesome duty. Here the Duchess of Manchester, Nazimova, a covey of missionaries from the foreign field, Professor

Hieronymous, on from Urbana (Ill.), all dutifully imitated the colony of great apes which Dr. Kellogg had recently visited in Algeria, with their wise, instinctive knowledge of roughage foods.

The new Main building was dedicated May 11, 1902, with impressive exercises. The procession of nurses and matrons formed on the old Battle Creek College grounds, marched across Washington Street through a waiting crowd of five thousand. Many an aging veteran of the Grand Army of the Republic, many a hero of '98 sat there, many a pioneer Adventist——all links with the disappearing nineteenth century—and applauded or wiped away a tear, as the Sanitarium staff swung starchily to right and left of the speakers' stand, matrons in cream white, nurses in blue and white, the gentlemen nurses in crisp white duck.

The dedication was a three-day, gala affair, with excursion rates on the railroads and reunions of old comrades in the battle for health. The occasion and the season—it was warm for May—gave the affair the ivied air of a college commencement, as did also the announcement of financial pledges.

There was a "health banquet" in the evening and the *New York Tribune* noted that "Everything passed off smoothly and most pleasantly . . . without accident . . . or incident." The *Tribune* had evidently heard something. It is difficult, more than fifty years later, to conceive of the tensions and passions which swept through Advent Town after the West End fires. Wild rumors went the rounds as the date approached for the "San" dedication. It was whispered, for instance, that the new Main would be dynamited at the Grand Opening.

The atmosphere is caught up in a *New York Tribune* headline:

DYNAMITE ASCENSION DAY

Planned for These Adventists,
but the Plot was Discovered
Through a Warning Letter

According to the *Battle Creek Journal*, an anonymous letter had advised the Sanitarium officials to search the building. Doing so, they found a large quantity of oil-soaked rags in the dormitory and two sticks of dynamite in the pipe that supplied the building with gas. The story was denied by the Sanitarium management, and, as the *Tribune* said, there was no incident.

Among the several issues over which Mrs. White and The Doctor were at loggerheads, was the reopening of Battle Creek College. Two years after the college moved out of Battle Creek, Dr. Kellogg announced the establishment of a new Battle Creek College at the old location. It was needed, The Doctor explained, because the medical work required a good college. The "San" continued to attract four hundred to five hundred young men and women to Battle Creek to take care of the patients. It was necessary to offer them educational opportunities. The coin also had another side. The college students provided the "San" with a reservoir of low-cost labor.

"It is not necessary for so many of our youth to study medicine," Sister White rejoined. "By fire, the Lord removed the great argument in favor of gathering many students to Battle Creek."

But The Doctor had a charter, the Board, and physical possession. He appealed directly to the Seventh Day folk for money, and got it. And so, a new Battle Creek College came into being. Here, then, a cook or vegetable scrubber at the Sanitarium could attend a liberal arts college fully accredited by the North Central Association, and prepare to head the medical institutions of the future.

Into the second Battle Creek College were combined the Sanitarium's School of Home Economics, the School of Nursing and the School of Physical Education. Since a kind heart and a strong back were not substitutes for technical training, Dr. Kellogg had organized these facilities back in the 1880's to prepare therapists, dieticians and physical education instructors to staff the "San" and to go out into the medical missionary field. Dr. Kellogg also established, in 1893, the American Missionary College in Chicago, carrying the work of Battle Creek College on to a professional level. Preclinical work was done at Battle Creek. But Battle Creek could not handle a full-fledged medical school: not enough cadavers. The Chicago medical school existed until 1908 when, with a gradual loss of Adventist support and heavy pressure from the American Medical Association for higher standards, this branch of Battle Creek College was absorbed into the University of Illinois.

As Founder, first President and Chairman of the Board of Trustees, Dr. Kellogg was the whole show at Battle Creek College, as he had always been at the Sanitarium. In 1925, he persuaded Dr. Paul Voelker, President of Olivet College, to assume the Presidency at Battle Creek, and at Dr. Voelker's insistence a liberal arts course for men and women was added. The principal source of income for the college, other than tuition, was the Race Betterment Foundation, which controlled the Battle Creek Food Company. Since Dr. Kellogg arranged all these ingenious interrelationships, he held the purse strings, for it was, actually, his book royalties, the profits from his foods and other inventions, to the extent of about sixty thousand dollars a year, which footed the bill at the end of each college year. And he had more than a million dollars invested in the physical plant of the College. According to Battle Creek folklore, W. K. Kellogg would have given the college a million dollars any time that John Harvey would humble himself to ask for it. That time never came.

The health gospel of the Kellogg Sanitarium was, of course, rigorously enforced at the Kellogg College. There was no smoking. Even the employment contract for professors contained some peculiar language, a kind of "biologic clause," which permitted their summary dismissal if it became publicly known that they smoked or shook up a cocktail. The faculty smoked in the back rooms of their houses, of course, chewed Sen-Sen and dispensed vegetarian hospitality when guests came to dinner. From time to time Dr. Kellogg, as President of the Board of Trustees, would convoke the faculty and lecture them on their posture. With a chair mounted upon a table, he climbed up to show his professors how to sit. Grizzled survivors acknowledge that faculty meetings at Battle Creek College were an unforgettable experience. The college closed in 1938 under peculiar circumstances which will be set forth later. The United States Army demolished it in 1943 in connection with some abortive, now-forgotten plan which left the old site bare and cindery.

Dr. Kellogg unwittingly stirred up a doctrinal hurricane in connection with the fund-raising plans for the new "San" building.

The church had agreed to get up five hundred thousand dollars with the understanding that Dr. Kellogg would write a book and contribute its earnings to the building fund. The Adventists undertook to put their canvassers to work selling the book, and expected to move five hundred thousand copies at a dollar each. Dr. Kellogg obliged with a manuscript entitled *The Living Temple*, a health work about the structure, function and care of the body, with religious overtones. The book was printed and put on sale by the Adventists, according to plan. The Doctor referred to *The Living Temple* as "this little volume." Actually, it was a big, fat, diffuse, 568-page octavo—a book agent's dream in weight and wordage. All went well for a while. Then Elder W. W. Prescott caught a whiff of pantheism as he went through the book.

"It is God in the sunflower that makes it follow the sun," he read, his eyes popping. God was in the drop of water, the snow crystal, the instinct which guides the wasp in building its paper cells. Sweet mystery of life—what next! The digestive process, the text continued, was itself a sign of divinity through the striking arrangement whereby the stomach is able to digest flesh identical with its own substance, yet does not digest itself.

Prescott hurriedly called together his associates. When the heads of the Seventh Day Church read that the ability of a cat to find her way home was the voice of God, they were sure The Doctor was off his rocker. Whatever this stuff was, it wasn't the Advent's Bible, the word-for-word and cover-to-cover literal voice of God. There was nothing in the Good Book about inspired wasps or divine cats.

Prescott hastily pronounced *The Living Temple* heretical. Mother White confirmed the verdict. The book was full of mysticism and "snares," she said. The "San" had become headquarters indeed for apostasy. This charge, the heaviest she could make, indicated that she was about ready to lower the boom on Dr. Kellogg. She had a nocturnal visitation about the book. There was a big meeting and "The Instructor" showed that Dr. Kellogg had misquoted the Bible for his own purposes, just as the Devil was known to do, using "smooth words and fair speeches"; and the speaker held up the Kellogg opus and said the author didn't understand it himself. Poor Kellogg! He wanted his new Sanitarium. So he humbly recalled the book, revised it, purged it and retitled it *The Miracle of Life*. The Doctor brought science into harmony with the old-time religion, endorsed the orthodox Seventh Day Adventist theology, subscribed to the idea of a personal Creator, abjured theosophy or Christian Science, and cast grave doubt upon the theory of evolution. No book primarily concerned with anatomy and physiology ever contained a higher content of traditional supernaturalist piety. Encouraged by The Doctor's compliance, Sister White requested the officers of the General Conference to examine the situation of the Sanitarium exhaustively.

"See whether the God of heaven can take control of it."

Mother White was getting old. Sometimes she nodded and repeated herself and had to be helped down from the desk on Sabbath mornings when she couldn't get on with her discourse. But she hadn't given up hope that her writ might run again up at the "San."

Mrs. White had once thought seriously of making Dr. Kellogg a reverend. There were precedents. Primitive medicine had always been sacerdotal. Any such idea evaporated after the "San" was rebuilt against Mrs. White's dictates, followed up with such a serious *faux pas* as *The Living Temple*.

If there had been any possibility of a peaceful coexistence, it vanished in the autumn of 1907 when a daring little pamphlet appeared, locally famous as the "blue book," because its cover was blue. It was entitled *Responses to an Urgent Testimony from Mrs. Ellen G. White Concerning Contradictions, Inconsistencies and Other Errors in Her Writings*. The authorship was generally attributed to Dr. Charles E. Stewart, one of Dr. Kellogg's most trusted associates. The background was this. Mrs. White had invited Dr. Kellogg and all who doubted the infallibility of her inspired communications, to inform her of their perplexities and specify their criticisms. The book manuscript was sent to her in private through Elder William C. White. But no explanations ever followed. After a month had passed with no response, the pamphlet was made public. It showed that Sister White cribbed from other writers and was, in general, a fraud and a hoax. The author did not call Ellen a plagiarist. He just printed the data in parallel columns.

The pamphlet was considered to represent the Sanitarium point of view.

Later, in response to questioners, Dr. Stewart described Mrs. White as "a good, kind-hearted old lady."

Did he feel she received visions from on high?

"Well—that is another matter. I believe she is a victim of auto-hypnotism. She has actually hypnotised herself into believing that these visions are genuine. I don't think she willingly sets out to deceive—she's gotten into this visionary habit—but I do blame those who foist upon the people a scheme which is nothing more or less than a gross fraud."

During the summer of 1907 a preliminary operation was carried out, which an elder described as "cleaning off the barnacles" on the church. Among the "barnacles" were W. K. Kellogg, Judge Jesse Arthur, and various members who had failed in financial support, choked at theological technicalities, or played ball on Saturday. Implicit was the split between the strict church party and the Sanitarium element. In October, a church committee inquired into Dr. Kellogg's views on Mrs. White's divinity. It was an ex parte proceeding, an ordeal lasting for eight hours. The Doctor was his own and the only witness against a marshalling of all that the elders could bring against him. The stenographic report came to 164 pages. The Doctor was fluent and pointed, handled himself superbly under unfavorable conditions and before a patently hostile group of the godly party. Speaking of Mrs. White, he allowed that she was, or wanted to be, a good Christian woman, but wasn't infallible and had always been used, first by her husband, later by others.

"I do not believe in Mrs. White's infallibility, and never did," said Kellogg flatly.

A month later, behind locked doors, at which some Adventists vainly knocked, Dr. Kellogg and his loyal Elder Tenney were expelled from the church. Reasons given ranged from leading a movement to undermine the tenets of the church to disrespect toward Mrs. White. The real intention was to cut The Doctor down to size.

Kellogg was unusually reticent about being disfellowshipped. "Not a word, sir, nothing at all," he said to a questioner, and added, "There will be no change at the Sanitarium; things will go right on just as before," as he ducked through a side door.

The famous family of Kellogg foster children withdrew from the church school, but continued to observe Saturday as the Sabbath. The religious atmosphere at the Sanitarium remained unchanged at the time, though later, by a gradual relaxation of Sabbatarian rigor, the management accommodated themselves to both Saturday and Sunday keepers.

Both sides disengaged with acrimony and bitterness.

"I wish they wouldn't tell lies," Dr. Kellogg finally said.

And the opposition pointed out:

"Dr. Kellogg's reputation and fame were made by Mrs. White and her husband and now he turns around to revile her. . . . Poor, is he? Well, I guess he has pots of money stored away, and we Adventists sold his books for him and helped make him rich."

The *Detroit Free Press* speculated: ". . . there are those who say he's glad because the severance with the church adds to his professional dignity and prestige, and that he has only kept silent regarding the frauds of Mrs. White so long because in his youth she befriended him and he does not want to see her reviled and humbled in her old age."

On balance, it was a relief to be free of the Adventist tag. The scattered church sanitaria abruptly ceased to be Battle Creek "branches." The Battle Creek Sanitarium, said The Doctor, "has no connection with any so-called Battle Creek 'Treatment Rooms.' " When he felt like it, Kellogg could play as rough as any elder.

It was a relief to be finally finished with theological quiddities. Now Kellogg would be able to question a fundamentalist, if he felt like it, and he sometimes did, in some such manner as this:

"Do you believe in a personal God? Can you picture Him to me? How tall is He? How old? What color is His hair? His eyes? Does He have bowels? Does he defecate?"

When The Doctor's shocked conversationalist whispered hurriedly, as he was apt to do, "No—no—" Kellogg replied triumphantly:

"Well, I do. So He is not as wonderful as I am."

For Dr. Kellogg, as for Leonardo long ago, the human organism was a marvel, astounding in its functions; "that true bible, the human body," as Vesalius, founder of modern physiology, called it, speaking out with the deep piety of the rigorous observer of fact.

With separation of church and Sanitarium, Dr. Kellogg would have the time to munch an apple, catch up on the latest work in physiological chemistry of Mendel, of Osborne, of McCollum down at Johns Hopkins, or try out a new hygienic candy on office visitors. More vigorously than ever, the Battle Creek Sanitarium would take the high, hygienic ground, a free, self-supporting protest, a unique reformatory enterprise. The Doctor was demonstrably not a good Adventist from the point of view of the Sanhedrin. But deep in him there remained forever something of the fervor of the millennial move of '44.

Down the hall he could see the boys who hopped bells sitting on the long benches in back of the main desk, clad in natty green uniforms, with "No. 2," or whatever the number was, inside a laurel wreath embroidered over the left breast. The alert bell captain sat at his tall desk on a high chair. "Ice water," he would sing out. "Boy for wheel chair." "Take a wheel chair from Main to Surgical." No. 5 was to carry a specimen across the street to the college laboratory for analysis. The parlors were crowded, bookings never better. Old-timers, patients who knew the old "San" before the fire, like Lucy Page Gaston, President of the Anti-Cigarette League, were faithful still. William Jennings Bryan was coming soon, full of grape juice and theories. A food broker had just checked in from North Carolina. He might like to meet Harry Byrd or William Gibbs McAdoo, and take on the Battle Creek Sanitarium line of dietetic foods, too.

There were still plenty of decisions and problems. Should The Doctor buy a rotary cooker for the food company? A linotype machine for *Good Health*? Brother Will was cutting up real rusty. John Harvey and Will K. were in a new venture together. The time had come, W. K. insisted, to push corn flakes, or C. W. Post, the big gun of the Battle Creek food industry, would run away with the idea—if, indeed, he had not already done so with his Elijah's Manna.

As a result of W. K. Kellogg's initiative, the Battle Creek Toasted Corn Flake Company was started. The Doctor was the principal—but this time not the sole—proprietor. This new circumstance was to make a great deal of difference. Already there were opposing points of view. It was a question, whether to conciliate W. K. or teach him a lesson, as the older Johnny had done many a time in days gone by.

Dr. Kellogg finished his apple, took off his eye shade, lay down on the floor of his office and raised his arms above his head. He could think better that way.

1. Sylvester Graham, whose name was once enough
to start an argument or a riot. He advocated the
"Grahamite" diet in an atmosphere of sublimated
puritanism; his memory is preserved in the terms
"graham flour" and "graham crackers."

2. The pattern for many developments later associated
with Battle Creek was cut at
Dansville, New York, by Dr.
James Caleb Jackson, notably
in his personal leadership, his
medical theories, his health
propaganda and his pioneer-
ing efforts to develop ready-
to-eat breakfast foods.

3. Miss Doctor Harriet Austin is shown modeling "The American Costume," her version of the bloomer outfit, which was "favored by patients in sanatoriums." Is it really so very different from what the fashion writers now recommend for a cozy evening around the television set?

Grunt tries Hydropathy. What-a-cure for a pain!

4. An expression of mid-nineteenth-century medical realism, hydropathy was taken up by many clever charlatans who made the treatment a cure-all. Satire was the inevitable result.

THE WATER-CURE JOURNAL.

36

Fig. 1.   Fig. 2.   Fig. 3.   Fig. 4.   Fig. 5.

5. When Mrs. Ellen G. White, the Battle Creek prophetess, railed against corsets, hoops and long dresses, numerous coterie journals joined in to reinforce the point with argument and ridicule leveled at the world of fashion. But the feminine heart still got a naughty lift at the swoosh of a bouffant skirt over a ruffled petticoat with that "stand-alone" look.

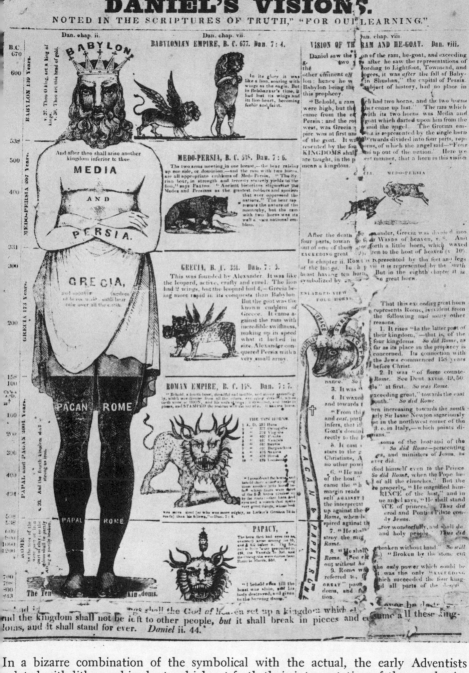

In a bizarre combination of the symbolical with the actual, the early Adventists selyted with lithographic charts which set forth their interpretation of the prophecies the Books of Daniel and Revelations; while the rugged elders unkindly predicted that sickle of the Lord would soon mow down the Sunday-keepers until the blood ran up the horse bridles.

7. Mrs. Ellen G. White in the days of her power and vigor, preaching from the desk
the "dime" Tabernacle where she frequently mingled comfort and reproof. She
remembered now for her extraordinary pretensions, her good work in promoting brea
fast foods, fresh air, frequent bathing, and swatting the housefly. One of her books so
over a half-million copies in 1956.

8. An early view of the Battle Creek Sanitarium buildings which burned in 1902. He
the spirit learned to soar, the mind absorbed information, and the stomach and bowe
got educated, too.

9. Surgeon, administrator, educator, health evangelist, inventor and founder of the breakfast-food industry of Battle Creek, Dr. John Harvey Kellogg was a man of high competence in many—perhaps too many—fields.

Battle Creek Sanitarium

DINNER

Sunday, April 28, 1912

		Protein	Fats	Carbo.	Oz.	Portion
SOUPS	Tomato Bisque	14	50	11	4¾	¾
	Savory Potato Soup	11	26	38	4¾	¾
ENTREES	Protose Fillets	43	46	36	4	1¼
	Nuttolene—Apple Sauce	29	56	40	3	1¼
	Rice a la Carolina	13	63	74	3	1½
VEGETABLES	Baked Potatoes	11	1	88	3	1
	Brown Sauce	3	64	8	2¼	¾
	Escalloped Potatoes	15	45	90	4½	1½
	Creamed Parsnips	7	16	52	3	¾
	Fresh Asparagus	5	15	5	1	¼
RELISHES	Lettuce—Lemon	2	1	7	1¼	1/10
	Tomato Jelly—Mayonnaise	12	6	32	3½	½
	Cabbage Salad	4	30	16	2	½
	Malt Honey	0	0	200	2¼	2
	Malt Honey with Butter	0	100	100	1½	2
	Malt Sugar	3	16	81	⅞	1
BREADS	Whole Wheat Bread—1 slice	12	2	61	1	¾
	White Bread—1 slice	9	4	62	1	¾
	Entire Graham Bread—1 slice	10	4	61	1	¾
	Breakfast Toast—2 pieces	4	12	34	½	½
	Toasted Granose Biscuit—two	7	1	42	½	½
	Toasted Rice Biscuit—two	4	0	46	½	½
	Bran Biscuit—two	21	31	73	1	1¼
	Nut Butter	28	105	17	1	1½
	Dairy Butter—1 square	1	99	0	½	1
COOKED FRUITS	Cherry Sauce	4	6	90	3	1
	Stewed Figs	6	1	143	3	1½
BEVERAGES	Apple Juice	0	0	50	3½	½
	Grape Juice	0	0	50	3½	½
	Caramel Cereal—1 teacupful	1	1	8	4	1/10
	Cream—1 pitcherful	6	107	12	2¼	1¼
	Sugar—1 sugarspoonful	0	0	25	⅓	¼
	Kaffir Tea	1	1	8	4	1/10
	Sanitas Cocoa	13	89	23	5	2¼
	Hot Malted Nuts	36	96	68	1¼	2
	Milk	23	67	35	6	1¼
	Yogurt Buttermilk	28	5	42	6	¾
DESSERTS	Date Cream Pie	42	87	171	4	3
	Oranges	4	2	69	5	¾
	English Walnuts	9	82	9	½	1

d

To ascertain the number of calories eaten of each element, add the figures in first, second and third columns, opposite the various articles eaten and put down the sums at the foot of the respective columns. Mark each article eaten, sign bill of fare, and hand to your physician.

A "portion" is that quantity of any food which contains 100 calories or food units. No food to be taken from the Dining-room.

NAME.................................... ROOM..................

10. Nut and grain preparations, scalloped, purėed, sprinkled with peanut meal, all the children of Dr. Kellogg's ingenious brain, dominated the "San's" cuisine under various coy disguises. They were measured out in exact quantities according to the new calorie system, against a background of mood music, beneath the motto—"Fletcherize."

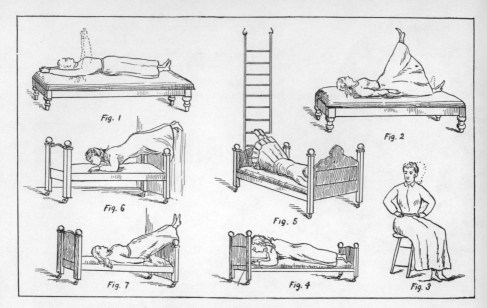

11. In his writings, Dr. Kellogg endeavored to arouse a new popular interest in physiolo[...]
and stir up the general indifference to diet, personal hygiene and exercise. The "Kell[...]
Sanitarium" emphasized procedures involving fresh air, sun, rest, sleep, simple fo[...]
Indian-club drills and calisthenics.

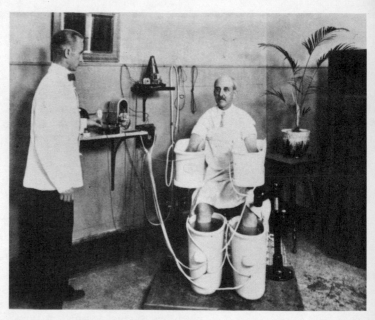

12. Electricity in the form of the "sinusoidal bath" joined the
therapeutic application of heat, the water treatment, meatless
meals and fiendish exercise machines from Sweden as curative
agencies at the "University of Health."

13. This drawing by John T. McCutcheon appeared when Battle Creek was booming wheat flakes and cereal stocks. W. K. Kellogg liked the cartoon so much that he reproduced it later in a cornflake advertisement. The building in the background was the Sanitas food factory.

14. "San" patients brought their anxieties to Dr. Kellogg's Monday-evening "Question Box" lecture, a dramatic high point in their ascetic week. Rising to inquire "How can you eat a thing that looks out of *eyes?*" the Doctor would whip out a shocker on diseased-meat statistics from the Chicago stockyards. "A man who smokes," he said with biting sarcasm, "*ought* to drink whiskey."

15. Ambulatory patients gathered at the end of the day for what was officially called the Grand March, sometimes in the gym, often on the roof, in which case the ceremony was known informally as "The Hop on the Top." But the Physical Education girls knew it as "Sterilized Dancing."

16. Pretty, wholesome-looking Fanny Bryant, a Kellogg Co. stenographer, was chosen in 1907 to personify the idea of "The Sweetheart of the Corn," and so set a national standard for feminine charm. Since the "Sweetheart" girl first appeared, she has been reproduced hundreds of millions of times, and has been slenderized and modernized by various artists.

17. By the time young Will Kellogg had had his first barbershop shave and attended his first oyster supper, he was out drumming up trade for the Kellogg corn brooms for his father. When he was eighty-four years old, he still remembered that the oyster supper cost twenty cents.

BILL OF FARE.

DINNER

Eleven o'clock, A. M.

Soups.

Chicken Soup	5	Mutton Broth	5
Oyster Soup	5	Vegetable	5
Clam Chowder	5	Bouillon	5
Fish Chowder	5	Pea	5

Fish.

Salt Codfish, boiled	10	Mackerel	10
Bass, Baked or boiled	10	Fried Tomcods	10
Salmon, baked or boiled	10	Fried Smelts	10
Tenderloin of Sole, with one Egg	10	Fried Clams	10
Codfish, Family Style, (on Friday)	10		

Boiled.

Beef, German Style	10	Beef, Oyster Sauce	10
Mutton, Mint Sauce	10	Corn Beef and Cabbage	10
Lamb, do	10	Corn Pork and Cabbage	10
Mutton, Caper Sauce	10	Pig's Head and Parsnips	10
Mutton and Turnips	10	Ham	10
Bacon and Cabbage	10	Calf's Tongue, Tomato Sauce	10
Mutton, Oyster Sauce	10		

Roast.

Beef, with Stuffing or plain	10	Beef with Lima Beans	10
Veal, " "	10	Lamb with Stuffing or plain	10
Pork, " "	10	Roast Hare	10
Mutton, with Lima Beans	10	Roast Duck	10
Turkey on Sunday	20	Roast Goose	10

Entrees.

Chicken Pot-Pie	20	Clams fried in batter	10
Chicken F.	20	Lamb Chops, Tomato Sauce	10
Veal Stuffed	10	Hamburg Steak	10
Pig's Feet in Batter	10	Veal Pot Pie	10
Sheep's Tongue, Pickled	10	Beefsteak Pie	5
Pig's Feet, soused	10	Fried Corned Beef Hash	10
Breast of Lamb, breaded	10	Stewed Lamb	5
Stewed Rabbit	10	Beef, Spanish style	10
Pickled Tripe	10	Beef a la Mode	10

Extra Vegetables.

Boiled Potatoes	5	Fried Potatoes	5
Mashed Potatoes	5	Cabbage	5
Lyonaise Potatoes	5	Tomatoes, stewed	5

Puddings. Pies. Cakes.

Puddings.	Pies.	Cakes.
Apple Roll	Cream	
Corn Starch	Apple	Pound
Apple Dumpling	Peach	Jelly
Rice	} 5c { Mince	5c { Wine } 5c
Sago	Custard	
Bread	Turnover Pies	Doughnuts
Farina	Squash	

BAKED APPLES		5 cts
Stewed Prunes	5 cts	Baked Pears ... 5 cts

CLARET WINE.   SONOMA WHITE.

CLARET WINE.		SONOMA WHITE.	
Bottle	20 cts	Bottle	20 cts
Half Bottle	10 cts	Half Bottle	10 cts
Glass	5 cts	Glass	5 cts

Chocolate	5 cts
Black or Green Tea, Coffee or Glass of Milk	5 cts
Glass of Chicago Beer	**5 cts**
WHITE LABOR CIGARS	5 cts

18. Compare the menu above with the cuisine of the Battle Creek Sanitarium shown on an earlier page of this section. To the old query, the food reformers gave a stern and unequivocal answer: We do, indeed, eat to live.

19. The man who knew the early austerities of Adventism attended upon Mother White in the 'seventies, walked with German naturopaths in the 'eighties, lived on into the age of publicity: Dr. Kellogg came to endure and then enjoy it. Always ready for a "gag" shot, he was photographed almost as often as a Hollywood celebrity.

20. The nondescript pet of W. K. Kellogg's youth, "Old Spot," is recalled in the affection which the taciturn cornflake manufacturer felt for his purebred Arabian twin colts. And through the fabulous Kellogg Ranch in California, W.K. enjoyed for a time an association with the famous and privileged of the entertainment world: Rudolph Valentino, Tom Mix, Gary Cooper, Will Rogers, Olivia de Havilland, Clara Bow, Douglas Fairbanks and Mary Pickford.

"Stomach Comfort in Every Shred"

❧ It is not how much we eat, but how much we digest that makes us strong. Indigestion is not confined to the stomach The starchy foods, such as bread and potatoes, are digested in the bowel. Millions of persons are unable properly to digest starchy foods. ❧ Whether it is stomach indigestion or bowel indigestion, what the sufferer needs is food, not medicine—the right kind of food Such a food is

Shredded Whole Wheat

❧ It is made of the whole wheat, steam-cooked and drawn into fine-porous shreds and baked. These delicate shreds are retained and assimilated when the stomach rejects all other foods. Thousands of persons—including many doctors—gratefully affirm this fact in letters to this Company.

"It's All in the Shreds"

❧ Shredded Wheat is not "treated" or "flavored" with anything—it is the whole wheat and nothing but the wheat—the cleanest and purest cereal food made. It is made in two forms—BISCUIT and TRISCUIT. The Biscuit is delicious for breakfast with hot or cold milk or cream or for any other meal in combination with fruits or vegetables. Triscuit is the shredded whole wheat cracker which takes the place of white flour bread; delicious as a toast with butter or with cheese or preserves.

THE NATURAL FOOD COMPANY
Niagara Falls, N. Y.

21. Shredded Wheat was invented by a man with stomach trouble for himself and others in a similar fix. Later the virtues of the wheaty little mattresses were advertised and merchandised to the whole world with boldness and skill. "If you can't sell them, give them away," the home office once wired its district managers. The plan effectively attracted paying customers to the novel food.

22. Early commercial ventures in the breakfast-food field often exploited the religious background of the Battle Creek cereals. In an unusual mistake of judgment, C.W. Post called upon the prophet Elijah and the raven to help sell his corn flakes. Ministers preached sermons against the modern Manna and the English had the law on him for his sacrilegious Elijah's Manna, which quickly became Post Toasties.

Patented November 23rd, 1915

Post (NEW) Toasties

REG. U.S. PAT. OFF.

IMPROVED

CORN FLAKES

New Post Toasties

are made of choice at Indian Corn—flaked and toasted—seasoned with sugar and salt. Their tiny "bubbles" are produced by a patented process that assures you of flakes as much different and better as their name is distinctive.

23. In 1908, with a new name and color scheme, the Postum Cereal Company's corn flakes found, especially in the Middle West, a veritable Garden of Eden of sales and profits. In a vivacious sparring match of 1913, when commercial manners were blunter than they are now, the Kellogg Co. described Post Toasties as a "spritely two-year-old, sired by Post and damned by the consumer." The new package portrayed a dainty sprite, eating cereal in front of an open fire.

24. C.W. Post was built on a far more spacious scale than the brassy pitchmen who used to set up their tripod and keister in front of Minty's Cigar Store on Battle Creek's Main Street to sell patented can openers to rustic visitors. But he applied their brand of salesmanship to a new kind of proposition on a world-wide scale, and became the first breakfast-food promoter to hit the jackpot.

25. This imposing structure is the former main building of the Battle Creek Sanitarium, a monument to the life and work of Dr. John Harvey Kellogg. It was later owned and operated by the government as an army hospital. It is now national headquarters for Civil Defense.

C. W. Post; or, What Is This Strange Power?

BATTLE CREEK didn't become "Foodtown" until sometime after the unheralded arrival in the early 1890's of an obscure new citizen, sick, approaching middle age, a discouraged health seeker in a wheel chair. There was, nevertheless, a cause and effect relationship between the rise of the man and the fame of the town.

The invalid who first exploited commercially the Battle Creek background, who made the city's name a synonym for sizzling enterprise, was Charles W. Post, formerly of Springfield, Illinois; Independence, Kansas; Texas and points west. Post called forth an industrial miracle, made Battle Creek's story one of romance and riches, that caused the *New York World* to poetize:

> Behold the belle of Battle Creek,
> Plump of form and pink of cheek
> Her beauty is a type so rare
> It causes comment everywhere.
> She needs no powder for her face;
> She needs no stays to give her grace
> Her days with happiness are rife
> The Secret of her health and life
> Is PURE FOOD.

"Now every home dominated by intelligence," observed the *World* "has adopted the flaked and granulated grain foods of Battle Creek, scientifically blended with various digestives and sweets, as the standard for the breakfast table."

C. W. Post was thirty-six years old. He had been around, was rich in his knowledge of rough-and-tumble living.

"I have hammered iron at the anvil," he said, "worked with wood-working machinery, and in a paint shop, from the color coat brushes to the coarse and fine line stripers. I used to be able to run and keep an engine in fair order, can line up shafting, figure the lines and pulleys, make a pattern so that it will draw out of sand."

Post had done some inventing—a bicycle, a mechanical piano, a suspender. His father, Charles Rollin Post, was a Vermonter who arrived in Springfield by way of Marietta, Ohio, the California and Pike's Peak gold rushes, Waverly and Jacksonville, in Illinois. One may speculate upon possible strains of inheritance in the son through each parent. C.W.'s mother, Caroline Lathrop Parsons Post, had a turn for words, wrote verses of conventional sentiment, celebrating the felicities of domestic life, handed on to her son a gift useful to an advertisement writer, a turn of expression—"plain words for plain people," as Post later described his own major literary effort.

The father had been an inventor in the farm-implement field. He was a grain dealer and a deacon in the Congregational Church. He supported the men and measures of the Republican Party having held, as the county history of Sangamon County says, "several local offices of trust in the gift of the people." Unsupported tradition has it that Post père was a friend of Lincoln. There is folk say to the effect that Lincoln once patted young Charley on the head, and Francis Bellamy, following an interview with C.W. at the Postum plant, wrote in "Little Advertising Journeys" that the child was present when Lincoln delivered his famous "Farewell to his Neighbors." "He remembers Lincoln's reaching down," Bellamy wrote, "to shake his hand goodbye the day before he left Springfield, in 1861, to go to his inauguration, never to return."

Charles W. Post was born in Springfield on October 26, 1854. He attended the local common schools and in 1869-70 did some college work at the Illinois Industrial University, predecessor institution to the University of Illinois. There he made no brilliant academic record, but enjoyed the athletics and military training. Back home, he joined the Springfield Zouaves, recently designated the Governor's Guard, was accoutered in baggy red trousers, yellow leggings, blue jacket and a small red cap. The Zouaves served at the scene of the Chicago Fire and at ceremonies unveiling the statue of Lincoln at Oak Ridge Cemetery in 1874, attended by President U. S. Grant and party. Post was present at both actions.

In the same year, C.W. married Ella Letitia Merriweather. They had one child, a daughter, Marjorie. Post spent a year in Independence, Kansas, as partner in a hardware store. He was a drummer for a farm-machinery concern, the Climax Corn Planter Company, of Springfield, and also for B. D. Buford, of Rock Island, Illinois. An instinctive entrepreneur, Post started up a small manufacturing firm in Springfield, with some local assistance, to manufacture "Post Capitol City Cultivators." It was a time of tremendous expansion in the use of farm machinery. But ill health, a stockholder fight and heavy liabilities reduced Post to a low state of fortune. He became bankrupt and went to Texas with his brother Carroll to make a fresh start.

At Fort Worth, C.W. dealt in city real estate, a congenial occupation "without the necessity of physical or mental labor." There was a brief California interlude. Then Post returned to Fort Worth and with Carroll developed a subdivision outside Fort Worth. During this period Post was also interested in a woollen mill which made blankets, projected a paper mill that would manufacture paper out of Texas cottonseed hulls. During the 1880's his health failed three times. Whenever opportunities seemed about to open up, every time Post threw himself into a promising new activity, he had another breakdown. He had tried sea voyages, summer resorts, ranching in Texas, mountain resorts, mineral springs, Swedish movements, special massage, gymnastics, dieting, will power. He had eaten scientifically. His gastric juices had been analyzed and tested. Even enemas lost their effectiveness. Post decided to find out what the Battle Creek Sanitarium could do for him.

C.W. arrived in Battle Creek in February, 1891, with his wife and small daughter, his white Stetson hat, a repertoire of good Texas cowboy stories, an interesting air of the West about him. But he was low in funds.

"I first met Mr. Post at the Sanitarium," said W. K. Kellogg. "He was in a wheel chair, greatly emaciated, and was wheeled about by his wife. For several months he paid his Sanitarium bills with the blankets salvaged from his Texas mill.

"He was quite inventive. He had invented a new type of suspender, and his wife sold them from house to house in Battle Creek to raise money to keep Mr. Post in the Sanitarium."

Post was indeed "quite inventive." In addition to the inventions already mentioned, he invented a fireless cooker, a paddle to generate electricity by water power, a plowshare still in common use, and the Post Currency Check, a substitute for express checks or post-office money orders, to be used in small denominations to send money safely through the mails.

The Posts lived as roomers in a private residence near the "San" for about nine months. At the Sanitarium parlor talks, Post absorbed all that he heard about diet, nutrition, materia medica, the manufacture of health foods and the astonishing possibilities of mental suggestion. But he didn't get well.

Dr. Kellogg had studied in Paris under brilliant, Napoleonic Jean Martin Charcot at the greatest neurological clinic of the times, which Charcot conducted at the Saltpetrière, and was quite familiar with Charcot's notable researches on hypnotic suggestion.

It is stated upon family authority that Post also "went to France to study," that he attended the clinics of M. Charcot, and that he looked into the cures of Father Sebastian Kneipp, the parish priest of Woerishofen, a hydropathic practitioner. The Kneipp Verein in New York had made the Kneipp regimen more popular than the bicycle, according to the enthusiastic translator of Kneipp's chief work, *Meine Wasserkur*. Father Kneipp had the ladies walk barefoot in the morning dew, as they had done for Preissenitz at Graefenberg. Kneipp was ready to tackle anything from asthma to tetters.

Since mesmerism swept over the Western world, the nineteenth century had had a voracious curiosity about psychic phenomena. One would be surprised and disappointed if Battle Creek, which had always appreciated the *outré*, failed to keep up with the progress of mental science. Battle Creek did not fall behind. It could boast of spirit mediums capable of giving the absent treatment, or revealing the past, present and future in such important areas as love and marriage, investments and health. Battle Creek, the old spiritualist and Adventist headquarters, was, in fact, always a congenial locus for soothsayers. The application of all this to the unsound body was what interested C. W. Post. He began to give close attention to emanations, radiations, Divine Harmony, and getting in tune with the Infinite. He read deeply in popular occult books, and learned to find his way about in their specialized vocabularies. "Hold the health thought," urged the uplift magazines, "and say I AM WELL."

Post is remembered as a melancholy roomer at the house where he boarded, lying wanly on the lawn under summer shade. The treatment given him at the "San" was an absolute failure, according to his own estimate, which may have marked the beginning of his antipathy to "Kelloggism." When he left the Sanitarium to seek other roads to health, they had, he said, given him up to die. The next stop was mental healing. He studied Christian Science with a Mrs. Elizabeth K. Gregory, and began to eat like a horse. He also did postgraduate work under a local medium, one Adams, and long afterward made a deposition that a Battle Creek healer, a Mrs. Agnes Chester, had cured him in two days when his appendix kicked up. She "vitalized in me the dormant forces," he said.

And so the sick man got up and walked.

"I suppose I was a sight, but the only way I knew to get well was to be well, however ill I looked, and I began walking around like a man who had business to attend to."

By this time Post had obviously put his confidence in other curative agencies than those of the Sanitarium; but he still sensed unexplored commercial possibilities in the Sanitarium health foods. He approached Dr. Kellogg with a proposal to work together in a program to promote Minute Brew. This was a health coffee about which Dr. Kellogg was currently enthusiastic. The Doctor refused flatly to have anything to do with the idea.

Post then went to the eastern limits of Battle Creek, and, in May, 1892, took title to the old Grenville Beardsley property, a picturesque ten-acre homestead with a small barn, situated in a grove of pine and oak trees with vine-clad hills and hollows and an orchard of ancient apple and pear trees. There Post established his own medical boardinghouse, La Vita Inn.

Entering into a contract to pay as the money came in, Post set La Vita Inn up as a place which would put into general practice the curative discoveries which had been effective in his own case; special diets and mental influence. The Inn provided light exercises, gadgets and games, music, a carefree atmosphere. Meat was not banned. But tea was; also coffee, whiskey and M.D.'s. In a wing of the Inn, the Post suspenders were still manufactured. C.W. had built up a mail-order business on the galluses which netted about ten dollars a day.

Asked if he was a doctor, Charley Post once said, "I did not take any particular titles. . . . I simply treated patients by mental therapeutics."

After Post became a mental healer, W. K. Kellogg recalled that Charley went to Dr. Kellogg at the "San," "and offered to pray for some of the 'San' patients for fifty dollars a week. The Doctor did not avail himself of the service."

Nevertheless, stories of some remarkable cures came out of La Vita Inn. A woman told C.W. that she had been to four or five Seventh Day Adventist meetings and got all fired up, so that in the night God appeared to her in person in shining garments and told her the Advents had the right slant on doctrine. But she still had her rheumatism. Post told her to forget her joints, because to feel the twinges any longer after the extraordinary favor which had been shown to her would be contrary to the will of God. Use the "energy of your divine self-hood," he told her solemnly. The mouth-filling language astounded the patient and her rheumatism did depart.

Usually the guests at La Vita Inn were discouraged Kellogg patients. Post liked to point that out. One young lady had been given up for dead at the "San." She came over to the East End and "Doc" Post had her playing tennis in ten days. A young man named Charley who had erysipelas of the face was on "the road to Wellville," a favorite metaphor of Post's, in less than five minutes by "quick mental negation" of the power of the disease. The purplish tinge left at once, the swelling in a day or so.

C.W. always remembered the circumstances of this cure. It was fixed in his mind because at the time he was sorting pears. Post told Charley to look at him while he got his instructions—and then to go into the house. Post would follow him.

Finding the patient standing at the corner of the house, the proprietor remarked, "Didn't I tell you to go around to the front and into the house?"

"Yes, but I have no reason to go in there."

"Why?"

"Because my pain has left me. I have none."

"Do you mean to say that you have no pain?"

"None at all."

Later this Charley returned, bringing his mother. She had an ulcerated tooth. C.W. looked at her too in a fixed manner and told her she was well. She was.

The erysipelas case came up some years later to plague the breakfast-food multimillionaire. In one of his court battles a trial lawyer for the other side, the redoubtable, rough-hewn James W. Osborne, went over the episode with a fine-toothed comb, happily waved Post's treatise on mental healing, "*I Am Well!*", in front of the jury, and roared out in his Southern accent, "Ah've been lookin' at him steadily for two weeks, and he makes *me* sick."

Again, there was the time that a businessman from Omaha turned up at La Vita Inn—but is it necessary to multiply instances? That same week the Nebraskan was eating pork and beans. Numerous other case histories are extant, the dyspeptic, the "living skeleton," the man with the bladder complaint who doctored with the former salesman of corn cultivators and was cured by the higher understanding.

Post liked to allude to the failures of "a prominent sanitarium," though he coupled his digs with virtuous disclaimers of malice.

"It is not our purpose to cast the slightest reproach on any physician, hospital, or sanitarium, who, while they fail in a great many cases, do honestly what they can for the alleviation of human distress."

Post read Gray's *Anatomy*, Pavlov, Doctors Cary and Ochsner. He extended his reading beyond the sciences to include Marcus Aurelius, Ruskin, Ella Wheeler Wilcox, Henry Ward Beecher, Amelia Barr and Anonymous. But his meditations always returned to professional interests, the Indian rope trick, the strange power by which a yogi could plant a mango fruit and materialize a fifty-foot tree; the ninety-odd recorded cases of the stigmata. There was an application if he could only find it. He shut his eyes, relaxed and whispered: "There is no such thing as sickness. . . . I am well."

As his reading widened, Post's own system took definite shape.

He began to do some writing. It is not generally known that before he became a master of the advertisement, C. W. Post had been an author. In later years he was shy about his ventures into belles-lettres. But, during his mental-healing days, he did place before the public a blue-backed, hard-cover vade mecum entitled, "*I Am Well!*", *The Modern Practice of Natural Suggestion as Distinct from Hypnotic or Unnatural Influence. Scientiae Vitae*, first published by the author in 1893 at $1.25, with a second edition brought out by Lee and Shepard in Boston in 1895. The title page carries a quaint by-line: "By C. W. Post, worded for Plain People."

A later condensation in pamphlet form (ten cents) was called *The Second Man*. The title is taken from I Corinthians XV:47. "The first man *is* of the earth, earthy; the second man *is* the Lord from Heaven." According to a puff appearing in the *Battle Creek Journal*, written in a style resembling that of C.W.'s signed work, and the attribution may safely be made to him, "It is said that either book possesses the peculiar quality of healing the sick while being read." *The Second Man* only hit the high spots. Those who wished to go into the higher branches were referred to the seminal work which preceded the pamphlet. The latter, however, gave a quick general view of the system.

Both of Post's excursions into literature are now great rarities. Alexander Woollcott, who investigated just how rare they were, reported that "the entire edition [of "*I Am Well!*"] had apparently evaporated . . . including . . . the copy which had mysteriously disappeared from the Congressional Library." But both works served their time and their purpose, which was to promote Charley Post's New Thought boardinghouse.

The ideas contained in these somewhat inaccessible writings did not wholly disappear from the stream of popular thought. Many phrases and whole sentences were later lifted from "*I Am Well!*" and put into an advertising leaflet entitled *The Road to Wellville*, a package insert for Postum and Grape Nuts. Divine Harmony was no longer enough. It was necessary to call on Mind, first, and then adopt a diet of Postum and Grape Nuts.

Relations between Post and W. K. Kellogg, while cool, were simply those of two hard-hitting competitors each of whom would like to be the autocrat of the U.S. breakfast table. W.K. never called Charley Post anything worse than the "Original Imitator" of his Toasted Corn Flakes. His comment at Post's death, while it fell short of eulogy, was not actionable, a comparatively mild remark that, "I hope when I pass on that I will have done more for the town than Mr. Post ever did."

Between C. W. Post and The Doctor there was real rancor. It started when Dr. Kellogg rejected Post's offer of a business alliance. After that, Post scoffed while seeming not to, at the Sanitarium. A man's intentions are hardly pacific when he says, as Post did, in delineating the plight of the dyspeptic: "Then some vegetarian crank tells him he must live on oatmeal and Graham bread . . . finally some sanitarium physician or some publication on health warns him that man should eat but twice a day . . . here he is surrounded with a web."

Post lectured his patients and served them a hot drink not unlike the Sanitarium's Caramel Cereal Coffee. C.W. said he got the idea while he was in the Southwest where he had often seen the ranch wives roast wheat and chicory for a homemade coffee substitute. He also could have read Mrs. Ella Kellogg's *Scientific Food Cookery*, which appeared in 1892 and was often reprinted. She gave nine recipes for coffee substitutes whose principal ingredients were bran and molasses, the same as Postum's. *Good Health* magazine recited this account of the origin of Postum:

> Early in his career, Dr. Kellogg noted that many patients who came to the Battle Creek Sanitarium seeking relief from insomnia drank many cups of coffee daily. When he eliminated coffee from their bill of fare, they demanded something in its place. He kept a man busy in the laboratory carrying out experiment after experiment, using a variety of grains. Mr. Post, who was a patient at the Sanitarium at the time, visited the laboratory frequently to watch the progress of this work. The laboratory technician one morning looked up the Doctor and said:
>
> "Mr. Post is keeping himself informed regarding every detail of your experiments. I believe the next thing that will happen will be that he will make a cereal coffee and put it on the market. Shall I keep him out of the laboratory?"
>
> "No, indeed," replied The Doctor. "Let him see everything that we are doing. I shall be delighted if he makes a

cereal coffee and wish him every success. The more he sells of
it the less coffee will be consumed, and this will be of great
benefit to the American people."

One must receive this burst of generosity with caution. After
The Doctor saw how fast the good ship Postum sailed he felt less
broad-minded about her skipper. For during the Battle Creek cereal boom he said:

"More than a score of these food enterprises have been
launched in Battle Creek and vicinity and as many more elsewhere
in the country. By ingenious advertising, much after the method of
medical quacks, some of these concerns have built up large business interests and have waxed rich by their ill-gotten gains. One
party in particular has made some millions by the sale of a cheap
mixture of bran and molasses. . . . The Battle Creek Sanitarium
has never at any time had any connection whatever with the manufacture of 'postum,' 'Grape Nuts,' 'Obesity Pills' or any other of
the nostrums made or sold by parties advertising from Battle Creek.
The prestige of Battle Creek as a health center has made this an attractive place for the operations of various charlatans, and not the
least pretentious and predatory of these are the numerous food
charlatans . . . posing as experts and discoverers."

"Dr. Kellogg never forgave Post," said Albert D. Lasker,
famed Chicago advertising man, who knew the Battle Creek of
1902 and 1903. "Kellogg felt that Post was a plagiarist."

How sharper than a serpent's tooth is the bite of an ungrateful
multimillionaire!

Finally, and with deliberation, Post started out alone on his
plan for manufacturing a cereal coffee. Frank Sherwin, known locally as The Redheaded Grocer, who employed seven carrot-topped
clerks and a red-haired cashier, and had six delivery wagons all
drawn by sorrel horses, was fond of Post and staked him to his first
molasses and bran. In December, 1894, the future Henry Ford of
the breakfast table made an investment, as follows:

    1 secondhand 2-burner gasoline stove—for roasting bran
    1 small hand-operated peanut roaster—for roasting wheat
    1 coffee grinder to grind the mixture
    Several mixers

This equipment cost $46.85. Post also acquired the following inventory of raw materials:

2 bushels of wheat
200 pounds of bran
10 jugs of molasses
50 packing cases
2000 cartons

The cost of these materials came to $21.91. The molasses was from Sherwin. Post ground, mixed and cooked up his bran, wheat and molasses in the little horse barn, searching for a palatable, caramelized grain "coffee." The town scoffed at such "puttering around." It held grain coffee in low esteem as "the harsh companion of poverty." When the strain got too great, C.W. went out behind the barn and chopped wood, returning refreshed to boil some more bran. The result was Postum Cereal Food Coffee. "When well brewed," C.W. proclaimed, "Postum has the deep seal brown of coffee and a flavor very like the milder brands of Java."

Charley Post, with one helper, Clark (Shorty) Bristol, started the first commercial batch—they hoped it would be commercial—on January 1, 1895. Postum Cereal was joined later by Grape Nuts and Post Toasties. Finally Post rounded out his creations with Instant Postum. In the early days Post was factory superintendent, bookkeeper, salesman, demonstrator and advertisement writer. As an early and massive user of national advertising, Post put a "halo" around Postum, using a powerful brand of farmer English: "If coffee don't agree—use Postum." Within less than a decade the Postum plant became a spectacular "White City" of wooden factory buildings painted white with green trim, recalling to thousands happy memories of their visit to the "White City" of the Columbian Exposition at Chicago in '93. Post gathered up all the yeasty forces which had been working in Battle Creek for a generation, some elements of religion, aspects of vegetarianism, Right Living, hydropathy and Christian Science, dropped overboard the altruism and turned the health crusade into an attractive businessman's risk.

Neither the East Enders nor the West Enders of Battle Creek could properly claim the idea of a coffee substitute for their very own. One can trace the idea back through a multiplicity of channels. At the same time that Post was experimenting in his little white barn, another picturesque character, out in La Crosse, Wisconsin, entertained similar ambitions. "Doctor" Frank Powell, or "White Beaver" as he was known among the plains Indians, did a shooting act in Wild West shows, was billed as chief medicine man of the Winnebago Sioux. Whatever his interneship or practice may have been among the Western tribes, he was definitely chief medicine man of La Crosse. He was mayor, proprietor of a patent-medicine business, and had a cereal coffee known as Panamalt. "White Beaver" touched his crony, William F. Cody, "Buffalo Bill," to establish the food business, with Cody as president, probably for the same reason that the boy who owns the ball gets to be pitcher. But the Cody-Powell Panamalt Company, lacking a C. W. Post to run it, lapsed into desuetude.

A generation earlier, mothers of the 1860's used "toast water" for sick children and knew from experience that it had some food value, that baking starch somehow increased digestibility. In 1868, Dr. A. W. Chase of Ann Arbor, published a book of recipes and miscellaneous household information designed to meet practically all of life's contingencies. In it appears a formula for "Dyspeptic's Coffee." The soldiers in the Civil War boiled up a similar concoction of bran and molasses. Earlier, E. T. Freedley, popular economist and writer on business topics, mentioned that there was a business opportunity in wheat, well dried and roasted, which "makes an excellent coffee."

Going back to 1835, Mrs. Lydia Maria Child, in her *Frugal Housewife*, described a number of coffee substitutes. She characterized them with unusual candor: "none . . . are very good." And her contemporary, Mrs. Asenath Nicholson, the Vermont school teacher and Grahamite, who took the Protestant Bible to the Irish poor, turned, when her "tottering fabric" was about to collapse, to "Bread Coffee"; and also experimented with a potato coffee. Edward Hitchcock, the President of Amherst, in his *Dyspepsy* (1830) recommended "well burnt rye" as being cheap, and "scarcely to be distinguished from it" [coffee]. The Shakers at New Lebanon, New York, had cereal coffees in the late eighteenth century, and back in Revolutionary times the wife and children of the Reverend Cotton Mather Smith, Congregational minister at

Sharon, Connecticut, rose at three A.M. to set the sponge for the bread, get the hickory coals ready for the johnnycake and boil the wheat coffee; "all we could get," Mrs. Smith's daughter, Julia, recorded in her diary, "in those days."

All this is reviewed not to detract from Post's accomplishment, but to change the emphasis. Whether he did or didn't borrow any formulas or procedures from Dr. Kellogg, the idea had been open to all from time immemorial. Post introduced a standard, uniform product, manufactured on a large scale. He contrived new methods of mass distribution, and he taught the public to use his product by a new kind of argumentative advertising. "It Makes Red Blood," the Postum advertisements proclaimed, and did not mince words about the "poisonous alkaloids" in coffee. Coffee was also tagged as a cause of rheumatism. "Coffee Heart" might send the palpitating reader "to his or her long home." Economy, comfort, health and red blood "speak out strongly for the natural drink."

Postum Cereal was first put up in paper bags and sold around Battle Creek from a handcart. But expansion came quickly. In February, 1895, C.W. went to Grand Rapids with a supply of Postum Cereal Food Coffee, a pot of cream and an alcohol lamp to demonstrate his new product. Post boiled his substitute brew for the prescribed twenty minutes in the office of Willis H. Turner, the editor of the *Evening News*, and demonstrated to Turner the fragrance, potability, caffein-free characteristics of his brain child. He left with a credit of one thousand dollars for advertising. Then he went to see E. J. Herrick, a Grand Rapids grocery jobber. Herrick was discouraging, as Post liked to tell the yarn later, "showing some big bale-like packages called Caramel Coffee which he bought a dozen or eight years before."

"Nobody wants such a thing," Herrick insisted. "There is absolutely no demand.

"Save your money, young man, have fun with it, or go into some business that there is some reason for. You simply cannot make anybody ask for an instead-of-coffee cereal drink."

But C.W. was insistent. He promised local advertising and consignment billing: no pay until the goods were sold. Thus a fundamental policy of the Postum Cereal Company was established, the guarantee of quality and sale. Post himself wrote all the advertisements, the product descriptions and company literature. A woman demonstrator was added to educate the housewives in how to brew Postum. Post filled the local papers with Postum advertising. It was a totally new kind of copy. By April total sales amounted to $856. In December they were $5,000. The next year they jumped again—$265,000 was the final figure. In 1898, sales amounted to $840,000. Growth continued at an almost geometrical ratio. La Vita Inn was quietly closed up. Sometime after 1909 the building disappeared to make way for corn tanks.

The nature of this evolution was brought out on one lively courtroom occasion. Post was occupying the witness chair. The time was 1910.

"And now," the examining attorney said, "you've reached the point where you propose to relieve pains, not by the use of mental suggestion, but by Grape Nuts and Postum?"

"It's much easier," assented the witness.

"At fifteen cents a pound?"

"Yes."

The lawyer then read from a book in his hand.

" 'If you go into the silence humble and trusting . . . you will be refreshed in every way and food taken will digest readily, as the stomach works smoothly when under the influence of the Higher Power.' "

"Did you write that?" the attorney inquired.

"I am proud to say I did," said Mr. Post, emphasizing his words by shaking a long finger at the lawyer in front of him.

The tormenter commented that "positive thoughts" were once the Post doctrine, but "Nowadays it's 'eat Grape Nuts, drink Postum, and think positive thoughts.' "

C.W. said he thought that excellent advice.

"And then it was just positive thoughts?"

"Well, they did eat," Mr. Post replied.

It is a paradox of mass manufacturing that cash is always short in a strong growth period. Post was put to his trumps to get up the money to pay for his advertising. On one occasion he went to Chicago to ask a newspaper publisher for a line of credit to be used to advertise in his paper, on the basis that the sales of Postum were certain to liquidate the loan. The publisher declined. Then his fishy eye fell upon a Postum letterhead which showed a red circle or bull's-eye in the upper right-hand corner of the sheet, bearing the magic words, "It Makes Red Blood." The imagination, or possibly the effrontery, of the idea exerted a strange power over the Chicago man. He reconsidered and Post got a credit of ten thousand dollars, later increased to forty thousand.

The C. H. Fuller Company, advertising agency of Chicago, was also unable to resist Post's powers of persuasion, and agreed to underwrite Postum advertising and place it in magazines and newspapers on a delayed-pay basis.

Industrious Charley Post invented a disease called "coffee neuralgia" and poured on more advertising. "Lost Eyesight through Coffee Drinking," Post wrote of a sad case reported from Aurora, Illinois. The moral: quit coffee. Take up well-boiled Postum.

When the Postum Cereal Company fell behind on its payments for advertising, Fuller demanded notes from Post for the amounts owed, arranged in weekly maturities. The anxious advertising men in Chicago sent representatives to the Postum main office each week on a collection trip. But Post's plain words for plain people were beginning to get results. Even so it was touch and go. "Charlie," said C.W. to Fuller, "my position is this. I owe you so much now that unless you see fit to extend further credit, it looks like the plant would belong to you." The Fuller Company was involved so deeply there was no way to back out. Within three years the Postum Cereal Company was netting three million dollars. Postum was the largest single consumer of molasses in the world.

When C. W. Post portrayed the frantic wife and mother, the wise physician, watching for the first signs of heart disease in a beloved coffee drinker, or the coffee fiend saved at the last gasp by changing to Postum, he was following the classic pattern of symptom-inducing advertising used by proprietary-medicine men. This is not to deny him his due for originality, for originality often consists in a new application of an old idea. No one had thought up to that time that a food could be advertised successfully as a medicine.

Being a hot drink, Postum developed a seasonal pattern of sales with the peak in the winter. Post needed another cereal product to sell in the summer. For several years he had prepared a granulated food for his own use and twice-baked it in his kitchen range, with the help of his little daughter, Marjorie. It was then ground up in a home coffee grinder. The result, Dr. Kellogg thought, strikingly resembled Granola. Some kind of circle was completed when The Doctor later brought out Nuttola which the *Chicago Vegetarian,* a friendly but objective publication, said "reminds one somewhat of grape-nuts."

Post's brown, hard-to-chew granules had been christened "Grape Nuts"; Grape because the product contained maltose which Post called grape sugar, and Nuts in honor of the nutty flavor of the new dish. It was in January, 1898, in the days of the dollar watch, that the new food product, mighty close to brown bread in content, but novel in form, a little more nutritious than graham bread because there was less water in it, made its bow in a small black and tan package, bearing Post's signature in facsimile. The box was small because the food was "concentrated." The little health classic, *The Road to Wellville,* was packed in every package.

Grape Nuts and Postum made an ideal team. They supplemented each other seasonally in sales, and the bran which had to be removed from the wheat in the manufacture of Grape Nuts was used to make the Postum. Grape Nuts received a generous infusion of the Post advertising magic. The new cereal food was advertised as an alternative to surgery for an inflamed appendix. It was recommended for consumption, malaria and loose teeth. It was a special food for the brain.

The mention of Grape Nuts as brain food naturally brings up the memory of Nick Cox's horse. Nick was a big, round, jolly man with white whiskers, who had an arrangement with Charley Post that he could have the sweepings from the Grape Nuts plant for his dappled horse. The horse may have had Adventist leanings. At least, he didn't eat meat and loved his Grape Nuts. On a Saturday night, Nick would go down to Ernie Chilson's saloon and get loaded, climb into his buggy, say "Giddap" and fall asleep. The horse would haul Nick home safely, lines dragging in the snow. He had to negotiate three railroad crossings to do it, too!

Nick liked to brag on his horse. He would call attention to how fat and sleek he was; and how smart. "That's because he eats Grape Nuts," Nick insisted.

Post depended heavily upon the testimonials of grateful drinkers of his liquid bran-and-molasses; and advertised for more letters of praise in *The New York Magazine of Mysteries*, his advertisement headed, "More Boxes of Gold and Many Greenbacks." Despite its title, this magazine was not edited for the whodunit market. The angle was health, happiness, prosperity and life vibrations. The advertisers were a raffish lot: diamonds on credit, "protect your watch" devices, hair restorers, sexology books. Be a lightning calculator, the advertisements suggested, learn jujitsu, sell a ten-cent novelty by canvassing and get an oak rocker.

It took a horse and wagon to haul the testimonial letters from the Battle Creek post office to the Postum works. The obscure admirers of Postum appeared a less brilliant team than were the endorsers employed by Dr. S. B. Hartman of Columbus, Ohio, who owned Pe-ru-na. "Doc" Hartman had a whole stable full of congressmen, General (Fightin' Joe) Wheeler, and three U. S. Senators with side whiskers. He even gathered in the great naval hero, Admiral Schley, to speak for Pe-ru-na. There was, on the other hand, a homely realism about the remarks of Postum's *aficionados*. That was because C.W. rewrote all of the letters; or, as he put it, they were "condensed to give the facts in a short space."

Post's absolute certainty of what he could do with advertising is itself an interesting phenomenon of social engineering. When he got it straight in his mind what he wanted to say, he felt as sure of the results as he was of any natural phenomenon in Nature—that spring wheat would sprout, that birds would sing, that steam would expand. He risked all of the money that he had and a good deal that he hadn't on that conviction.

Frank Lauhoff of Detroit, who made flaking mills for the ready-to-eat cereal companies, was talking with Post at the time the Postum Company had made a net profit of $260,000 which was considered a pretty tidy sum. Lauhoff asked C.W. what he was going to do with all that money.

"Frank," the Battle Creek advertiser confided, "I'm going to stick it all right back into advertising. After all, it's not enough to just make and sell cereal. After that you get it halfway down the customer's throat through the use of advertising. Then, they've got to swallow it."

Post used advertising so familiarly as an instrument that later, when his combativeness led him into various controversies—with the American Federation of Labor, with *Collier's* magazine—he used paid advertising as a means of circulating his views. He handled his opponents roughly, in the admired Rooseveltian style. C.W. was quite titillated when a Westerner described him as "all cat, part wild and not quite safe to cuddle." He often repeated the compliment.

An important ingredient in Grape Nuts advertising was mystery, not dispelled by the famous slogan "There's a Reason," which never disclosed what the reason was. If an angel guided Dr. Kellogg's curette when he operated, surely the spirit of the late departed Dr. S. Andral Kilmer, of "Swamp Root" fame, must have perched on Charley Post's shoulder as he transferred patent-medicine hyperbole to the field of grocery advertising with consummate skill; a "hypnotic advertiser," Elbert Hubbard called him.

Post was so adroit in the composition of his advertising copy, in inserting the limiting phrase, the incomplete comparative, the unobtrusive operative phrase, in suggesting a good deal more than he ever actually said, that the line grew indistinct between untruth and truth. And, indeed, as an advertising colleague, Bert M. Moses, the Omega Oil man, said, restating Pilate's ancient query, "What is the truth, anyhow?" Grape Nuts did not originate either with grapes or nuts. But was Beechnut Bacon made from beechnuts? How much cream was there in Cream of Wheat? Could a nutritionist take the stand and affirm that Grape Nuts did not make red blood? Or deny that coffee adversely affected the health of some people? "Just whisper health," ruminated a student of Post methods, a moody coffee merchant with a bad case of Postum jitters. "That is the open sesame to the public's purse."

Others have carried on from where Post laid down his burden. To him is owed a debt of gratitude from every cultist and dietary-food lecturer, every manufacturer of inorganic salts, every mahatma who ever sold ground-up alfalfa, blackstrap molasses, or employed food folklore to scare the customers.

Is fish a brain food? Do fruit seeds cause appendicitis? Is it dangerous to eat ice cream and sea foods at the same meal? Are bananas hard to digest? Are aluminum cooking vessels poisonous? Do eggs create a predisposition toward cancer? Does garlic purify the blood? Is salt a cause of Bright's disease? All practitioners of dieto-mysticism, who desire to attract attention by raising these or similar questions, all who feel the urge to do something quick about their health, are under obligation to the methods pioneered by C. W. Post. Joining the zeal of the reformer to the profit motive, and adding a shrewd understanding of popular psychology, C.W. showed how it was possible to generate fads in eating. Thus a new form of social power was made available.

In time, a group of associates was formed into what C.W. called his "Cabinet" to help in the direction of the business: Marshall K. Howe to watch the money; Harry Burt, plucked from a downtown jewelry repair shop; Henry C. Hawk, especially close to Post in later years; and others. Unlike Dr. Kellogg, Post could organize, delegate and supervise. Where The Doctor lost himself in a morass of detail, where Will K. Kellogg went it alone, Post preferred to work through Howe, Hawk, or Harry Burt. Each was able and respected. But the method was significant of the gradual withdrawal from the Battle Creek scene of C. W. Post; and the Postum profits went with him.

In 1901, Post was an exciting figure to his fellow citizens, the most enthusiastic booster for Battle Creek who had ever stepped off the train at "the food pole of the merry old earth." That was the first year, according to the newspapers, that he cleared nearly a million dollars. Post's interests reached out in all directions. He put up the Post Tavern, the Post Office Building, the Marjorie Block. There was a Post Sugar Company, a carton and container plant to manufacture his own packages, the Post Gardens out west of town. The Post Addition, eighty acres of homes on the heights of Postumville, housed Post employees. The elegant new Post Theatre with two balconies gave Battle Creek visitors the impression that Post was a princely patron of the local drama.

C.W. didn't exactly build the theatre which bears his name and he didn't exactly give it to anyone. Some one hundred and ten citizens had financed over half the cost, and then lost their nerve. Post stepped in with a characteristic offer to have the Postum Cereal Company take over the bonds of discouraged holders, with a time limit. Thus he saved the theatre. Thus the house got its name. Post declined to enter a philanthropic race in Battle Creek.

Quietly insisting that giving was a privilege not to be confined to the few, but open to all, C.W. often made his own participation in good works contingent upon the observance of this principle by his fellow citizens.

"The welfare work that I believe in," said the Founder of the Postum fortune, "is that which makes it possible for the man to help himself, but it does not include the holding a milk bottle to his lips after he is weaned. . . . I never give people anything, but I put them in the way of getting what they want for themselves."

C.W. hated "High-Muck-A-Muck-Unionists," Samuel Gompers and "sociologists." It is not determinable now whether he meant what he said, or "socialists." Perhaps he felt the terms were interchangeable.

Post retained a real feeling for his bread cutters and cookers, the boys who drove his wagons and "peeled" the pans of Grape Nuts dough in and out of the brick ovens on long-handled paddles. C.W. paid the highest average wage for work of like character. But there wasn't any other work of like character, except at Kellogg's. There were, however, bonuses for faithful service, and a gold-washed pin to look forward to with a sheaf of wheat on it and the inscription, "Postum Veteran." But Post opposed bitterly the closed shop, the boycott, restrictions on machinery except for safety, the sympathetic strike, compulsory use of the union label. He fought for the right of the unorganized man to bargain with his employer on an equal basis, one to one.

The inventor of Postum respected all loyal Postum Cereal Company employees; and in one instance respect ripened into a more tender emotion. In 1904, he divorced his wife, with whom he had not lived for some two years, and married a poor girl who earned her living in his office, his "typewriter." This last word may not be immediately intelligible. In the roll-top desk era the "literary piano" and its operator were known by the same name.

Charley Post's typewriter was Leila Young, twenty years his junior, both interesting and pretty. Her father and brother worked in the milling department of the cereal works, so the marriage was endogamous—all in the Postum tribe. The ladies of Battle Creek's upper crust received the second Mrs. Post with some reserve at first; but she was so tall and trim, so graceful, so cultivated and well-

turned-out, that all hesitation was soon swept away. Mrs. Post out-
lived her husband by many years, married again, and carried out
many of the benefactions which might have been C.W.'s, too, had
he lived to break ninety.

At a Postum employees' banquet Post plunged into the whole
question of his divorce and remarriage with extraordinary explicit-
ness. He explained how Leila's presence "with Marjorie and I
meant peace." The public would perhaps have chosen for him "a
wealthy society woman," but Leila, he said, had "a fairer hand
than any society women I ever saw . . . a hand that for five years
has helped me, when work was needed. A lot of people talk about
the dignity of labor, but I believe in it. . . . Ladies and Gentlemen, I have the honor and pleasure to introduce to you the captain's wife, Mrs. Post."

Sometimes Post was brusque with his Battle Creek neighbors.
One said to him when he started to build the Post Tavern, "C.W.,
that is going to be far too big for this town."

"Why," he replied, "that is so. But I have the money to pay for
it and I think I shall go on with it notwithstanding your opinion."

On another occasion two men were talking on Main Street. "I
wonder why anybody would build anything so pretentious," one
remarked. C. W. Post, overhearing, stepped up to them and told
them why he built the Tavern.

"When I come downtown I like to have something to look
at."

Ever since his Fort Worth days Post had had a yen for real estate. As a Battle Creek subdivider, he offered lots for sale and built
houses, selling both on liberal terms, laying out new streets with
commemorative names, such as Post Avenue, Grenville, named for
Grenville Beardsley whose farm home became the mental-healing
Inn, Marjorie Street, named for his daughter, and Lathrop Street,
honoring the maiden name of his mother.

"Homesick," sang a local lyricist of the man who had no place
in Battle Creek to lay his head except a whole-floor suite at the
Post Tavern, "he dreamed of homes for other men."

During 1906 and 1907, C.W. acquired 213,324 acres or about
333 square miles of high plains land in Garza, Lynn and Hockley
counties, Texas, with the idea of operating the vast property as a

cattle ranch, and then when emigration pressed closer, cutting it up into farms. In connection with that venture he founded Post City, Texas. It was at first a tent city, called familiarly by its denizens, Ragtown, but later a solid community with a Baptist church and a hotel where they changed the bed sheets after each guest.

The return of the cereal magnate to scenes he knew in his youth offers valuable insights into the psychology of the self-made man. We see C.W. hacking across his vast holdings to a barbecue, rising for a speech in "black cowboy boots, silver spurs, black corduroy trousers, a maroon shirt, and in his hand was his white Stetson hat." On other occasions, Post would appear "in his white tengallon Stetson, blue shirt, yellow corduroy pants, and black cowboy boots," looking like Roy Rogers. He would watch the stonemasons working on a building, ask for a "chew" and lay a few courses himself. And sometimes he wielded his axe on the mesquite to supply fuel for his kitchen range. Post loved to hit the trail with a congenial party in a couple of two-cylinder Reo cars, pick up old buffalo chips for a fire, and toast the cheese for the midday snack that always included Uneeda Biscuits, sardines, gingersnaps and canned peaches. Flocks of Western meadow larks ran along ahead of the Reos in the old ruts, as prairie dogs barked with alarm. It was a landscape of cactus, pear, the coyotes, accented with the white bones of cattle which had drunk alkali water.

C.W.'s mastery of detail was amazing. He issued instructions in a steady stream. "Mr. Alexander's house: Stain roof and side shingles Moss Green; paint siding Colonial Yellow, trimmed in white. House where Mr. Hill lives: Stain the roof dark brown; side shingles, much lighter brown; paint siding Light brown, and trim all around with Dark Brown." The hotel's halls were to have strips of carpet sewed double. Stained floors outside the strips of carpet. No stain under the carpet.

Coffee and tea were served at the Post City hotel, but the waiters were instructed to tell the guests when the Postum was ready. Grape Nuts was kept on the table in a covered glass dish, and the cream was free, too. Some of the hotel guests thought the rates too high. For their benefit, C.W. had a card printed up by Stockton Henry, editor of the Post City *Post*, a man without the slightest taint of socialism. The card, placed behind the desk, said:

"The rate at this hotel is $2.50 a day. There are plenty of good boarding houses in town and plenty of room in the mesquite. Four-flushers, kickers, and other suspicious characters find board with the sheriff. When in doubt, hit the mesquite."

Post loved the hotel business. In it his passion for detail seemed unable to exhaust itself. He was inexpressibly pained one Sunday to find upon the bill of fare, "Fricassee *aux pois*" and "roast beef *au jus*." He issued peremptory orders.

"I want to cut out all that monkey business."

Like some great patroon in the days of the Hudson Valley proprietorships, Post ordered each phase of life over his vast messuage; what shade trees were to be planted, what orchard varieties. Chicken wire was to be used to keep the ivy from blowing off the store building. For his own use, Post built a bungalow, revealing again his love of beauty in its decorations and furnishings—hand-painted leather wallpaper, chairs covered with stamped leather.

Lack of water made it impossible for Post to develop his Texas lands as he had hoped. This defeat he took as only temporary, and launched forth on large-scale experiments in rain making.

"I don't undertake the task of rain-making as a disciple of science," said the Battle Creek empiric, "but because the crops . . . need rain."

C.W. was a trial-and-error man. He had confidence in the method. It had paid off handsomely in Postum making. C.W. assumed no more kindness or altruism in the phenomena of nature than he did among men. He simply sought practical ways to impose his will upon the clouds.

As an old Zouave militiaman, Post had talked with scores of Civil War veterans about their experiences in the late war. He concluded that artillery fire and rain were connected. Rain followed thunder. Cannon made thunder. Why not complete the syllogism and find out if cannon didn't make rain? Sitting in his English half-timbered office in Battle Creek early in 1910, Post outlined to his Texas managers the preparations they were to make. They were to provide themselves with fifteen to twenty kites, capable of carrying two pounds of dynamite each, and one hundred and fifty sticks of dynamite with five-minute fuses. Long since, they had become accustomed to such bizarre adventures. His letters read like a general's order of battle. The results turned out to be difficult to evaluate. There was a tendency among the Post general staff to construe any showers that fell from thirty to a hundred miles away as being favorable to the experiments. On one occasion there was a sky bombardment at Level Park, a Battle Creek real-estate subdivision, with the public invited to witness the spectacle. "Umbrellas will be for sale all over the field," it was announced confidently.

The dynamite was exploded.

It rained, a good soaker. *Post hoc, ergo propter hoc.*

There were also showers in Marshall and Kalamazoo. In fact, it rained that day from the Great Lakes to the Pacific Ocean. The ingenious food manufacturer died before any conclusive results had been obtained. His successors did not press the matter.

Since 1902, Post had been partially retired from the food factory. He had his suite at the Post Tavern, a summer home at Greenwich, Connecticut; spent time in New York, London and Washington, with offices in each city. He subsequently added another home at Santa Barbara. His legal residence was Washington. Local tax authorities found it an exciting adventure when they tried to levy upon his personal property. His elusiveness in such matters fully matched Dr. Kellogg's with his tax-free Sanitarium.

For the greater part of the time Post was in Washington, operating a publicity bureau which he called his "Sentry Box." The Sentry Box sent out material dealing with issues in which Post was interested. He was felt on the national scene in connection with unionism, as spokesman for large advertising interests and for the economic and social views of the National Association of Manufacturers.

Possibly no man starting out absolutely from scratch ever made more money in a shorter time out of a legitimate business than did C. W. Post; a New Thoughter in 1895, a multimillionaire seven years later. *The World Almanac* put in several months around 1901 or '02 compiling and checking a list of American millionaires. Battle Creek got two into the league, Edwin C. Nichols and David Shepard, proprietors of threshing-machine fortunes; but Post's name did not appear, although his fortune was estimated at ten million dollars in 1903. Events had moved too fast for the almanac people to catch up with the cash flow at the Postum works.

Battle Creek watched Post's comings and goings with pride; also with gratitude, *i.e.*, a lively sense of favors yet to come. Millionaires were more interesting in the social climate of 1900 than they are today, and they weren't so common. We may catch a glimpse of C.W. in the year 1903, relaxing in male company at Battle Creek's Athelstan Club.

"Yes, gentlemen," said the capitalist to a deferential group, "I will briefly tell you how near I came to being interested in the great Servian railroad scheme . . . there were millions in it. But . . ."

At last, after many disappointments and false starts, Charley Post had "the world by the tail and a down-hill pull."

Post's spectacular career symbolized what benign, paunchy Russell H. Conwell said on the lecture platform: that it was a sin to be poor when it was so easy to be rich. The great opportunities in life lie near at hand. Learn taxidermy. Get up a collar button. Raise trout. Invent a wooden toy. Read *System* magazine, and post up on the new business tricks and office wrinkles. Be a good talker. Train your memory by the Pelman System. Find out a need and fill it. The application was clear. That's what C. W. Post did. The richer man was the better man and Post was richest of all in Calhoun County, Michigan.

Post acquired yards and yards of oil paintings in Europe, bits of old armor and Italian marble. The aesthetic movement represented by William Morris reached C.W. in dilute form by way of Elbert Hubbard. Fra Elbertus often dropped in on C.W. for a chat, hoping that he could be of some service, possibly whip out a "Little Journey to the Home of a Great Breakfast Food Manufacturer." Post advertised in *The Philistine*, bought the Roycroft treasures. He found Hubbard's ideas congenial—the East Aurora Philosopher's respect for the power of advertising, his admiration for men who got things done, like Andrew Taylor Still, founder of osteopathy; John B. Stetson, who made the Texas hats; Horace Fletcher, the hard chewer; and motherly Lydia E. Pinkham, confidante of millions who thought they had GY complications. Hubbard, in turn, gratefully lent his son, Sanford, to appear with a torso as bare as Bernarr Macfadden's, in Grape-Nuts advertising, with the note, "Diet principally Grape-Nuts. Never ill a day."

The Posts' rise in fortune was accompanied by an equal social mobility. To those they left behind in their rapid progress it seemed that they "put on cornstarch airs," with their houses and intercontinental travels and fleet of automobiles including a Loco-mobile with black and orange top. Post was a bit stage-struck, too. It was probably the high point of his contact with the arts, when Nat Goodwin and Maxine Elliott dedicated the new Post theatre, appearing in the farce, "When We Were Twenty-One."

Twelve hundred fashionables saw the Goodwins—it was made plain early in the game that they were man and wife, though actors —heard C.W. deliver the entr'acte speech, well aware that they owed the Post Theatre to his intervention, and that Nat and Maxine were his personal friends. There were enthusiastic curtain calls, endless bouquets handed up over the footlights, while the Germania Orchestra played with unusual vigor. Hon. Edwin C. Nichols, the certified millionaire, had his box on the left. The Ed-ward C. Hinmans (steam pumps) with their party of six were in the next box. The Post box was the first on the right, Mrs. Post wearing an elaborate creation in light blue crepe de Chine. Miss Marjorie also chose a light blue crepe de Chine frock, handsomely trimmed with rose appliqué. Between the second and third acts she presented each and every one occupying boxes with a rose and went backstage with a dozen long-stemmed American beauties for Miss Elliott.

The Goodwins had entertained the Posts as soon as they got in on the Grand Trunk. The Posts responded with a trip to the Pos-tum works where the party enjoyed a dish of Grape Nuts ice cream. Again, after the play the Goodwins were guests at a select dinner party given by the Posts. Later there was a grand ball at the Athel-stan Club, with the Germania Orchestra expanded to twelve pieces. A certain number of gentlemen, as usual, sneaked off to play pool, while the proletariat repaired to the Green Moon Café for their after-theatre snack, to muse upon Miss Elliott's fair face, Mr. Post's munificence and the drop curtain portraying Ann Hatha-way's Cottage, invoking memory of the Bard:

Ann Hathaway's Cottage a mile away
Shakespeare sought at close of day.

It was the most brilliant social event staged by the Battle Creek Edwardians.

Next night Goodwin and Elliott played Bay City.

In the entrepreneurial environment of the late nineteenth century Big Business stood high on God's list of approved callings, the great preachers of the day said. But the self-made man often looked back, with tangled emotions, at the simpler past he had left behind him. Thus, C. W. Post, when guest of the Lord Mayor of Dublin, or when coaching between London and Windsor, and exchanging polite salutations with Queen Alexandra and the Princess Victoria, could say "Rats," and scoff at "all the hunky, punky, flunky trappings." He could say with the sincerity of the moment that he would rather be out at Postumville, shooting the breeze with one of his "boys." Or sharing a "chaw" with a cowpuncher under the Texas stars, listening to the Texas philosophy and the point of view of the plain people.

Once Post wrote wistfully from Warwickshire, "These days in England make me think of the cool, crisp days in Michigan, when apples are ripe and the bob white whistles in the stubble fields." And then the elegiac spell breaks as he recalls that King Edward VII uses the Kellogg electric-light bath: "We are going to have the king and the Royal Family eating Grape-Nuts before long."

In 1914, C. W. Post became the first of the trio of cornflake crusaders to die. Dogged throughout his life with a stomach ailment, the man who made millions pointing out The Road to Wellville never found the way himself. Post made a spectacular dash from Santa Barbara to the Mayo Brothers Clinic at Rochester, Minnesota, for emergency surgery, by special train, followed by an extra engine as a precaution against delay. A "Race with Death," as the newspapers called it. And so it was, in a way. Post returned to Santa Barbara. There were encouraging reports of his condition. But the industrialist fell into spells of melancholia, involving a horror of weapons of all kinds. Firearms, once his hobby, were removed from the premises. One rifle was overlooked. On May ninth, the breakfast-food manufacturer killed himself with the 30-30 hunting rifle which stood in a corner of his bedroom. The coroner's jury returned an open verdict, but it was generally believed in Battle Creek that Post faced months of suffering and the certainty of death.

C.W.'s body arrived on the Michigan Central's Wolverine on its last journey back from the greater world in which he moved during his later years. He was given a titan's burial. Photographic blowups, draped with lavender ribbon, were displayed in the windows of business houses, stores were closed, the ball game was called off. There was no matinee at the Post Theatre. Reverently, the founder was carried to a temporary tomb by Veteran Postum employees, in the presence of the family, the Cabinet, Postum workers, advertisers and food brokers.

Like William H. Vanderbilt, who was buried in a three-hundred-thousand-dollar version of the Romanesque chapel of Saint-Gilles at Arles, guarded by watchmen who punched a time clock every fifteen minutes, C.W. also was considered to be a possible object of interest to grave robbers. So Postum guards stood through the watches of the night beside the tomb until the permanent resting place was prepared and C.W. was placed under seven feet of concrete in the largest and most magnificent mausoleum in Oak Hill Cemetery.

There was, following the death of the Founder, a caretaker government at the Postum Cereal Company. In 1925, Postum united with the Jello Co. in the first of a series of mergers and purchases which led to the development of today's giant General Foods Corporation. Thus the Postum Cereal Co. merged its identity into a new kind of food company, based upon new techniques of distribution and selling.

Post's career was one of the most colorful which lay between the days of the railroad builders and the automobile tycoons. He was a satisfying figure to a generation which, above all others, placed a high valuation upon material success and men who were fighters. Two-fisted. Graduates of the University of Hard Knocks. Capable. Carried the message to Garcia. No stopping to ask, "Where is Garcia?" Entrepreneurs of the age were delighted to learn that accumulating spondulics was, as Carnegie put it, "an evolution from the heterogeneous to the homogeneous." A man with a wealth-winning idea, such as C. W. Post, famous for achieving success following failure, for his public quarrels and his singular methods of advertising, was the chief ornament of the classless society of the U.S. The frontier was gone. The supply of free land was exhausted. But Post's career proved that the new industrial age offered opportunities of a different sort. With his sure touch on popular psychology, Post might have become a Dowie or a Mrs. Eddy. But he chose the manufacture of breakfast foods as his métier and found in advertising an outlet for his versatile talents.

There is now scarcely a man alive who knew C. W. Post as a contemporary, fewer still who could claim to know all of the Big Three corn flakers well—Post, The Doctor and W. K. Kellogg. Each had his admirers and critics. But a good many rank Post first among the three for personality, presence, a sense of dynamism and personal power. Broad-shouldered, slender, usually courteous and slow of speech, with a cordial handshake, Post was a commanding figure. Even in a casual meeting, men sensed a magnetism in his needle-sharp gaze. He had dash and faith in himself and bulldog determination. For a while it seemed as though Battle Creek might become a one-man town. But a good many people were determined to share in the grain-given fortunes of the Postum king. After all, what had he done—invented a couple of products, given them oddish names, constructed appliances to produce them, and convinced the nation it needed to drink and chew healthfully? It looked easy. Drug clerks and invalids, internes and preachers, the men usually found leaning against the side of the depot, all started to think up names which sounded just as good as Postum and Grape Nuts. In revery, they saw themselves as "the wise and good and rich," riding in Locomobiles, with a footman to open the tonneau door and put on the side curtains, their wives rivalling Mrs. Post with rows of diamond rings over their long, gray suede gloves.

The great Breakfast Food Boom was on. . . .

XII

Our Stock Salesmen Meet All the Trains

THE first important commercial exploitation of flaked breakfast foods was launched by the Battle Creek Pure Food Company which made Malta Vita. Malta Vita was a wheat flake sweetened by the addition of barley malt syrup. It could trace its ancestry on one side to Dr. Kellogg's Granose Flakes. On the other it was indebted to C. W. Post who introduced the malting process and the concept of selling "health" foods to well people. Malta Vita flakes were particularly curly and crinkled.

Since technical knowledge was new, and certainly scarce, the first requirement for a food factory was a production man who knew something about the business. There was only one source of supply, the men who worked for Dr. Kellogg. Malta Vita got its start by what became a commonplace method. Two promoters hired Jesse D. Bordeau, a former bakery foreman at the Sanitarium Food Company. Bordeau added malt extract to Dr. Kellogg's Granose Flakes and the Malta Vita people obtained patents on the mechanical malting of the grain which they contended made the product itself patentable.

Soon Malta Vita, "the concentrated malted food, ready to eat, Pure, Predigested, Thoroughly Cooked, Scientific and Hygienic," was selling at a fast clip. A second factory went into production at Toronto for the Canadian market. The wheat flakes went to England and Germany. Then out-of-town interests purchased the company, reincorporated and changed the name to the Malta Vita Pure Food Company, with an authorized capital of five million dollars. But when the articles of association were filed in Lansing, the Secretary of State could find only one hundred twenty-five thousand dollars invested in Michigan, which struck him as odd, since the principal factory was in Battle Creek.

All of the United States was exposed to Malta Vita advertising. Mexico was taking the patent food by the carload. Cartons were printed in Spanish, German, French, Norwegian, Swedish and Czech. The atmosphere of success was infectious. The day clerk at the "San" threw up his job, headed for Benton Harbor to be a Malta Vita salesman. Frank Sherwin, the redheaded grocer, who had passed up the opportunity to make a fortune with Post, regretted his decision and invested in Malta Vita. Five big ovens, three stories high, dropped their appetizing shower of hot, crisp, wheat flakes—day and night. A second brand was added, Vim Wheat Flakes. The market seemed insatiable.

Short on equipment, the company resorted to improvised methods. Men, in rubber boots, spread the cooked wheat on factory floors and shovelled the wet, mushy grain over and over until dusty mould filled the room as the product slowly dried. The workmen said, "They will take it." But the flakes became mouldy and the consumer said "No." Malta Vita disappeared from the scene as swiftly as it had risen, a memorial to the dangers of absentee ownership and shortsighted policies. Making and marketing breakfast foods, it turned out, called for no less business sagacity than running a department store or a wagon factory.

Treading on the heels of Malta Vita came Force, a wheat flake produced by the Force Food Company of Buffalo. Force pearled the wheat to remove some of the bran. This made it possible more readily to cook the sugar and maltose into the starchy endosperm. The promotional genius behind Force was Edward Ellsworth, brilliant prototype of the breakfast-food king. He was a tall, distinguished-looking executive with gray hair and moustache and a commanding presence. Known locally as "the Duke," Ellsworth cut quite a swath in Buffalo, driving through the streets behind a matched pair of handsome bays. But Force, too, was a Battle Creek brain child. Charles Rhoades carried the technology of flake making eastward, from the Sanitas Nut Food Company.

There were certain factors operating in American life which were of potent assistance in developing a public for Battle Creek's food creations. The prepared cereals and the newer knowledge of dietetics came along about the same time. The Battle Creek foods combined the appeal of crispness, the flavor of maltose and dextrin, the lure of economy with the cachet of "scientific" eating.

The flaked foods were also associated in the public mind with purity and progress for the negative reason that they were clearly *not* involved in certain scandals which arose in other branches of the food industry during the last decades of the nineteenth century. The first generation to manufacture foods in factories had abused the confidence of their customers. Calling upon the resources of analytical chemistry, they stopped the processes of nature and sometimes tried to improve upon them. Thus formaldehyde, borax and boracic acid, coal-tar flavorings, copper salts, sulphite bleaches, benzoate of soda or salicylic acid appeared unannounced and unidentified upon the United States home table. "Vermont maple" syrup was made from cane sugar; potted chicken came from young veal. There was alum in the bread, a coal-tar dye in the cheese, flour and tumeric in the mustard, methyl alcohol in the ice cream. Butter could be renovated in at least five ways. The consumer could not distinguish an honest manufacturer from a rogue.

The confused situation and the indignation of aroused housewives brought down upon the food industry Dr. Harvey W. Wiley, the great "pure food" crusader of the early 1900's, and the federal Food and Drug Act which became the law on January 1, 1907. "Pure food" was on the public mind. Battle Creek produced it by the trainload.

W. K. Kellogg and George C. McKay, a trusted lieutenant, once figured up that forty-four breakfast-food concerns started up in Battle Creek during the early 1900's. Whole families put their lifetime savings into a fanciful trade name, a recipe and some old machinery. Manufacturing was started in sheds, even tents, and "cappers" met the trains to accommodate any stranger who would like to take on some stock in a food factory.

A tent on a hillside, a make-do shack, the half-finished framing of new dwellings, the skeleton walls of partially constructed factory buildings—that was the visible aspect of the new Battle Creek. At night the stranger's rest was disturbed by the flash from a lantern, the bang of a hammer, the snarl of a crosscut saw in the hands of an indefatigable camper building himself a home.

The campers were not necessarily poor. They were just in a hurry. Factory construction came ahead of housing.

"Don't know where all my people are," said Lewis G. Stevenson, father of Adlai Stevenson, then secretary of the Javril Coffee Company, Ltd., which had a product, Javril, and hoped soon to have a place in which to make it.

"I've told them to get tents and camp on the pasture lots around the factory," explained Stevenson. "There're no houses to be had."

There was an air of New England about the fine old homes along the avenues, a bizarre touch of Indian Territory about the tent colonies. Reaching for a way to express his impressions, a visitor said of Battle Creek, "It looks as though a cyclone had dumped Guthrie, Oklahoma, down on Boston Common."

Battle Creek was a city, said the *Detroit News*, "filled with women who grind out breakfast foods of all sorts and drinks of a sort." Such levity met with a stony response from the local citizens. Edward C. Hinman, a leading businessman, said that there wasn't any boom, just the natural growth one would expect, considering local brains and push.

"The food is good, people seem to want it, and it pays to market it."

The health foods, in two or three years, lifted men from obscurity and modest means to wealth, a measure of fame and a carriage.

"Battle Creek, Mich. has a population of 21,647 persons," said *Jabs*, a Chicago humorous magazine, "all of whom are engaged in the manufacture of breakfast cereals.

"One street car conductor is president of eight companies and has four more all capitalized as soon as he can think of names to call the manufactured article."

"The bill of fare at the Post Tavern," continued *Jabs'* correspondent, "has had several extensions and a bay window built on it in order to make room for the various foods that the guests are supposed to eat at the morning meal.

"I spent a Sunday there lately, noting that they had Grape Nuts, Grip Nuts (for commercial travellers only), Postum Cereal, Hullo Boena, Hello-Billo, Cero-Fruto, Shredded Wheat, Fruito-

Cerro, Malt-Ho, Flake-Ho, Abita, Tryachewa, Corn Crisp, Korn Kure, Korn Pone, Oatsina, Hayina and Strawina . . .

"And it is surprising the amount of nourishment that some of these foods possess. A dyspeptic drummer who sat opposite from me at breakfast, and who from all appearances was not long for this world, ate three ounces of Malt-Ho and one and one-half ounces of Griplor, and then moving the automatic player up in front of the agony box played 'On the Banks of the Wabash' until 12:59 P.M. without batting an eyeball."

In Battle Creek homes the guest was led to express some flattering sentiment about a tempting dish.

Said The *Chicago Tribune:*

And then you are informed that you have eaten desiccated this or that, or shrouded, or shredded, or macerated, or predigested, or beforehand assimilated something or other. And you are estopped during the rest of your visit from speaking disparagingly of health foods.

"Glad to know you," said any Battle Creek entrepreneur upon being introduced to a stranger. "$$$$ $$ $$$$$ $$$$$."

"Indeed," says the visitor.

"You bet your life," the local promoter says with emphasis. "$$$$ $$$$ $$$$ $$ $$ $$."

"Can that be possible?" the stranger says meekly.

"Possible! You bet it's possible. Why, $$$$ $$ $$ $$ and there's old Well Chewed Popcorn, he $$$$$ $$$$ $$$$ $$$ and then $$$$$—wait a minute, I want to tell you $$$ $$$ $$$$ $$ $$ and $$$$$ and over there $$ $$ $$$$$ and this coming year they won't make a cent less than $$$$$$$$$$-$$$$."

The boy in the cigar store said the Detroit papers haven't come in yet, and then he starts "$$$$ $$."

You sit out on the front porch at night with your host [the *Tribune* continued] and as the cigars turn into ashes he tells you of the fortune that waits the man who can invent a near cigar, full of near tobacco, or almost tobacco, which will look like a cigar, and smoke like a cigar, and sell for ten cents like a cigar, but which will not be a cigar at all, but some pure, sweet, wholesome combination of noninjurious ingredients, having all the characteristics of a cigar, but none of its harmful and debilitating effects.

"Make tobacco," the man says, "just like we have made coffee and breadstuffs of all kinds, retaining the good qualities and striking out the bad. There's a fortune for the man that can do it. Somebody in Battle Creek will do it some day. Sure thing. He'll make his million out of it in two years' time or less.

"Yes Sir-ee . . . $$$$ $$$$$$$ $$$$ $$$$$."

The business section of Battle Creek on a July evening during the boom days looked like a street carnival. There was a patent-medicine "doctor" working one corner, a curbstone orator on another, a pitchman hawking knife sharpeners on a third.

It was along Main Street, between Minty's and the Williams House and the Marjorie Block, that the fever of breakfast-food high finance took hold. Anybody, it was said, could go along old Main and say, "I am starting a food factory" and turn a sober druggist or mortician into a Get-Rich-Quick-Wallingford, eager to risk his savings.

W. I. Fell, founder of the Hygienic Food Company which made Mapl-Flakes was a clothing-store man from Ypsilanti. W. H. Hamilton sold out his grocery store to put his money into Per-Fo, a coined name meant to suggest Perfect Food. John E. Linihan had been a druggist and hay, grain and feed man. Linihan, a likable Irishman, made a fortune out of Cero-Fruto, sold his interests, and moved to Quincy, Illinois, to manage a food-company plant there.

Niel S. Phelps was head of a printing and publishing business, very much the Ellsworth type. Involved with Malta Vita from its early beginnings, Phelps, in association with his brother who was a doctor, also promoted a sanatorium which tried to challenge Dr. Kellogg's. He was president of a grape juice company, too. ("A small block of stock . . . can be had by the right sort of investor.") A. C. Wisner, Phelps' partner in Malta Vita, had sold pianos and organs, taught school, found himself at the age of thirty-six with a fortune estimated at two million dollars, all made in two years' time. E. P. Boggs, who saw several fortunes come and go, had owned a livery stable, herded cattle in Nebraska, ranched in California.

Most of the breakfast-food entrepreneurs were somewhat like the professional Chautauqua manager, a mixture of altruism and cupidity, of organ music and hard cash. They were all optimists. A breakfast-food promoter was the kind of man who always took the parlor stove down too soon in the spring. Aside from the Kelloggs and C. W. Post, they were more interested in stocks than in flakes.

The customary form of company organization was the limited liability partnership. It resembled a corporation, could sue and be sued as a corporation. But the members incurred no liability beyond the amount of their subscription. It was a good scheme for a speculative enterprise. The stockholder could still lose his money. Most of the companies counted only on smooth sailing, had no reserve in case of a storm. The key words in the articles of incorporation were "fully paid up." If it said so, the stock was worth par. But it often didn't say so. Complaints about irregularities were presented at Lansing from time to time, and rumors came from the capital that the attorney general might crack down with *quo warranto* proceedings against food firms whose stock was sold for less than par value, or not all subscribed for. Sometimes the stock was issued regularly enough, but someone forgot to transfer the property to the new concern. There were no "blue sky" laws. The market for food-company equities was the classic market, what someone was willing to pay. It certainly separated the men from the boys.

A few from among the many cereal names which flourished for a time during the exciting first decade of this century may be cited. They are representative of all.

Cero-Fruto was wheat flakes sprayed with apple jelly. The trustee in bankruptcy was listening to bids on its elegant factory by the end of 1904.

The University of Michigan football team, with the aid of Mapl-Flakes, which gave the old Yost team its power and drive— the Mapl-Flakes folks said—clobbered Minnesota, 23 to 6, on Thanksgiving Day, 1902. Michigan fielded a squad of only sixteen men. But one of them was the mighty Willie Heston, at right half. And Heston ate Mapl-Flakes. Despite such glories won on the field of honor, the assets of the Mapl-Flakes concern passed on to Cero-Fruto, and then to the Armour Grain Company; finally to the Ralston Purina Company.

Norka (Akron spelled backwards) Malted Oats, "Richer than wheat, better than meat," was a cooked oat food. It was extruded through a perforated disc in a meat chopper, while a revolving knife outside the disc cut the ductile bars of oats into various lengths. The irregular crumbles were then baked and went to the packing line a mottled gray in color, bland and sweetish in taste. Lacking appeal either to the eye or tongue, Norka Oats grew even grayer on the grocers' shelves. Norka became the memorial of men who did not know their oats, the plant a place of bleak walls, broken window lights, sparrows chirping and endlessly mating, fluttering and nesting through the gaunt four-story building. Tryabita, in 1902, was "peptonized and celery impregnated," made a few miles out of town at Gull Lake, the only Battle Creek breakfast food to carry the union label. The Postum Cereal Company provided, involuntarily, the superintendent who got Tryabita into production.

Vestiges of the religious background of the pure-food crusade appear in such names as Food of Eden, Golden Manna and Elijah's Manna, the original name of Post Toasties. Post at one time also put out a cereal coffee called Monk's Brew, a pseudonym for Postum. The Golden Manna people—it was a yellow meal product —sold town lots along with cereal shares. They had an auto named "Morgan Park," a three-seater with a fringe on top. Old Morgan Park chugged from the front of the Phelps Sanatorium out to a real-estate development. The fare was a nickel, round trip; or one auto-ride ticket to be found in every package of Golden Manna. Another company had a combination deal, a health food and rheumatic sanatorium stock combined, at fifty cents on the dollar.

The Hibbard Food Co., Ltd., announced that it would manufacture cereal coffee just as soon as they could think of a name. With the Battle Creek Food Co., Ltd., it was just the opposite. They had a name, but no plant.

The occurrence of "Food," "Pure Food" and "Battle Creek" in corporate titles leaves one today in utter confusion. The Battle Creek Breakfast Food Company, the Battle Creek Flaked Food Company and the Battle Creek Food Company were three quite separate entities, one not even located in Battle Creek. They had nothing in common except their indebtedness to Battle Creek cooking, cooling, tempering, flaking and promotional genius.

The Malt-Too Food Co. was not connected with the Malta Vita Company except in a me-too way. The Battle Creek Sanitarium Food Company, of which Dr. J. H. Kellogg was president, with offices at the "San," was far removed in every way from the Battle Creek Sanitarium and Health Food Co., Ltd., with offices down-town in the Penneman Block.

There was a good deal of preoccupation in cereal coffee ad-vertising with what was called "coffee intoxication." According to a medical writer in *Current Literature*, the victims of "chronic coffee-ism" were particularly apt to be actors, commercial travel-lers and "men connected with the news departments of the daily papers." Around 1900 there were six firms making health drinks in Battle Creek.

In general, what the food factories did in making flakes was to separate the bran coat and the germ from the starchy grits. The processing of corn flakes has varied little over the years. Bulk yellow hybrid corn is unloaded from boxcars, weighed, given a preliminary cleaning, and funneled into storage tanks. In the milling stage, the kernels are slightly steamed, the germ and hull removed, and then cracked into "flaking grits." The grits move on to the "cook room." There they are steamed in rotary cookers with a flavoring derived from sugar, salt and malt. In recent years most manufacturers of corn flakes restore to whole-grain levels vitamins and minerals lost in milling—mainly thiamine, niacin and iron.

After cooking, the flaking grits go through a drying and cooking process, then pass over to the storage area where they stand in bins. This causes a mellowing, a development of flavor. After this pause, the grits can be rolled into thin flakes under forty tons of pressure between water-cooled rolls turning at different speeds. It then takes only ninety seconds in the toasting ovens un-der high heat to bring the flakes up to a rich, golden brown, and they are ready to cool and pack. Variations exist between the flakes made by different companies as to the degree of toasting, the thick-ness of the flakes and the kind and amount of flavoring. The rest is merchandising, business management and advertising.

The rolling and toasting required new machinery and methods

calling forth new subindustries to serve the food factories. Adolph Johnson, a Battle Creek engineer, developed much of the new cereal machinery. Johnson designed retorts which were used until around 1918 when the rotary cooker was introduced. He also built the early travelling or "flight" ovens for the toasting operation. The old Sanitarium Food Company plant contained such an oven. The Postum Cereal Company, Quaker Oats and Egg-O-See used Johnson ovens, and W. K. Kellogg was a customer after the establishment of his Toasted Corn Flake Company. The larger companies made adaptations and improvements, but it was Johnson who eliminated the small batches and mechanized the industry. Lauhoff Brothers of Detroit introduced improved methods of flaking. All these developments meant higher output, a more satisfactory article, tighter control over quality, and a lower consumer price.

With the words "Battle Creek" acquiring a secondary meaning connoting health and hope, there were efforts made to divide up the sanitarium field as well as the manufacture of the city's characteristic foods. An ambitious challenger was the Phelps Medical and Surgical Sanatorium. A large colonial building, cobblestone on the outside, Flemish oak on the inside, the new medical center opened with a splash. The full Germania Orchestra played, with pretty nurses flitting about in pink uniforms and white aprons. There were pianos in the parlor, and plenty of meat in the icebox.

Dr. Kellogg noted the Phelps development with interest. During the construction he drove by in his carriage, watched the busy scene for a while and then addressed the workmen.

"Do a good job," he said. "I may need it some time."

Phelps' central theory was simple: It was to put the Battle Creek Sanitarium out of business. The method: to adopt every idea antithetical to the methods practised by Dr. Kellogg. The "San" emphasized health foods. So Phelps didn't serve them. The "San" opposed smoking. So Phelps had smoking rooms. The "San" was vegetarian. So Phelps featured roast beef, missing completely the canny economic idea that bran was a lot cheaper. The Doctor was calm. He was morally armed. And he had spies everywhere, who knew all that went on at the Phelps institution.

The Phelps Sanatorium was in receivership within four years

after it opened, and C. W. Post picked it up at auction. Post leased the operation to Bernarr Macfadden, who also failed. The property fell inevitably to Dr. Kellogg, as he had always thought it would. During World War II, through a series of swift-moving events, it became *the* Battle Creek Sanitarium, which it still is.

The arrival of "Professor" Bernarr Macfadden in Battle Creek was inevitable. A remarkable hillbilly from southeastern Missouri, Bernard Adolphus McFadden, developed his muscles on a wrestling mat in a St. Louis gym, and arrived in New York as a rubber. He gave health lectures, showed a flair for weird but effective publicity. He became a kind of freak, teased good-naturedly by the press, who could always count on him for a good Monday story.

"I'm just a Huckleberry Flynn," Macfadden said simply. The general outlines of his career are sufficiently well known. It is perhaps less well known that the Bare Torso King had a hot breakfast food of his own, called Strengtho. Macfadden lavished faith, affection and real money on Strengtho. But Strengtho proved to be ungrateful and turned rancid faster than the public would buy it. Confident that Strengtho would someday supersede the Kellogg cereal foods, Macfadden's devotion to Strengtho was the impelling reason why he wished to enter a sanatorium race with The Doctor. The Phelps Sanatorium, renamed The Macfadden Health Home, was to provide the background for Strengtho.

At the Health Home the manipulative procedures took a prominent place. Meat and surgery were dropped. A California naturopath headed the medical staff. There was exercise and dry friction bathing. Great stress was placed upon deep breathing, as anyone could see who met Macfadden on the street, striding along, barefoot, in shorts, long hair streaming, inhaling and exhaling rhythmically.

The physical culturist customarily delivered a Friday evening lecture. The big moment was when the proprietor himself did "Living Statues" before a black velvet curtain in the dining room. The curtain was raised and lowered with block and tackle backstage by a local kid, Frank Northrup. Frank never forgot the time when the "Professor," his body dusted with white powder, and nearly nude, struck a particularly difficult pose. That night the rope caught.

Macfadden coughed delicately. Frank jerked frantically. But the rope was stuck fast, and Bernarr had to break his pose. Northrup got a cussing that he never forgot. The old gymnast hadn't been a roustabout at the Columbian Exposition in Chicago without learning how to chew out a rube.

Unfortunately for the prospects of the Health Home, little Mac—he was only five feet six inches, the last six inches of his six feet was a lighting trick which the professor had picked up from Sandow, the Strongest Man in the World—around the end of 1907, *Physical Culture* printed a lurid two-part article about syphilis, entitled "Growing to Manhood in Civilized (?) Society." The article described clinically how youth sowed its wild oats. It was the work of a Macfadden pal, John R. Coryell, creator of Nick Carter and also active in pseudonymous literature as "Bertha M. Clay." Although the Coryell piece was presented as an urgently needed social tract, the U. S. Post Office saw no analogy between the *Physical Culture* tribute to Venus and, say, *Uncle Tom's Cabin* as social documents. Macfadden, who usually had been able to keep on the right side of the law, got two years in jail and a two-thousand-dollar fine for obscenity.

"It will not affect the Health Home here at all," insisted Macfadden's Battle Creek spokesman. But it did. The victim of American prudery left the States precipitately. His affairs were in reasonably good shape. *Physical Culture* stock was in escrow. His Chicago Healthatorium was in his secretary's name. But Mac felt distinctly like "a scrapegoat."

The Home at Battle Creek closed up. The rent was too high anyway. And the advocate of walking on all fours had become a little bit sour on Battle Creek since the cold winter night when he appeared at his local establishment, unannounced, in a Davy Crockett cap, wearing a bearskin coat, wristlets, gauntlets and carrying a hot Chinese stove in each hand. The staff took one look at the spectre before them and tossed The Father of Physical Culture out into a snowbank. They thought he was a nut.

Among the noncereal enterprises which located in Battle Creek to share the glitter of the Health City was that of a Burleigh Salisbury, who originated what he called a "system" for "hygienic dressing." A resourceful genius named Hoyt, shipped turtles from the Verona millpond to Philadelphia, where they became Battle Creek Health Soup. Advertising doctors called themselves "Battle Creek Specialists" and opened institutes in such places as Dayton, Elmira or Mattoon, Illinois, moving on when the supply of gullibles ran out. There was a Jebb Remedy Company, selling cures for rheumatism, eczema, and the ever-present catarrh. A Mrs. E. E. Taylor, Celebrated Indian Doctress, practiced medicine according to botanic principles next door to the knitting factory on South Jefferson Street. Among the ancillary enterprises which thrived on Adventism and the fame of the "San" was Joseph Lambert and Company, dealers in peanut roasters, family-size nut grinders and nut butter. In a town where every elder was an author, Mrs. Lambert entered the teeming literary scene. Her métier was the nutfood cookbook. The authoress glorified mock oyster patties, deplored the effect of protein food which was, she said, to "benumb the brain, cloud the conscience, and render man unfit to meet the vesper hour." Dr. James M. Peebles, with his long white beard, was quacking it in the Minty block with his "epilepsy cure"; and also had a nerve regenerator competitive to the malt tonic put out by the Battle Creek Beverage Company, Malta Pura. There was a Davray Neuropathic Institute, not osteopathic, not magnetic, not hypnotic, and no medicine either; just "Absolute Science"; also an Institute of "Mental Physical Culture," whatever that was.

An especial trial to the cornflake Kelloggs was Frank J. Kellogg. He was no relation. But he did bear the magic name. This scalawag, known locally as "Anti-Fat Kellogg," made a million dollars out of thyroid extract, pokeroot and toasted bread. His nostrum was known to the overweight as Kellogg's Safe Fat Reducer. The Battle Creek Flesh Food Company offered a catarrh remedy, promising investors a return of 22 to 27 per cent. It was pointed out that "There is more catarrh in this section of the country than all other diseases put together." In a special sense, that was true; because catarrh was the vogue word for whatever ailed you.

In the mood of the early 1900's it seemed that there was someone in Battle Creek who was ready to take a flyer on almost any industrial proposition; and some of them clicked. But it was the grain foods, created in Battle Creek especially for "a great blood and sinew-using age," that made the town a metropolis, where the news-boys were said to work off local stocks for change.

When a man could make his pile in a couple of years, many felt the call to supply the world with a better breakfast.

Many were called; but . . .

XIII

... Few Were Chosen

BATTLE CREEK's expansionist dream centered upon markets. If every one in the U.S. ate an ounce of breakfast food every morning the way Battle Creek folks did—and why shouldn't they?—they would chew up five times the day-and-night production of all the food factories. When the question was posed that perhaps the breakfast-food business was being overdone, the answer always came—more consumer education was needed, brought about by "judicious advertising." Look at the foreign market—practically untouched. Only the Postum Cereal Company and Sanitas Nut Food Company were shipping any quantity of goods overseas. Why, New Zealand alone —a nice country and filled with intelligent, progressive people, but not the largest nor the most important country in the world by a long shot—could easily consume the entire output of a whole factory. There were over one hundred glove factories in Gloversville, New York; and who thought there were too many gloves, asked *The Daily Journal* at about the time the number of dry-cereal foods on the market passed one hundred.

The optimists could point in 1903 to the ten million dollars a year being spent to promote the Battle Creek doctrine. It was to the effect that our high civilization, with its emphasis upon brain vocations, called for new foods. One cereal maker paid five thousand dollars for the right to paint a comic figure and some rhymes on a big chimney in lower New York that could be seen from the North River ferryboats. Such theatrical stunts attracted not only breakfast eaters, but also prospectors, drawn to a new kind of gold mine. They were to find that the market was not to be had just for the asking. Possibly only Post and W. K. Kellogg clearly understood that it cost from five hundred to eight hundred and fifty dollars to make and sell a thousand dollars' worth of prepared cereal.

So of all who felt the urge to agitate "the food question" at a profit, the greater number proved to be inadequate in the areas of finance, of production or of merchandising. In a memorable cartoon published early in this century, John T. McCutcheon hit off the climate in Battle Creek. He sketched a capitalist breaking ground with a spade under a sign reading "A Battle Creek Food Company will be established here tomorrow. Capital $4.00." The artist slyly satirized the Battle Creek products by drawing a side-show spieler beating his drum under the legend "You Have Heard of the Famous Battle Creek Health Foods. We Make Health Foods and We Are in Battle Creek. Try Us." Another along the breakfast-food midway was shown hawking "Bita-Pieca," the product of "The Noisy Battle Creek Food Co."

As it turned out, about all that most cereal-stock investors ever got back from their venture, beyond experience, was some samples and a free lunch at an annual meeting.

"I am sorry you are having such bad luck with the Mapl-Flakes stock," W. K. Kellogg wrote to a Detroit friend. "Would have been very glad indeed to have given you a tip had I been asked for one before the purchase was made." At the time, the stock was offered at $1.75 a share. There were, it is hardly necessary to say, no dividends.

One always turns back to C. W. Post as the man who knew the ropes. Money, product, distribution, advertising; he understood the importance of all, and their interrelationships. Business, like diplomacy, has its *Real-Politik*. C. W. played the game consummately according to the rule book in force at the time. He kept his engagements. His name on commercial paper was good. But there was no turn-the-other-cheek nonsense about him. If the manager of the Sanitas factory, a hard-boiled Irishman with a flaming red beard, was willing to visit the Post plant at night and bring along the Sanitas employee who knew how to make the malt flavoring for corn flakes, C. W. was willing to make it worth his while. If the Kellogg factory burned down, Post could promptly buy up all the cereal machinery in Battle Creek and store it while loading the grocery trade with his corn flakes. In the early days when cash was short, Post could also charm a farmer into dumping his wheat at the Postum works and driving off without getting his money. C.W. could handle a workman as deftly as he did a farmer.

L. W. Pratt, an old-time employee, remembered Post's visit to the factory.

"Often times he would find the men waiting for an oven to be pulled. Mr. Post would say, 'I see you have a little idle time on your hands.' So he would call us bread cutters with the rest of the gang together, and say, 'I have a good story I want to tell you.'

"We would all gather around Mr. Post while he told his story. We would have a good laugh. Then he would say: 'Boys, we have killed enough time. Let's all go to work.'

"Then he would walk away and we would go at it again *like wildcats.*"

Post's abilities present an interesting antithesis to those of Dr. Kellogg. Where The Doctor was diffuse, Post was concentrated. He put his all, or the Fuller Advertising Agency's all, on one, two, never more than three or four products. Dr. John was always economizing, resulting in much slow handwork and high costs. Post purchased the best machinery available, and made thousands of cases of goods on a few items while The Doctor made a few cases on his many.

Post was a superb judge of the main chance. Tough, bull-headed, often prejudiced and violent, there was a dynamism about him. People were attracted to C.W. and told stories about him and admired his hustle.

"If Post were to be dropped from an airship on a desert island on uncharted seas," said *Pearson's* magazine, "he would begin at once to take note of the things about him which were of utility. If the island were inhabited, C. W. Post would proceed to round up the natives and teach them to use his special brand of coconuts. . . . In six months the natives would have adopted fig leaves— 'grown only on Post trees'—and inside of a year he'd be mayor of the island and king of the Lululoos. Later on he would introduce shoes and sandals made from 'Post cocoa bark,' and when the rescue party finally found him he'd be in a position to buy the ship and sail it home as master."

So far as "truth in advertising" was concerned, Post did not lag behind his time. But he wasn't ahead of it, either. Business ethics required a man to tell the truth. But they did not require him to tell the whole truth. Postum advertising was based upon a sound half-truth: *some* people slept better, felt better generally, when they stopped drinking coffee, whether they drank any Postum or not. The spirit of the times is pretty accurately expressed in the remark of a Maine storekeeper who said he didn't see why people told lies when the truth could be just as misleading; or the Cohoes, New York, horse trader who sold a mare guaranteed to be sound of wind and limb, and without fault. When the buyer returned and wanted his money back on the ground that she had a very serious fault—blindness—the seller said virtuously, "Blindness is not her fault, but her misfortune."

Before Post, much advertising was flippant.

"Why is good advice like Piso's Cure for Consumption? Because everybody ought to take it!"

But advertising done the Post way was deadly serious. Addressing "highly organized people" (are you highly organized or are you a *clod?*), he counselled the reader, and one can almost see him waggling that long forefinger: "Remember, you can recover from any ordinary disease by discontinuing coffee and poor food, and using Postum Food Coffee and Grape Nuts."

So potent was the advertising tradition that C.W. established for his first-born product that it was not until 1951 that his business heirs agreed amicably with the Federal Trade Commission not to advertise that drinking coffee discourages marriage, or that it results in ". . . divorces, business failures, factory accidents, juvenile delinquency, traffic accidents, fire or home foreclosures."

As it became evident that the priceless ingredient in the future success of the Postum Cereal Company would be advertising, C.W. erected a special building for the production of his advertisements, presided over by debonair, dressy Frank Grandin, himself the creator of many catchy advertising phrases. The building was a half-timber replica of an English inn, furnished in mission oak, with a cozy corner or "thinking room" for the Chairman of the Board.

Publishers and salesmen of white space gladly journeyed to Battle Creek to make their reverences to the millionaire advertiser, and hear him say again, "All I have I owe to advertising." The

Michigan Press Association came to honor the man who "made the editor independent of store pay and farm produce." Carriages and tallyhos hauled publishers out to the White City all day long to see the advertising building, taking East Main Street to Post Avenue, then down Marjorie Street to the works, along the macadam drive to the *porte-cochère;* while the Postum band discoursed lively tunes under the gnarled trees of the old Beardsley orchard.

The publishers manfully downed their luncheon of oysters escalloped with Grape Nuts, their Postum muffins, Postum coffee, and Grape Nuts dessert with Grape Nuts wafers on the side; and gave a standing toast to C. W. Other manufacturers took up the new Post way to advertise food. Ralston Health Food, for example, said that when you opened the package, you could see thousands of tiny grains "full of the Vegetable Phosphorus that makes *children* grow like magic and develop strong mentally," giving the brain "all the phosphorus it can use in *heavy thinking.*"

The American Cereal Company, predecessor of the Quaker Oats Company, said of Apetizo, the Great Hemoglobin Producer and "physiologic food," that it made red blood, which distinguished it from all other foods; except Grape Nuts, of course, which also made red blood. And said so first. Hardy-food was "brain, nerve and muscle food," a nutritional concept which Dr. Harvey W. Wiley described as being the equivalent of saying "little toe food." Orange Meat was "absolutely digestible," although both the microscope and analysis showed the presence of bran, which *isn't.*

When Postum was spending about a million dollars a year to admonish the sufferers of "coffeedom" that their ills—real, imagined, or advertising-induced—would disappear when they drank baked wheat, other makers of similar products quickly appeared on the scene, their hearts also torn by the nervous troubles of the people. To C. W. they were not colleagues in a great health crusade. There was no outstretched hand of fellowship from the man who got there firstest with the mostest. They were viewed, rather, as "buzzards roosting on the fence watching for some choice bones to lick"; pirates "commercially seeking my life's blood," imitating Postum, the standard twenty-five-cent product, and offering their inferior article at fifteen cents.

"I concluded to twist the wrist of some of these pirates," said

Post. "I organized a new company, produced a new package, and called the product 'Monk's Brew,' announcing on the package that the cereal coffee therein was the equal of any cereal coffee made, and to be sold at five cents per package. . . . I simply filled these packages with genuine 'Postum,' but under a different name." This price was less than it cost to make the product. The imitators had to retire back into the woods, the Founder noted with satisfaction. "They died promptly and violently on all sides. . . . The slaughter was a massacre, plain and simple, although no one could complain under the circumstances."

Post always regarded the demise of cheap competition with a certain relish. When people trespass on a businessman's property, as he saw it, ". . . he has a right to mark the boys with bird shot when they come into his orchard and try to steal his apples." Dr. Kellogg watched Charley Post's anguish over his imitators with amusement.

"The Sanitarium rejoices that our reformatory ideas . . . have reached such a point of public esteem as to acquire commercial value."

When the Maine Agricultural Station said that the strengthening and vitalizing ability of a cup of Postum was that of about half an ounce of solids including 1/100th ounce of protein, equal to the protein in a dessert spoonful of skimmed milk——

When *Hygeia* pointed out that the amount of starch digested in the preparation of ready-to-eat cereals was a small percentage of the whole, hardly justifying the claim of "pre-digested"——

When the U. S. Department of Agriculture observed that "a novel appearance and quasi-scientific name do not necessarily represent any unusual food value. Unless something is added during the process of manufacture, all brands must have just about the same composition as the cereals from which they are made——"

When Dr. Harvey W. Wiley commented that "Cereal foods are flaked or rolled, so as to occupy an immense bulk with light weight, and while there may be no intention of deception, there exists the general impression of receiving more than one gets——"

When one rolls these observations over his tongue, the question naturally arises whether the new breakfast foods rendered a service to society commensurate with the rewards. To provide an answer it is necessary to dig deeper than advertising or chemical analysis of the common grains; deeper than saying simply that the manufacturer modified the grain's appearance, texture and flavor, producing something higher in price than the unelaborated goods such as farina and corn meal.

Despite the fact that in the early years of the industry there was no relationship between nutrition and price—Granose Flakes were among the most expensive—the ready-to-serve foods did offer definite advantages. They added variety in taste and appearance. They were fresh and clean. They were storable. They could be eaten right from the box. They were in line with the trend in food processing begun by Gail Borden and his condensed milk.

Adulteration was not a problem. The Pennsylvania Department of Agriculture looked into that. It found no bran masquerading as whole wheat, no corncobs or stalks, no bleaching agents. Thus an old joke fell to the ground, that the Battle Creek health foods were fostered by the Michigan lumber interests as a means of utilizing sawdust. Some readers of the perfervid preachments of the cereal gospellers wrote in that the only thing which could make people feel as frisky as the ads said would be a drug. So the Pennsylvania food analysts looked for strychnine as well as corncobs. The results were negative. No "tonic materials" were found.

What microscopic examinations couldn't reveal, what tests for moisture content, ash, protein, fibre, starch and fat could not show, was the fact that *the public was glad to pay a generous price for an attractive article.* The deeper reason why the breakfast foods so largely took over the morning meal was that the housewife was buying not just food but a shorter kitchen workday. This was something different from what the food dollar had ever purchased before. The flakes were among the first of the modern convenience foods, marking a trend later extended by dehydrated soup mixes, reconstituted milk and fruit juices, and frozen foods; a development in the utilization of foodstuffs that is still incomplete.

The idea persisted for a long time that there was sales appeal in a name with religious connotations. When C. W. Post wanted an alias for Postum he selected "Monk's Brew." When he launched his third important product in 1906 he called it Elijah's Manna. Elijah's Manna was corn flakes. Of Post's corn flakes it may be said that they were the first modern-type corn flakes to become popular on a large scale. There were also physical differences which a technician would consider important. The Post flakes were thicker than others, with bubbles on them which were said to cause the flakes to stay crisp longer in milk or cream. The Elijah's Manna carton was green and white, the color scheme of the White City. The package front carried a picture of the prophet, Elijah, seated on a rock in the wilderness, with a raven on his shoulder, scattering the manna which was supposed to have supported the Israelites.

Post was perplexed when a howl went up in the Bible belt over his new trade name, dismayed when he learned that it was against the law in Britain to register Biblical names for commercial purposes. So, in 1908, Elijah's Manna became Post Toasties, packaged in yellow and red cartons, cheered up with a picture on the front of a young miss warming herself in front of an open fire with a bowl of corn flakes in her lap. W. K. Kellogg's journal for the grocery trade mentioned the arrival of the new product: "Post Toasties—spritely two-year-old sired by Post and damned by the consumer," an interesting example of business amenity as it was practiced by our fathers.

The effect of the health-food boom was adverse upon the affairs of Dr. Kellogg. In 1895 he made $22,242 out of the Sanitas Food Company. By 1902, Sanitas was losing money. The merchandising policy was timid while The Doctor starved the business as to equipment and advertising. Some food brokers carried the line, but the interest was diffused over fruit crackers, oatmeal wafers, water biscuits, nut products and so on. There was vastly more charm for The Doctor in developing a vegetable egg made out of a tomato base, or a new Fruit Cocoa, than in finding a winner among his products and giving it a chance to run. Kellogg always had too many irons in the fire. Or, as Will Kellogg put it: "My brother is the best disorganizer in the world."

While C. W. Post was riding high, W. K. Kellogg continued to be the faithful drudge. He did the shirt-sleeve work, got up the money when The Doctor found it necessary to raise the wind, weighed in the local wheat at the Sanitas wagon scales, answered the mail, wrote to the Bureau of Chemistry in Washington as Dr.

Kellogg told him to do: "Can you furnish me with any information in regard to methods for producing oil from cottonseed, peanuts, or linseed meal?" After the Sanitarium fire, W. K. handled the financing of the new building, an important achievement which was not marked by any special notice.

Caustically, he recalled: "I had nothing to say about how the money was spent, but I had to raise the money to pay the bills."

The junior Kellogg saw all too clearly what was going to happen to the last and the greatest of the ready-to-eat cereal foods; and many a time he gave The Doctor a wigging over the future of corn flakes.

Early in 1902, W. K. had told Dr. Kellogg that he was leaving. Then came the "San" fire. In that extremity he stayed on to help rebuild and refinance. In 1903 he tried to advertise more aggressively. But Dr. Kellogg got a stern warning from the medical profession. Already under fire in orthodox medical circles over his attachment to massage and hydropathic methods, Dr. Kellogg froze right up every time W. K. broached the subject of commercializing corn flakes.

The situation dragged along in an atmosphere of brotherly incompatibility. Sometimes there were quarrels. Sometimes there was a truce; and sometimes the two Kelloggs wouldn't even speak to each other. In 1905, Charles D. Bolin, a St. Louis insurance man, came to the "San" as a patient, saw the corn flakes, and caught the vision. He urged W. K. to start a company for their manufacture. It was clear enough then that The Doctor was unwilling to undertake an operation on the scale that was being proposed; and, really, the entire food business was secondary to his major interest. The "San" was still heavily in debt as a result of the fire, and The Doctor deeply preoccupied with its financial problems.

Since The Doctor refused to go ahead on his own account, Bolin and W.K. put forward another proposal, the purchase of the right to make the flakes. The flake patents were invalid. This had been determined when Dr. Kellogg sued Malta Vita and Force for infringement. But W.K. expressed his willingness for The Doctor to be properly compensated for his invention. The Doctor found this idea interesting.

"I was worried," he explained later, "and thought it best to dispose, if possible, of the toasted corn flakes, so as to relieve the Sanitarium."

A deal was consummated. The cornflake business was separated from the Sanitas Food Company and placed in a new corporation, the Battle Creek Toasted Corn Flake Company, incorporated February 19, 1906. The new concern, under the management of W. K. Kellogg, took over Dr. John Harvey's rights, and began the manufacture of Sanitas Corn Flakes. The corporate name was changed later to Toasted Corn Flake Company, then to Kellogg Toasted Corn Flake Company and finally to the Kellogg Co. The actual cash in the business was thirty-five thousand dollars, raised by Bolin in St. Louis. But Dr. Kellogg was the majority stockholder. He distributed part of this stock among the Sanitarium doctors in lieu of salary increases, and trotted off to Europe to see Pavlov.

W. K. was well aware that his distinguished brother did not think he had much gumption, but when The Doctor returned to Battle Creek he got a sharp surprise. Will had bought in the stock that Dr. John had given away, patiently following the "San" physicians around, picking up their certificates like a chicken pecking at corn. Tirelessly he worked for the day when he would personally own a majority of the shares of stock. All of his life's savings were pledged for this purpose.

"Make no little plans," he muttered, and if he said it once he said it a thousand times. As he settled into the presidency of the cornflake firm, W. K. placed upon the carton a bold legend: "The Genuine Bears This Signature—W. K. Kellogg." The move was symbolical. At forty-five, an old man in his own view, the Kellogg whose name is now inseparable from corn flakes, began his independent career.

XIV

None Genuine Without This Signature

W. K. KELLOGG was a round, plain-looking, solemn man, a "single-footer" in business and in life. Completely bald, he seemed always to be staring with owlish surprise through his tortoise-shell spectacles. Since his life was a sort of votive hymn to corn, it may be apropos to consider for a moment this remarkable and abundant grain. Botanically an absorbingly interesting American plant, its genes are located, its chromosomes well mapped. Through knowledge gained from corn, the science of genetics has been applied to agriculture with conspicuous success. Our present strains of hybrid corn are one result, adding half a billion bushels to the annual grain supply.

Corn "has become the *Drosophila* of the vegetable kingdom," a leading biologist remarked recently. Corn, the gift of the Indians to the New World and the whole world, became the chief energy food of hundreds of millions of people, the source of late summer's delectable roasting ears, of the white confection which keeps our movie theatres solvent, of meal and breads, of pork and beef, indirectly, of an infinity of sugars and syrups, of starches and industrial products, of cob pipes and bourbon whiskey. Corn means griddlecakes, johnnycake, dumplings, fritters, hominy, muffins, mush, pones and puddings. Flaked, it is, above all, a crunchy breakfast food of unsurpassed flavor.

There would be no corn without man to perpetuate it, for corn cannot seed itself. Yet with a little help it thrives under a wider range of ecological conditions than any other grain, from clearings in the tropical rain forests to the St. Lawrence River Valley with its truncated growing season. Eve ate the apple and lost her heritage. The American colonists ate corn, and found theirs. "Corn fed" means a sturdy, provincial, healthy, hustling American. Corn means, in the slang of our time, a poem, picture, play or sentiment that is sincere, direct and unashamed. Corn is the familiar, the tried and true.

As early as 1878 young Dr. J. H. Kellogg had given some attention to the nutritive values of corn, its unapproachable economy, its possible wider use as human food. The brewing industry was using corn grits in the '80's, as has already been mentioned, in the form of uncooked flakes. Dr. Kellogg was well acquainted with this fact. These brewers' flakes were known as malt flakes or Cerealine. The latter was a trade name for tiny raw flakes made from small grits by the Cerealine Manufacturing Company of Indianapolis. But "Cerealine" was sometimes used in a generic sense. Mrs. Ella E. Kellogg, for example, spoke of cooking Cerealine in a double boiler.

Dr. Kellogg took up the matter of a flaked-corn breakfast food seriously in 1898. His "Sanitas Toasted Corn Flakes" were put out at that time under the Sanitas Nut Food Co. label in a blue package with a view of the Sanitarium on its face. For several years corn flakes created little stir. The interest in breakfast foods was all concentrated in wheat. There was another discouraging factor; the corn flakes were not very good.

These first corn flakes were made from the whole kernel of white corn. The "San" patients found them crisper than wheat, but the product would not stand up on the grocers' shelves, as the Sanitas people found out to their sorrow when a whole carload came back home—rancid.

In 1902, Kellogg tried again. This time he achieved a stable flake. Between these two different Kellogg approaches to the problem of flaking corn, Korn Krisp flakes appeared in Battle Creek during the summer of 1901. Korn Krisp was made by Fuller Bros., who came over from Kalamazoo. They got off to a fast start with a light, crisp flake which had a malt flavoring. But there was still too much corn oil in the flakes and they spoiled. Thus Korn Krisp joined the doleful procession of the bankrupts. The flake that established corn as a major grain type in the breakfast food field was the 1902 Kellogg corn flake. With its secret formula for the malt flavoring, this corn flake became the chief asset of the Battle Creek Toasted Corn Flake Co., the predecessor of today's cereal giant, the Kellogg Co.

W. K. Kellogg, who rather fancied the trade name Korn Krisp, and used machinery, if acquired at the right price, picked up the Korn Krisp assets in the fall of 1906 at a receivership sale. He thought seriously of adopting the name as the brand designation for the new Corn Flake Company. Dr. Kellogg insisted that the corn flakes should be called Sanitas and they were for a while. But W. K. hadn't given up on Korn Krisp. To his ear the connotation of Sanitas was plumbing, washable oilcloth, wall covering, refrigerators. A design was actually made up for a new name—"Kellogg's Toasted Korn Krisp"—plates engraved, and Korn Krisp cartons ordered. But the decision shifted at the last minute to "Kellogg's Toasted Corn Flakes" with the W. K. Kellogg signature line. The Doctor could hardly object to the continuation of the W. K. facsimile for a number of reasons. W. K. was, after all, the president of the company. The line made it clear which Kellogg was endorsing the product, the layman, not the ethical physician. A further reason why The Doctor could not object was that he was in Europe at the time.

The Battle Creek Toasted Corn Flake Company started up in an old frame building on Bartlett Street near the Grand Trunk depot. It was equipped with a 6-horse-power Corliss engine and had a travelling flight oven left over from the days when the Hygienic Food Co. had made Mapl-Flakes on the premises. A converted dwelling house served as office.

"It was an old fire trap," W. K. said later.

At the time the country was in the grip of a financial panic. W. K. didn't know the grocery trade. Wheat cereals still had the call with the consumer. But the younger Kellogg had an unshakeable faith in the future of corn. Like C. W. Post, W. K. plunged on advertising. At one time, he said that he had invested one third of his funds in a single page in *The Ladies Home Journal*. In addition to the little plant on Bartlett Street, W. K. was manufacturing corn flakes at two other locations. He had leased the Norka factory. (Oats. Did not keep. Failed.) He also leased some space and equipment at the Sanitas factory.

Thus, during the first year of operation, there were three small factories turning out corn flakes. Altogether they got up to a production of about 2900 cases a day, with a net return of about one dollar a case. The time had come to emphasize merchandising.

"I didn't know the difference between a food broker and a jobber," W. K. said of this era.

He knew enough, however, to hire Andrew Ross, blue-eyed Scotsman off a Canadian farm, who was then Philadelphia district manager for Shredded Wheat. Ross did know the cereal business; but he demurred when Kellogg visited him in Philadelphia and suggested that he come to Battle Creek.

"I hear strange things are done at the Toasted Corn Flake plant," Ross objected. "Open on Sunday, down on Saturday. Is it a commercial, or a religious institution?"

But sixty days later W. K. was back with a proposition that could not be refused.

Installed as sales manager, Ross first thing came up against a Seventh Day Adventist salesman who wouldn't work on Saturday, and found that about ten per cent of the factory help were Adventists. The plant operated, as Ross had heard, on Sunday, was closed on Saturday. There came a time when the company hired thirty Sunday-keeping girls from the Mapl-Flakes factory. What to do? W. K. was away, Ross in charge. He decreed that Kellogg would work on Saturday and keep the Sabbath on Sunday. It stayed that way.

The Kellogg concern embarked upon a strenuous, long-term effort to appropriate "Toasted Corn Flakes" as a distinctive part of its brand name. This program involved the company with the legal risks inherent in a descriptive name. Any relaxation in alertness would expose the trade-mark to the legal dangers of acquiescence or laches, *i.e.*, failure to maintain a right. On this "toasted cornflake" issue the Kellogg Co. sustained one of its rare defeats. Kellogg sued the Quaker Oats Company seeking to enjoin Quaker from selling corn flakes under the name "toasted corn flakes." The decision, upheld by the federal circuit court of appeals, was in favor of Quaker Oats. It was determined that the words were generic or descriptive. This litigation was to have a direct bearing upon the Kellogg Co.'s greatest legal dispute which arose when Kellogg started to manufacture and sell, under the name "shredded wheat," a product similar to Perky's original strawlike biscuit. Kellogg history bristled with crises arising out of patents, copyrights, trade practices and antitrust action.

"We were fairly active in the courts," W. K. recalled.

At the beginning of the cornflake venture Bolin thought that he had an option to sell corn flakes all over the world. The Doctor, regretting his generosity, insisted the sale of the rights was confined to the U.S. He had begun to see the Toasted Corn Flake Co. as a continuing source of revenue. There would be other products coming along. He could sell the rights to each one, product by product, country by country. For example, The Doctor started to flake rice, forming once more a new company, the Toasted Rice Flake and Biscuit Company. Dr. Kellogg also set up a Yogurt Company, evolved out of Bulgarian "yhoghoart."

Dr. Kellogg's idea about yogurt was to put lactic acid into constarch tablets for oral use. He brought a corps of old ladies into the plant to operate machines that filled capsules with sour milk and cornstarch. Not every Kellogg creation was a success. The rice flakes turned rancid, and whatever good the yogurt product did was not due to any power in the tablets to change the intestinal flora. For The Doctor had made a slip. He put in some acetic acid to produce a slight taste. Later it was discovered that the acid had killed the yogurt ferment. The therapeutic value of the pills was confined to whatever medicinal powers there were in plain cornstarch. But the yogurt company boomed for a while and made a substantial contribution to the support of *Good Health* magazine.

With his ingenuity and his flair for trade names, Dr. John Harvey was always incubating little proprietary businesses. He had a certain amount of commercial acumen, but he was not, as he thought, a captain of industry. In The Doctor were combined, strangely, a high inventive faculty, and an actual indifference to money. It was not the equipment likely to produce an industrial leader. To The Doctor the Toasted Corn Flake Co. was just another one of many schemes. He thought of closing up the Sanitas business, then decided that all he wanted to do was to change its name. So Sanitas adopted the business style of the Kellogg Food Co. Thus there was a

Toasted Corn Flake Company over on the East side of Battle Creek operated by one Kellogg, and a Kellogg Company on the other side of town run by another Kellogg. Both used "Kellogg" brand names on their goods. Both claimed to be "the original" and "the genuine." The nut foods carried the legend "the genuine bears the signature of W. K. Kellogg." But they belonged to Dr. J. H. Kellogg. The situation effectively confused the consumer, the food trade and even the U. S. post office, which delivered a substantial portion of The Doctor's mail to W. K. and vice versa.

The little cornflake business encountered one difficulty which W. K. could not charge against his mercurial brother. On the Fourth of July, 1907, after a little more than a year's operation, the Bartlett Street plant burned to the ground. The cause was never determined.

"There had been a number of fires in Battle Creek," W. K. remarked, "apparently a fire bug was at work."

The fire might also have been due to an overheated oven; or to the carelessness of some night-shift workmen who had been celebrating Independence Day by setting off firecrackers.

Already behind in filling orders, the lost production put the infant firm in grave danger of losing its markets. Such limited production as remained in the old Norka plant and the leased facilities at the Sanitas factory were allocated to strong territories. The heaviest blow, however, was the damage the fire did to the patented, water-cooled flaking rolls made by Lauhoff Brothers, in Detroit. Before the ashes were cool, W. K. appeared in the office of Frank Lauhoff with tears in his eyes.

"Frank, my plant has completely burned down," he said. "I'm falling behind on my orders. What can you do for me?"

With every disposition to help, Lauhoff was in an awkward spot himself. The Toasted Corn Flake Co. was a good customer. W. K. Kellogg had been buying flaking mills since 1905, first for the Sanitas Nut Food Co., later on his own account. But C. W. Post was also buying the rollers. The rivals were constantly jockeying to get delivery on flaking mills ahead of each other. At the time of the fire, Lauhoff Bros. had already accepted a large order for rolls from the Postum Cereal Company under a stipulation that no mill should be shipped to any other party until their own order was filled. All that Lauhoff could do at the moment for Kellogg was to promise to rebuild the damaged mills.

Lauhoff saw the Postum people about relaxing their contract. All day long Frank Lauhoff and M. K. Howe went up and down the subject. Howe pointed out that the contract had been placed in good faith, that they needed their rolls badly. (Most of them went into storage.) It was unfortunate that Kellogg had had a fire, but Postum could not in fairness to their hungry customers allow any deviation from the agreement. There were other things in the background; such as the time when Post ran short of coal and Kellogg had a number of loaded coal cars on his siding. When the Postum Company asked if they could buy a car to tide them over, the offer was refused. So . . .

At the end of the long day, the Post people escorted Lauhoff to the railroad station and put him on the train. He always thought that this extraordinary courtesy was to make sure that he was headed for Detroit, not the Kellogg factory.

Only one possibility remained. Perhaps the Post contract could be fulfilled and some additional production of flaking mills could be squeezed out of the Lauhoff machine shop. As it turned out, Lauhoff did make and ship to Kellogg some extra stands of rolls at the time Charley Post was trying to corner the supply. On one occasion, just to be sure he got what was coming to him, W. K. Kellogg, while visiting in the Lauhoff plant, took some acid and etched his "W. K. Kellogg" signature on some mills so they would be sure to find their way to the right home.

Any roller which Lauhoff shipped to the Corn Flake Co. at this time was known under a euphemism as "A Diamond in the Corner." The "Diamond" was a flaking mill packed in the corner of a box-car billed out as Crystal Malt Flakes. The mill did not appear on the bill of lading.

"I am sending you another car load of Crystal Malt Flakes," Frank Lauhoff would notify W. K. Kellogg. "Unload it at night and you will find a diamond in one corner."

All Postumville knew that Kellogg was getting malt flakes from Detroit. But the "diamond story" remained a well-kept secret for years. Long afterwards the Postum people heard about the "Diamond in the Corner."

"Even after all those years," Frank Lauhoff said, "they gave me hell about it."

Before evening on the day of the fire, W. K. Kellogg had an architect on the phone. Rough plans for a new factory were in a form to be approved three days later. A new location was purchased within a week, ground broken before the end of the month. The new plant was in operation in January, 1908.

Following the completion of the new plant, there occurred a series of developments which resulted in the termination of the thirty-year association between the Kellogg brothers. In 1908, W. K. relinquished his interest and position in the Sanitas Nut Food Co. Soon after The Doctor resigned as a director of the Toasted Corn Flake Co. Another tie was broken when W. K. removed the picture of the Battle Creek Sanitarium from the face of his corn-flake packages. Corn flakes were to be promoted thereafter for their appetite appeal rather than as a dietary food.

As a result of these moves there developed a series of legal controversies between the two brothers over who had the right to use the Kellogg name in the manufacture of breakfast foods. The conflict lasted for some twelve years. Did Dr. Kellogg, when he adopted the business style of the Kellogg Food Co., hope to benefit from the extensive advertising of W. K.'s company? Will Kellogg thought so. The Doctor had never shown any desire through the years to use the Kellogg name until W. K. did. Perhaps vanity was a factor, or W. K.'s success, or the simple desire to thwart Will. Certainly The Doctor believed with a great sincerity that he was *the* Kellogg. To J. H. Kellogg, the Toasted Corn Flake Co. was using "his" name.

Dr. Kellogg, when challenged, gave an ingenious explanation of why he changed the name of Sanitas Nut Food Co. to the Kellogg Food Co. He said that W. K.'s son, "Lenn" Kellogg, told him that Frank Kellogg, the patent-medicine Kellogg, was about to enter the food field. The Doctor rushed in to copper the Kellogg name and save the family honor. But W. K. didn't believe a word of it. In 1910 he brought suit charging that Dr. Kellogg's food company was trying to create the impression that its products were made by the Toasted Corn Flake Co.

The issue was settled out of court in 1911 under an agreement whereby Dr. Kellogg's company was permitted to use the Kellogg name on flaked cereal foods subject to certain sharp restrictions. There was also a Canadian aspect to the struggle, with the embattled brothers each claiming the right to make and sell corn flakes in Canada on an exclusive basis. In 1916 the controversy flared up again, resulting in a sweeping victory for the younger Kellogg, the judge ruling that the Kellogg Toasted Corn Flake Co. was the exclusive owner of the trade name, except for the restricted use granted to The Doctor by the 1911 agreement. This ruling was sustained by the Michigan Supreme Court in 1920, and a court order in 1921 ended the case.

W. K. bought out the last of The Doctor's holdings in the cornflake company in 1911. To do this he went into debt for a third of a million dollars. Later, when he found himself able for the first time to write a check for a million dollars, he said that he had never wanted or expected to be rich, but that other people had made him rich by trying to push him around. Much of the credit for W. K.'s prosperity, then, must be given to John Harvey, an artist in the push-around. With stock control, W. K. was able to establish his own policies and see that they were pursued—inviolable trade practices, highest product quality, expansion of facilities financed by the plow-back of profits, relentless advertising, one-man management and an impregnable financial position.

W. K. would repeat to his associates: "Attack boldly. Crack it or quit. The trouble with you men," he would say, "is that you don't know how to lose money."

There were interludes of pacific relations between the Kellogg brothers when nothing more ruffling occurred than "San" patients addressing W. K. as "Doctor," or mail coming into the Sanitarium addressed to "Dr. W. K. Kellogg." W. K., if indisposed, would enter the Sanitarium as a patient, though reserving the right to complain about everything. Dr. Kellogg would address W. K. in correspondence as "Dear Brother Will," and sign himself, "As ever, your affectionate brother—John Harvey Kellogg." On one occasion The Doctor grew positively effusive, and complimented Will on his "good judgment and good sense in business," acknowledging that Will got no fame or prestige during the years when he worked for him.

And then something disturbing would come up. There would be ugly rumors about how the cornflake company had defrauded the Sanitas concern out of five thousand dollars, and W. K. would accuse The Doctor bitterly as the source of the libel. Once again Will wouldn't even talk to J. H. on the phone without taking the precaution of having Andrew Ross listen in on an extension.

"W. K. never in the world came to visit his mother," a niece, Priscilla Butler, remembered, "that he didn't hunt up J. H. and have a good quarrel."

"Now, Doctor," W. K. would start out satirically, "if you will again refresh your memory . . ."

And, again, in exasperation:

"I have your six page letter. . . . I am getting very tired and sick of this controversy and think it very unprofitable for either you or I."

Sooner or later a fast buck or a trade-mark came between the loving brothers. Or a Kellogg Toasted Corn Flake Co. salesman would find some Kellogg Food Co. export goods that The Doctor could not legally sell in the continental United States out on the shelf in Port Chester, New York. Then the fur would fly again.

"I served your interests, tried to be you, to see with your eyes, think as you thought," said Will K. Kellogg, sharply, "and now——"

When W. K. Kellogg founded his company on corn flakes, dire predictions of disaster were made on all sides. But pretty girls demonstrated the dainty flakes in food shows. There were baby picture contests for the most beautiful cornflake baby. Canvassers followed the advertising with samples, and advertising went *ahead* of distribution. W. K. went into the field himself. He was told by Southern jobbers that he couldn't sell corn flakes in the South. He replied that he wasn't trying to sell them. He was just telling what the boys in the North were doing. He sold thirty-five carloads in thirty days.

Premiums, cut-outs, games, package inserts courted the tots and teen-agers. There were contests for grocers. Sandwich men dressed as ears of corn, or as cornflake boxes were loosed upon the downtown streets, clad in the Kellogg colors—red, white and green. Remarkable "inside" advertising deals were consummated with publishers when the money ran short, according to the fireside recollections of surviving peddlers of white space. W. K. hit the market from all sides, even with blotter ads. Took five carloads of blotting paper to do it, too.

"Wink at your grocer and see what you get," said one promotion. All kinds of things happened as a result of *that*.

A trade character was devised; a pretty "typewriter" from the office force served as model. Personifying Kellogg's toasted bits of maize, her likeness became as familiar as the "Sweetheart of the Corn," the eidolon of the wholesome American girl. W. K. put up a large electric sign on Broadway in New York City, showing a small boy's face and the word "Kellogg's." When the words "I want" appeared, tears rolled down the boy's face. Then the spectacular flashed "I got," and the boy stopped crying. W. K. said he was poor at writing advertising copy, but "I was good at criticizing."

The Kellogg Co. begged the public to stop eating the toasted corn flakes, please, so that their neighbors could have some.

"It was only human nature," John L. ("Lenn") Kellogg, mused, "for people to buy more when such advice was given to them."

By such tactics corn flakes won out in popularity over wheat, assisted by the circumstance that corn flakes actually stayed crisp longer in milk or cream, and that the goods were always fresh. W. K. would never load the trade with more flakes than they could sell.

W. K. inspired, guided and decided; and he had a promising son in the business, a point of prime importance to the founder of an industrial dynasty. "Lenn" Kellogg had worked as a boy in his Uncle John Harvey's various businesses. He had been an odd-jobs helper around *Good Health*. He and another trusty had mixed up the malt extract used in making Caramel Cereal Coffee. He had stirred steaming wheat flakes by hand long before travelling ovens were introduced. Open, outgoing, friendly, "Lenn" was liked by all. He had some of The Doctor's inventiveness; at least in collaboration with a good research department, he brought out products similar to articles already on the market, though he often lacked the patience to do sufficient testing before launching them.

The younger Kellogg was effective in arousing enthusiasm at

sales meetings. There were regular Wednesday night sessions. The old man would get up and goad the salesmen by saying that Kellogg could make eight thousand cases of corn flakes per day—*if* the sales department could sell them. Then "Lenn" would provide an inspirational moment in the spirit of the old-time drummer who gloried in the lines:

> When you call on the trade and they talk "Hard Times,"
> "Lower prices" and decided declines,
> But you talk and you smile, make the world look bright,
> And send in your orders every blamed night,
> Then you're a SALESMAN!
> By gad, you're a salesman.

Both C. W. Post and W. K. Kellogg validated the maxims of the success manuals sold by book agents in every city, town and hamlet in the land. Millions waved the Chautauqua salute at the Reverend Russell Conwell as he launched into his famous lecture, "Acres of Diamonds," moved smoothly into the parable of Al Hafid, and how he searched the whole world over for diamonds, only to find them in his own backyard.

W. K. Kellogg found his diamonds in the corner of a freight car. Post found his in a steamy cup of seal-brown Postum. Such men deserved, in the catch phrase, to become "as rich as Jay Cooke": and they did.

X V

The Golden Rule and
Other Good Ideas

THE first advertisement W. K. Kellogg ever published was about chickens. When he was in his twenties, working fifteen or more hours per day, handling the billing and shipping of Sanitarium health foods, buying printing, filling in as a hospital orderly, W. K. supplemented his slender income (nine dollars a week, three children) by dealing in breeding stock and eggs as a side line. "Regular egg machines," he called his Brown Leghorns.

"As I recall, I did not receive a single reply," W. K. admitted, in looking back at this early venture into advertising. "Since that time I have been responsible for the expenditure of something in excess of one hundred million dollars for advertising," he said, "some of which did pay."

The first advertisement for W. K.'s corn flakes identified the product only as "Toasted Corn Flakes," and appeared in the Canton, Ohio, *Repository* in a test campaign that cost $150. Within nine years the Company was spending a million dollars a year for advertising. In 1931, its twenty-fifth anniversary year, W. K. put three million dollars into advertising. This was the first year, incidentally, in which extensive use was made of radio, which was quickly to become as essential to the conduct of a cereal business as corn grits or cardboard and glue.

Especially through "The Singing Lady" program broadcast over the NBC network, Kellogg led the way toward a major shift in emphasis which focussed the attention of the cereal promoters upon the dream world of the younger set. Capable men, to glance ahead for a moment into the longer future, have carried on the sizzling

"Sorry—I bought it for a client. It's not for sale."

"Well," The Doctor countered, "I'll think up another name just as good. I'll call my product 'Zep.'"

"If you do," W. H. Crichton Clarke warned him, "you'll be infringing on our trade mark and we'll sue you."

Dr. Kellogg then had to return to Battle Creek and destroy thousands of Pep cartons which had already been printed up.

"We weren't very sympathetic," W. K. said.

True to his threat, The Doctor renamed his product "Zep." The Kellogg Co. promptly filed a trade-mark infringement suit against him. He changed again to Zo. But by that time the damage had been done. His product was dead.

"That was characteristic of The Doctor," John L. Kellogg commented. "Here he had a product on which he was netting about two thousand dollars a *day*. He lost the whole thing while he was haggling with a little New York manufacturer about a twenty-five-hundred-dollar difference in the price."

W. K. Kellogg took no chances. He purchased a business in Washington, D. C., which had trade-marked the word "Pep" as the name of a laxative. Out in Humboldt, Iowa, he found a soft drink called "El-Pep." That, too, was gathered in. With the Pep trade name securely nailed down, W. K. began marketing a Pep cereal of his own, a granulated product similar to Grape Nuts. The product is now a whole-wheat flake. The name alone has been worth a fortune.

Nearsighted from boyhood, when he could scarcely see the schoolroom blackboard, W. K. Kellogg experienced a gradual loss of vision in later life. In July, 1935, he underwent a first operation for glaucoma. A second unsuccessful operation was performed in 1937. Thereafter, he had only partial vision, decreasing until he could barely see a hand held close in front of his face, or recognize an old associate. During his last years he was totally blind, unable even to walk from his car to the door of his apartment without the aid of his white cane and his faithful German shepherd dog, a son of Rin-tin-tin.

The impression is held generally that W. K. didn't get much fun out of life.

"I've tried to recollect if I ever saw W. K. smile," one associate has said. "I believe he tried to one day when about twenty men were crowded into a small conference room for a meeting and his Seeing Eye dog developed a resounding flatulence."

However, it has definitely been established that W. K. did smile once, apologetically, behind his hand, at something Will Rogers said. Rogers was getting off some of his cracker-box philosophy at the dedication of the Kellogg Arabian horse ranch when W. K. gave the four-million-dollar show place, with certain strings attached, to the University of California. Differences in point of view on the management of the ranch did develop between the University and the aged donor. W. K. took the property back, and it was used by the U. S. Army during World War II as a cavalry school remount station. Later there was a second bestowal. The Kellogg ranch is now owned by the state of California and operated by California State Polytechnic College as a southern unit of the San Luis Obispo institution.

The W. K. Kellogg stud farm was such stuff as a cornflake magnate's dreams are made of. Here, at the foot of snowcapped mountains, on the northern slope of the San Jose hills, in luxurious barns arranged around a quadrangle and gleaming white in the California sunshine, was not just one Old Spot of possibly aristocratic lineage, but fifty pedigreed Arabian brood mares. Here, too, were Rossas, son of Skowronek, and Jardaan, the beautiful gray stallion used in parades and the movies, Jardaan with his three-hundred-year-old genealogy, who was insured for fifty thousand dollars when Rudolph Valentino rode him in his last picture, "The Son of the Sheik." Before the movie producers' interest in his horses petered out, W. K. enjoyed for a time the titillation of Hollywood contacts. He went on location with his Arabians, visited in the movie colony, chatted with technicians and cameramen and dined in style at the Brown Derby.

Kellogg himself never learned to ride his steeds. But it pleased him to preside at the regular Sunday ring exhibitions when he was in residence. Riders in native desert costume opened the exhibition. "Bedouin sheiks" dashed about madly in a blaze of color. Clever Rossika stole the show in operating a cash register. Rossika could, and did, discharge a rifle and wave a flag; and sometimes W. K. himself genially consented to hold Raseyn's bridle long enough for a picture to be snapped. It was at Pomona, according to Albert W. Harris, the Chicago banker and horseman, who saw W. K. on a horse only once, that Kellogg made a try at horsemanship, only to slide off the animal's rump and break two ribs.

"He is not the type of man we regard as a lover of horses," said Harris. "He went into the Pomona Ranch enterprise, I think, with a view of taking a problem and working it out in his own way." The project was the thing, not the horse.

W. K. went to the movies as long as he could see the pictures. Sometimes, on lodge night, he attended Battle Creek Masonic Lodge, but the boys froze up when they saw him coming. W. K. was not the gabby type. Perhaps, before his sight failed he had read the books in his library, its four walls filled from floor to ceiling with standard sets and special bindings. He must have consulted his Mark Twain because he quoted Twain in support of the dim view he took of a possible biography of himself: "When I was young I had difficulty in remembering anything with accuracy, from day to day. Now, it seems, I am able to remember everything— whether it ever happened or not."

The hard-driving old cornflake king in the black, baggy suit and neat bow tie, was not a brilliant conversationalist. His reliance upon the cliché was notable even among corporation presidents. "Once seen, never forgotten," he would say; or, "What cannot be cured, must be endured." Perhaps his abiding sense of his own inadequacy dried up the springs of a freer communication. At any rate, he was a man of few words, and those mostly borrowed. The only subjects Kellogg would talk about with animation were Kellogg Co. plant problems and the grocery trade. W. K. did not inquire after the comfort of his advertising men when they came to Battle Creek. But he never failed to ask where they were staying, and financed the construction of a hotel so that people in town on Kellogg business would not spend money at the Post Tavern. W. K. was a voracious reader of sales figures and balance sheets, and liked nothing better than to chew the fat with some visiting jobber. When he mentioned the product of a competitor, W. K. always cited the price per case.

An illustration of W. K.'s extraordinary tenacity appears in the curious relationship he maintained with Andrew Ross. Kellogg never forgave Ross because he had believed around 1913-14 that the cereal industry had reached its ceiling. Yet, from 1914 on, until the rough old solitary's death in 1951, W. K. wrote regularly to his former vice-president. About twice a year, W. K. composed a long letter in his own hand, giving Ross the kind of breakdown of operations which might appear in a company's annual report, developing the theme of the wonderful progress which had been made, the limitless horizon ahead. He went into the same kind of detail about the W. K. Kellogg Foundation and its princely benefactions. That was his life, sitting on top of a complex, the hundred-million-dollar Kellogg Co. and the fifty-million-dollar Foundation. He wanted to show Andrew Ross, over a period of more than thirty-five years, that his judgment had been wrong.

Perhaps W. K.'s most human side is illustrated in a little game he liked to play when making important financial decisions. For example: there was a time when the Kellogg Co. had an all-bran product. W. K. believed that the opportunity was limited. However, he asked his advertising agency, N. W. Ayer and Son, to work out a merchandising plan under which bran could be sold in interesting quantities. The result was a well-reasoned proposal which deeply impressed W. K. But the cost was six hundred thousand dollars. This sum appeared to be as much as the total sales would amount to in a year. The cost was high, perhaps too high. W. K. went over the plan with a fine-toothed comb, then reached in his pocket, flipped a coin. He covered it with his hand, leaned over and peeked. He announced it was heads. Clarence Jordan, the Ayer representative in the meeting, spoke of the incident to Arch Shaw. Shaw explained that W. K. always flipped, always peeked, always announced the turn of the coin as he wanted it to be. R. O. Eastman used to say that he was going to eliminate the monkey business by getting Mr. Kellogg a nickel with heads on both sides.

During the early years of the Corn Flake Co., Kellogg got out a lively, brash house organ, called *The Square Dealer*, edited by able, uninhibited, young Eastman. Its character was that of "a monthly message of good cheer from the Home of 'The Sweetheart of the Corn' to the sales force of the Company and their customers." It was devoted to "a Business Application of the Golden Rule and Other Good Ideas." When W. K. told the sales force that the factory could manufacture so many cases daily if the sales department could only sell them, Eastman's little magazine rubbed the point in. If the Postum Company was caught in some misbehavior, the dereliction was reported by Kellogg's censorious *Square Dealer*. If the Quaker Oats plant had a fire, Kellogg sadly reported the fact to the grocery trade. The magazine publicized the vital connection between a healthy agriculture and a healthy breakfast-food company, by stories about the annual award of the W. K. Kellogg National Corn Trophy for the Grand Champion ear of corn. The trophy was a thirty-inch-high urn of no great usefulness, but turned out handsomely by Tiffany in gold, silver, bronze and enamel, with a picture of the Sweetheart of the Corn on the side. All through this period the chief problem was to get the goods made fast enough.

"During several years there were more orders than we could fill," says George C. McKay, who rose from the ranks to become vice-president and treasurer. "We cut down the orders, not as a scheme, but from necessity."

With short supplies and quick turnover, the corn flakes were always crisp and fresh; and that kept the stocks continually turning. W. K. filled his magazine with business-building ideas for retailers —counter-display suggestions, layouts for advertisements. He conducted an idea exchange. In return he expected a *quid pro quo* from the retailers—adequate display of Kellogg's Corn Flakes, eye-level shelf position, the maximum of "front facings." The bigger the display the greater the sales. And the less room there was left for competing cereals. It was a practical application of The Golden Rule.

The Kellogg Co. had in its early and middle years looked at Shredded Wheat with admiration and envy. Recall that The Doctor had tried to get the shredding machines in the early days but Perky had eluded him; that Andrew Ross had come to the Kellogg Co. with laurels earned in merchandising Shredded Wheat. In addition, the exploits of Shredded Wheat continued to attract attention. And time was running out on the Shredded Wheat patents.

After the patents did expire, what was the status of the pillow-shaped biscuit? That was the multimillion dollar question. Anyone could make a similar product, provided he did not try to pass it off as the article made by the original manufacturer; and he could call his biscuit by the name under which it had become known to the public, *if* the name had become generic. A famous case involving this issue arose over the name "cellophane." The word "linoleum" likewise passed into public usage when the patent expired. One way the courts could tell when a privately owned trade-mark had fallen into the public domain was to observe whether the newspapers and the dictionaries printed the name in lower-case letters. In such instances, the public associated the trade name with the goods, but not the maker of the goods. The owner then had one more chance. He could proceed under the broader unfair competition principle of "secondary meaning"; *i.e.*, the trade name had come to denote the source so that in the case of Shredded Wheat, the name recalled the company located at Niagara Falls whether printed in upper- or lower-case letters. But secondary meaning was hard to prove.

In 1927, W. K. Kellogg challenged the claim of the Shredded Wheat Company that it, and it alone, could make a pillow-shaped biscuit out of wheat shreds and describe it as "shredded wheat." The result was a series of complicated legal battles. There were moves and countermoves, diversions and disengagements. The National Biscuit Company bought the company which made Shredded Wheat (in 1930) and inherited the controversy. The fighting ranged through four United States District Courts, two United States Circuit Courts of Appeal, two English courts, the King's Privy Council, and the House of Lords. Finally the case came before the United States Supreme Court (1938). The Court, by a seven to two decision, rejected the doctrine of secondary meaning that the name of the well-known biscuit necessarily meant a product manufactured at Niagara Falls by the National Biscuit Company. The Kellogg Co. was upheld.

W. K. "retired" on numerous occasions, a little drama of renunciation and withdrawal which was played out in a series of repeat performances between 1924 and 1939. There was in him a fanatic drive to work, to amass, to dominate, which even blindness and four score and seven years could not subdue. Various men had risen in the Company since the early days—Andrew Ross, followed by the younger "Lenn" Kellogg, George and Eugene McKay, Lewis J.

Brown, James F. O'Brien, Walter Hasselhorn. "Lenn" Kellogg and Brown each had borne uneasily and briefly the title of President. In the end, none were chosen. The parade of ex-officials from the Company never disturbed its progress. Perhaps that was why W. K. never felt it necessary to give credit to other men for contributions to his success.

The old President or Chairman of the Board, or whatever he called himself at any particular time, would come to the victim and sit and twitch. He would finger his old-fashioned watch chain and fidget, darting glances to the right and the left, nervous as a witch, talk of this and that. Finally he would whisper in a weak voice, "I've bad news for you. You've lost your job."

After much tribulation, W. K. Kellogg found his man in Watson H. Vanderploeg, a vice-president of the Harris Trust and Savings Bank of Chicago. "Mr. Van" became president of the Kellogg Co. in 1939 after a two years' preparatory period of service and continued as the operating head of the Company until his death in May, 1957. In 1946, W. K. declined re-election to the Board of Directors, but, as it said in his obituary, "retained an active interest in the administrative affairs of the Company." That was a euphemism for saying that the old food manufacturer would die, but never surrender.

There is reason to suppose that the passing of the nonegenarian, when it finally occurred, brought relief and refreshment to the Company's management. The best evidence is that the progress of the Kellogg Co. has been accelerated. A new vitality showed itself when it was no longer necessary to reckon with the founder's opinion on each advertising idea, his requirements on package design, on new products, his viewpoints on executive salary and titles. Wall Street pays its own special kind of hardheaded tribute to the Kellogg Company's latter day progress in words such as these: "Common stock is of good quality. Leading breakfast cereal company. Good management. Sales growth above population growth."

"Nothing succeeds," as John Finley once said, "like successors."

W. K. always kept a sharp watch over his personnel, encouraged private confidences about his executives and even second-string employees. It is related of him that once, when his train was crossing Iowa on the way to California, he looked out of the car window as the train passed through a town. It was early evening. He saw a Kellogg Co. automobile parked on a street. At the next stop a telegram was sent back to Battle Creek. It called for identification of the salesman who operated the truck and a check on his next expense account to see if he charged up garage rent that particular night. An attitude of suspicion based upon a low conception of human nature was one characteristic of The Doctor's which W. K. had borrowed and carried on with refinements of his own. The more he saw of men, the better he liked German shepherds. A sparrow couldn't fall, a heart interest couldn't blossom on a packaging line, the wife of a Kellogg white-collar employee couldn't smoke a cigarette in public, but what W. K. would hear of it.

Perhaps the quality of this granitic man can be wrapped up in a single incident. The time: 1932. The directors of the Kellogg Co. were in a dither. They decided to pull in their horns, cut the advertising, the house-to-house sampling, the premiums, pare all costs no matter what the cost. Word of the decision reached W. K. in California where he had settled down for the winter. He wired that he would be back in Battle Creek on a certain date, called a meeting of all directors, executives and advertising men. W. K. walked in, spoke to this effect:

"If we knew this entire country was going bankrupt on Saturday, we would fight right through Friday night, wouldn't we?"

And walked out.

The meeting voted to *add* a million dollars for advertising and a full-throttle selling drive. Once more W. K. had demonstrated solid-rock courage in a long career of pluck and luck. The greatest development of ready-to-eat cereals came *after* this dark time.

W. K.'s fond hope of developing a successor in the Kellogg family line to carry on after him was never realized. His family relationships ended in disorder, disharmony and disaster. One son, Karl H. Kellogg, a physician, lacking both physical robustness and the characteristics of a businessman, spent his life in California. W. K. quarrelled with "Lenn," the other surviving son, who tried to make a go of it with his father. W. K. became estranged from his second wife, the former Dr. Carrie Staines, a one-time physician at the Sanitarium, whom he had married in 1918. The aging capitalist tried to bring a grandson into line for the succession; but the business relationship ended up in a tangle of lawsuits. Loneliness was W. K.'s final portion.

John L. Kellogg made many contributions to the business. He once took a wax-paper wrapper off the outside of the corn flakes package and put it on the inside. This eliminated an inner paper bag and required about two inches less of paper than had the outer wrapping. A trifling innovation, it would seem. But wax, ink, glue, cardboard and paper rank high in the costs of a breakfast food factory. Two inches less of waxed paper meant $250,000 saved in a year. On another occasion John L. suggested treating bran with the Kellogg malt flavoring. Out of the suggestion came a valuable product, Kellogg's All-Bran. Here again the humble kitchen stove, so often encountered in the Battle Creek story, comes into prominence. "Lenn" said he read every book extant on the human colon at that time: a book in one hand, a spoon in the other, a health-giving mixture bubbling on the back of the kitchen range.

Less fortunate was "Lenn's" experience with a hot cereal called New-Ota. The American Hominy Company was in bankruptcy. Among its assets was a comparatively new rolled-oats mill at Davenport, Iowa. At a time when W. K. was in Europe, the mill was up for auction. J. L. bought it in his own name, persuaded his father when he returned to have the Kellogg Co. take over the oatmeal mill. But W. K., a cornflake man through and through, wanted nothing to do with the oats game. The Company took a heavy loss on this operation and the plant was sold finally to the Ralston Co. For this mistake, and for divorcing his wife to marry a girl in the Kellogg office, W. K. threw "Lenn" out of the Company.

John L. Kellogg was a reasonably good businessman, but a thought on the risky side. Like Edsel Ford, he never really had a chance. Perhaps he just didn't measure up. His subsequent career suggests that this was so. He went to Chicago where he started several promotional ventures. These enterprises went into receivership and disappeared. John L. died in California in 1950, suddenly, while standing by Dr. Karl Kellogg's fireplace. His body was returned to Battle Creek for burial, not in the place prepared for him by his father but at Memorial Park, in the Roman Catholic faith of his second wife, farthest removed of all Christian creeds from the ancestral Kellogg Adventism. But so it was; John L. Kellogg came to see the hand of Our Lady guiding the Cereal City on its high road of destiny, and found in Rome a balm and solace after the extraordinary rigors of being W. K.'s son.

The old cornflaker then turned his attention to a grandson. He would bring him up in his own image. John L. Kellogg, Jr., was the apple of W. K.'s eye. Tall, slender, attractive, artistic, somewhat diffident in manner, John L., Junior, prepared for his business vocation, became a lively participant in the social activities of Battle Creek's horsy set, and made the grand tour. He entered the Kellogg Co. where he was quickly elevated to a seat on the Board of Directors and a vice-presidency. The theory was that he was to learn the business from top to bottom. It turned out to be more top than bottom. His duties were chiefly those of "assisting" his grandfather who had a handsome desk but never used it, and needed an assistant the way he needed a hole in his head.

When Grandpa reduced young Kellogg's salary from ten thousand dollars a year to forty dollars a week to toughen him up, the second John L. stormed out of the Company in an overwrought nervous condition, and like his father, went to Chicago. There he made a start at manufacturing confections and coated-cheese products. Despondent over the news that a patent application for a popcorn machine on which he had been working for three years was rejected, he went to his office on a blue Sunday. After bidding a fond farewell to the machine on which he had lavished all his hopes, and tasting one knows not what bitter dregs of despair, he took his own life, at twenty-six years of age.

Possibly W. K. did not cause this tragedy, though an infringement suit he brought against his grandson must weigh heavily in the balance. Probably W. K. could have prevented it. But to do so he would have had to be born again. Father of five children, three preceding him in death, W. K., like Croesus, knew the sorrow of outliving his children. We never miss the water until the well runs dry.

None of these personal matters appear in W. K.'s own account of the important experiences of his life. He prepared a sixteen-sentence autobiography, interesting for its brevity, its emphasis and its omissions:

Born 1860. Less than high school education. Supported
self after 14. Purchased from earnings most of clothing after
10. 1879 went to Texas for a year to get experience. Attended
commercial school four months, graduated 1880, took a job
in April, 1880, continued same 25 years. Organized company
in 1906 at age of 46. Established business by selling $35,000
worth of stock to people in St. Louis. Factory burned 1907.
New factory constructed same year. Only money from earnings
reinvested in business. Business built on advertising. Numerous
law-suits. From 1906 to 1941 more than $100,000,000 ex-
pended for advertising, wholly from earnings. Dividends paid
during the same period about the same amount as spent for
advertising. Selected new personnel and retired from business
in 1939.

When it became evident that the life of W. K. Kellogg might
become a matter of interest as an expression of U.S. industrialism,
plans were made to put a writer in the ring with W. K. But he
proved to be a tough fighter against any biography.

"I am not going to start my memory spinning," Kellogg declared at Pomona. "I live in the present. Don't ask me questions
about what has gone before."

Perhaps it was just as well.

W. K. Kellogg over his middle years made many small-to-
moderate-sized gifts—say from fifty dollars to five thousand dollars
—to individuals and good causes, often anonymously, sometimes
with the advice of his friend, Arch Shaw. The particulars of Kellogg's early charities were known to only a very few persons. The
operation was very simple. A bank would make a telephone call to
some person who was having financial difficulties. There would be
a summons to appear, when the information would be conveyed
that the mortgage or the doctors' bills had been paid off, but not
a word disclosed as to the source of the relief.

Later there came a program of larger benefactions. It became
an organized procedure after 1925 when The Fellowship Corporation was established. The Corporation systematized Kellogg's giving,
surveyed needs and opportunities, at that time emphasizing those of
a nearby character. In 1930 the W. K. Kellogg Foundation was

organized and took up the task of awarding large sums on a broad, national pattern.

W. K. had a particular aversion to being tagged as a philanthropist. One does not need to look far for the reason. Once, as a witness in a lawsuit, The Doctor was asked to state his business. He could have made many answers. But he saw them all as one: "All my life my business has been philanthropy."

When W. K. gave the Youth Building to Battle Creek he refused a newspaper request for a picture and a story.

"Print The Doctor's picture," he said sourly.

After an extended parley, W. K. gave way on the story. But he made this a condition: "Agree not to call me a philanthropist."

W. K. would not sit upon a stage or dais, while The Doctor would not sit anywhere else. Always, on his rare public appearances, W. K. asked to have a seat reserved for him in the last row. When Mr. Kellogg gave the W. K. Kellogg Auditorium and Junior High School to Battle Creek, he attended the dedication ceremonies and instructed the Superintendent of Schools not to mention him. When he did so in one sentence, W. K. got up and stalked out.

"I don't like applesauce," he insisted, "not any kind of applesauce. My mother used to give me quinine in applesauce. And the modern kind I can't stand either. I DON'T LIKE APPLESAUCE."

George Darling of the Foundation staff, on one of his boss's later birthdays, took his job in his hands, as he thought, and ordered a cake with candles sent to W. K.'s California home from the Foundation staff. W. K. was delighted.

Legends which purport to demonstrate W. K. Kellogg's recessiveness, his painful shyness, his passion for anonymity are a part of the folklore of Battle Creek capitalism. But George Darling understood the old lone wolf better than most. He found the deeply buried id.

The bulk of the Kellogg cornflake fortune passed to the W. K. Kellogg Foundation; to which may be added W. K.'s personal "out of pocket" benefactions approaching three million dollars. The Foundation's program was the application of knowledge rather than research or relief. The variety of the approach is suggested in such projects as a tuberculosis-control program for Detroit, diagnosis of speech defects in children, the construction of schools, pools, hospitals and gymnasiums, camps and playgrounds, the enrichment of life in rural areas. The majority of the expenditures during Mr. Kellogg's last years, and since, have gone into national and international activities through seven operating divisions: Dentistry, Education, Medicine and Public Health, Hospitals, Nursing, Agriculture and the International Division. The W. K. Kellogg Foundation is now one of the largest in the United States, with assets of $128,-670,144, ranked only by the Ford and Rockefeller Foundations and the Carnegie Corporation.

Without denying the possibility that W. K. was moved by a simple, warmhearted desire to extend a helping hand to his fellow man, one cannot but notice other circumstances which help, at least, to explain a benevolence which was atypical. First of all was a great unsolved problem of gerontology—You Can't Take It With You. W. K. felt, certainly, no disposition to leave fifty million dollars to the family with which he had quarrelled and feuded and which he had already largely survived. Especially as he had long before made what he considered to be adequate provision for them. He could not, in good conscience, see the cornflake millions gobbled up by the government. He certainly could not allow John Harvey to go down in history as *the* humanitarian Kellogg. In this context, then, there came into being the Ann J. Kellogg School, the W. K. Kellogg Bird Sanctuary, the Kellogg Experimental Farms, a Kellogg Reforestation project, the Kellogg Radiation Laboratory at California Institute of Technology, the Kellogg Center at the then Michigan State College now Michigan State University, the School of Dentistry at the University of Michigan, the W. K. Kellogg Municipal Airport, and special research programs and fellowships in various universities abroad and at home.

The minister who committed W. K. to his last resting place said that Mr. Kellogg's monument was "the numberless men and women, boys and girls, and little children whose lives were enhanced by Mr. Kellogg's plans." The plans included a high per-capita consumption of corn flakes and the return of most of the profits, for a complex mix of reasons, to socially useful projects serving the people who ate the flakes—a kind of gigantic cereal premium on a world-wide scale.

"There was a lot of good in W. K. Kellogg," mused a leading citizen of Battle Creek, looking out over the winking lights of the cereal city, "buried way down deep."

XVI

The Simple Life in a Nutshell

THE LOCAL Chamber of Commerce estimated in the mid-'twenties that the health seekers were worth six million dollars annually to Battle Creek. By 1935 more than three hundred thousand patients had come to seek "The Simple Life." This was a slogan of great repute after President Roosevelt had praised enthusiastically "La Vie Simple," a mediocre treatise on right living by Pastor Charles Wagner, a French clergyman and uplifter.

Many patients came for two weeks and stayed for the rest of their lives. According to Stewart Holbrook, historian of the westering New Englander, "The influence of the Battle Creek Sanitarium on migration to Michigan has never been estimated but the institution has perhaps attracted more visitors and possibly more permanent settlers—both Yankees and others—than did the Jackson, Lansing & Saginaw Railroad Company."

Dr. Kellogg was himself not only the exemplar of The Simple Life but also of another favorite slogan of the Rooseveltian epoch, The Strenuous Life. He performed up to twenty surgical operations in a day, dictated to a whole battery of stenographers, jotted down a note for a food experiment, dashed off to Paris to look at the latest developments in X ray. Between times he was busy with the problems of sanitarium administration and the metabolic disturbances usually found at a watering place.

At the breakfast table at The Residence, Dr. Kellogg carried on experiments with beta-lactose, more soluble than the alpha type, which he mixed and sipped with various fruit juices. Later The Doctor received staffers, heard reports, issued instructions, while an orderly administered his daily enema, and an Adventist laid out his snow-white clothing. One can see The Doctor in his gown, the nurse fluttering and whispering that the patient is waiting in the operating theatre, and what should be done about the lateral anastomosis, Dr. Kellogg beating his stomach with annoyance while he horse-traded with an Oldsmobile salesman. Doctors and heads of departments gathered around to get in a word. The Doctor shot his instructions to various functionaries:

"Tell Marshall I want his report on the bonds and the annuity proposition."

"Tell Russell to bring over the last experiment I asked him to make."

"Phone Gould I want to make a slight alteration in the plans he is preparing."

"Get from Attorney Mason a copy of the new brief in the will-case."

"Get me three hundred dollars from the treasurer."

"Tell the operating room I can't come for fifteen minutes; yes, the laparotomy comes first."

"Ask Dr. Maxwell if the specimen removed in the case of Mr. Blank showed malignancy."

"I want to see all the laboratory reports including strength and metabolism graphics in the case of Mr. Epstein."

"Wire Benson, Marks and Schaeffer to meet me tomorrow noon in New York."

"Wire that man in Chicago that I will be there to examine him at four this afternoon."

Thousands of Kellogg alumni and alumnae can still easily invoke their memories to bring back the busy scene as it existed between, say, 1910 and 1930. Crowds, carriages, automobiles, flowed to the main entrance of the "San." The lobby was as busy as a bus station. The Palm Garden and the acidophilus milk bar buzzed with rumors of a gigantic new fifteen-story tower to be built at the south end of the new building, facing the corner of Washington and Champion Streets.

To the left, was the business office, the cashier, the bell captain, Colonel Dumphy's little telegraph cubicle, a step across the corridor.

A long corridor stretched to the right, flanked by medical

offices. Directly ahead through the lobby lay the oval, glass-domed Palm Garden. Bananas ripened twenty feet overhead, and a rubber tree towered above the splashing pool. There the patients often preferred to take their tray luncheons, down beneath the sheltering palms.

To the left again, in the north wing, the guests gathered for relaxation. There the superannuated foreign missionary who had staked his all on the rewards of another world mingled with those who had achieved high place in this one—Professor Irving Fisher of Yale and family; Edmund B. Ball, the Muncie, Indiana, capitalist; a marchesa, "charming member of the Italian nobility," as the publicity department described a woman guest of Italian nationality, or Mr. Cheek, up from Nashville. How did Joel E. Cheek, the Maxwell House Coffee man, one wonders, regard the Caramel Cereal Food Coffee, the Health Koko? To some the "San" gave sanctuary—Mrs. Anne U. (Fifi) Stillman, for one, after the ordeal of her celebrated divorce suit. Also in seclusion was Harry M. Daugherty, Attorney General in the Harding Administration, a patient for several months in pajamas and wheel chair, while a New York grand jury sought vainly to question him about the American Metals case, and especially about a particular fifty thousand dollars' worth of Liberty Bonds found in the safety deposit box of his intimate, Jess Smith.

Recognition of the Sanitarium as a sort of temple even took this form: many couples chose to be married there. Among many couples of hygienic tastes, a honeymoon trip to Battle Creek was definitely preferred over the conventional visit to Niagara Falls which offered, after all, only a waterfall and the Shredded Wheat factory. At the "San" there was something exciting doing every minute, the arrival of the U. S. consul from Morocco, the opportunity to form interesting new friendships to the music of "Billy" Drever and the Sanitarium Philharmonic Orchestra. At the "San," a cat could always look at a king, whether it was Frank Buckman in the Men's Bath Department, giving a gracious interview to the press in *le nu intégral*—no news hens present—or Harvey Firestone, feet up on a radiator, telling a group what it was like to rough it in the great outdoors with Warren G. Harding.

Dr. Kellogg was quite well aware of the importance of mingling diversion with treatment. An overweight lady from St. Louis found comfort and camaraderie in being able to discuss with the wife of a Topeka lawyer the disagreeable facts developed by her posture-shadow photograph. It was exhilarating to enjoy an easy familiarity with Congressman Bill Yates of Illinois, "And how are your deltoid muscles today?"

The names of new arrivals were posted in the lobby, like the passenger list on shipboard. It was eagerly scanned by the devotees of "organized rest without ennui," who looked forward to pleasant associations while correcting their pelvic obliquity. Every two weeks a "new arrival" banquet was held, with speakers. Lucy Page Gaston, in her brown dress, frightened the patrons out of their Kellogg physiologic chairs with her graphic diatribe against the cigarette. Dr. Kellogg, if he was in town, mentioned some famous vegetarians of history who got things done: Lord Byron who wrote a lot of poetry, Newton and Franklin and Wendell Phillips, the silver-tongue.

It was a sound tenet of sanatorium management that a busy patron was more likely to be a contented one. There were side trips to the Bird Sanctuary at Gull Lake. Many of the customers were interested in the lettuce fields at the "San" farms, or a visit to the greenhouses where admirers of the esculents could gaze upon two thousand heads of Chinese cabbage.

There was always some pleasant surprise turning up. After lunch, Homer Rodeheaver, the gospel singer and golden trombonist, might sing impromptu to the whole "San" family, packed into the rotunda and hanging upon the stairways. On Sundays the bill of fare carried notices—after Saturday-keeping was no longer official at the institution—of no less than four opportunities to attend divine but nonsectarian worship.

More fun than the laughing exercise in the gym, more exciting than an encounter with George Palmer Putnam, more awe-inspiring than the Adventist God, more colorful than Frank Vincent, the explorer, wiser than Dr. Frank Crane, the newspaper philosopher, was the Sanitarium's own little wizard in white, Dr. J. H. Kellogg. Dr. Kellogg's skill as a host was proverbial. He was, among many other things, a superb hotel man. When a well-to-do repeater showed up at Battle Creek, Dr. Kellogg could take him by the hand warmly and confidently. There was no fumbling around with: "The face is familiar . . . Now don't tell me . . . Just give me a minute . . ."

The Doctor could call the name right off.

All through the week the guests deposited in a "Question Box," queries which Dr. Kellogg answered in his parlor lecture. Kellogg averaged out as the fastest talker clocked since John C. Calhoun. He threw in ad lib comments upon whatever might be uppermost in his mind at the moment, something out of the day's practise, or last night's glance at *Vegetationsbilder*, just arrived from Jena, or an idea gleaned from the *Annales de l'Institute Pasteur*.

"The decline of a nation," Dr. Kellogg would begin, rising on his toes, and teetering to emphasize the point, "commences when gourmandizing begins. Rome's collapse was well under way when slaves were thrown into the eel-pots to increase the gamy flavor of the eels when they came upon the table.

"Tobacco," he declared, and a visible shudder went through his audience, "destroys the sex glands."

Dr. Kellogg's language was sound King James Bible English plus Noah Webster with here and there a flash reminiscent of Mark Twain. There was no rust on his vocabulary.

Dressed all in white, a fashion he adopted some time after 1902, even to white shoes, white overshoes, hat, overcoat, gloves and spectacles, The Doctor explained that the costume transmitted the healthful light of the sun. It became a kind of trade-mark. When The Doctor was photographed between S. S. McClure and Gifford Pinchot, he made his point neatly that dark clothing is depressing. Only tall, bearded George Bernard Shaw, who also wore white suits, could challenge Kellogg photogenically.

Although Dr. Kellogg practised the arts of the necromancer on his audiences, he used the language of the medical scientist. When addressing the laity, he referred casually to the work of Van Noorden, Lusk, Zuntz "and others," as though of course his auditors had the medical literature well in mind. "Recent experiments by Hindhede and others have shown . . ." he would say. There was a mild air of health fanaticism among his hearers. Many had read up on their own cases, had learned to listen attentively for sounds within their own bodies. The passionate light of the health hunter flashed in the stranger's eye, as he looked at his neighbor and silently speculated, "I wonder what is wrong with *you?*"

In the dining room every portion was weighed on balances in the serving pantry. A dietician cruised the premises to help the puzzled customers choose their menus wisely and check off their calories. And oft she had to raise the wise, restraining hand of science against ravenous appetites which might produce eructations or anabolic toxins. The dietician could also point out who that was over there—Upton Close by the wall, and Upton Sinclair on the other side, with his special milk-and-honey concoction. She knew Emil Fuchs, Henry L. Doherty, Sir Wilfred and Lady Grenfell, just back from Labrador. There was Madame Marie Sundelius of the "Met," and that, of course, was Henry Ford in the quiet gray suit, blue striped shirt, a buckwheat blossom in his lapel.

"I like Mr. [sic] Kellogg's philosophy," the inventor of the high, black spidery Model-T declared, and sent a bag of water-ground buckwheat from his own grist mill over to The Doctor.

From 1904 on, caloric values of the portions were shown on the menu card. This was fast work, since Professor Wilbur O. Atwater had only a few years before carried out his classic researches with the bomb calorimeter and compiled the first tables showing the contributions in energy of the basic-food groups.

Most of the staff and students at the "San" in the 1920-1930 decade were not Seventh Day Adventists. The Doctor was enough of a realist to know that a girl educated in home economics couldn't get a job if she didn't know meat cookery. So he taught his students how to cook meat and then taught them not to eat it. The girls learned to lay out a high-protein diet for three cents a day, hoped to teach dietetics on the Chautauqua circuit, to discover a new member of the *Genus Plantago*, or become a travelling demonstrator for Malted Nuts. The scene of their operations, the meat-cookery laboratory, was tucked out of the way in North Lodge, where the smell of roasting, grilling, baking, braising would not infuriate the patients. The Home Ec. girls sat in the peanut gallery at the Post Theatre, got their extra snacks at the Good Health Café, bought their muslin underwear at The Roberts Shop on North Washington Street. With their class motto—"Service"—

in their hearts, the girls of '18 dreamed of the A.E.F. and being commanded to go abroad by Mr. Hoover as angels of mercy bearing soybean meal.

Across the street from the "San" was a shanty restaurant called the Red Onion. It was conducted by a sinner, William Gammanthaler, who specialized in steaks and chops with French fries on the side and steaming cups of strong, hot coffee. The clientele included the patients who couldn't take the nut-butter regimen any longer. Even the staffers often fell off the peanut wagon. And many a guilty "San" physician was flushed on a Michigan Central dining car, enjoying a pork chop on his way to a medical conclave in Chicago, when, by coincidence, Irene Castle was dancing at the Blackstone Hotel.

Dr. Kellogg's efficient Central Intelligence Agency reported to him upon such defections. But he took them with philosophic calm.

"They'll come back," he insisted, "to biologic living."

A frequent "San" visitor was Horace Fletcher, a remarkable man who, when old, did a double back somersault from the high diving board into the "San" pool, and once sent Professor Atwater, down at the U. S. Department of Agriculture, a sample of his feces in an envelope by first-class mail. Chubby in person and in personality, a eupeptic millionaire, Fletcher passed through a New Thought and Yoga phase. Recovered, he wrote a series of warmhearted, inchoate books against child labor, and died of overwork in connection with World War I refugee relief. Fletcher won enduring fame for his theory that the more one chews the less he needs to eat, and the more he enjoys what he does eat.

Get a crust of old, dried-up whole-wheat bread, chew it à la Fletcher, thirty-two times, one chew for each tooth in the normal human complement. You will find that Fletcher was right when he said that bread tastes sweeter when well-chewed. But Atwater showed that he was wrong when he thought that the nourishment was greater. Fletcher got 2.6 calories per gram from his whole-wheat bread, or 3.6 from his corn flakes, even as does the breakfast-bolter, or you and I. Fletcherism was an old idea. Luigi Conaro described it four hundred years ago. Dr. Franklin advised that one rise from the table as hungry as when he sat down. Count Rumford tried to make the Bavarian army save food by thorough chewing. Gladstone masticated furiously before Fletcher was ever heard of. But Fletcher dramatized "mouth thoroughness" so effectively that "Fletcherism" and "Fletcherize" are well-established Americanisms which appear even in the small desk dictionaries. One of Fletcher's innumerable books is catalogued by the Library of Congress as: "1. Optimism. 2. Mastication. 3. Nutrition." It is a good characterization of the gospel of health according to Fletcher.

Kellogg and Fletcher respected each other as fellow workers along the American Alimentary Canal. A large sign, "Fletcherize," was displayed at the head of the Sanitarium dining room as a part of the "San" discipline, and Fletcher's books were on sale in the main lobby along with stamps, picture post cards and acidophilus milk. But The Doctor noted with regret that Fletcher liked his coffee. And it was a cause of genuine sorrow to learn, in the exchange of sanitary confidences, that Horace held radical—or was it reactionary?—views on evacuation: he considered a periodicity of eight to ten days as normal and quite healthy. Upon this important subject the two colleagues in the food protest regretfully parted company.

Dr. Kellogg was of medium height, with a slight figure, his head large for his body, hair retreating back from a broad forehead. His presence made an interviewer think of David Garrick, Napoleon and "Little Phil" Sheridan. In middle life, Dr. Kellogg was rather plump and wore a full beard. Later, when his hair had whitened, his beard was trimmed down to a Van Dyke and he looked remarkably like Santa Claus. Seated in his office, Kellogg wore an eye shade to conceal the expression in his eyes. On his walls hung many pictures, including the Greek philosophers who, he remarked, "were preaching the simple life two thousand years ago." In among the Greeks were scattered Metchnikoff, John Wesley, Luther Burbank, David Starr Jordan, Henry Morganthau, Irving Fisher, John D. Rockefeller, Lord Lister, Lincoln, Grenfell, Pavlov, Sylvester Graham and Thomas ("Old Parr") Parr, the English centenarian.

Dr. Kellogg was a hard man to pin down. There was in him a genuine idealism. That aspect of The Doctor showed to advantage in his delight at screening a film for a responsive patient, showing the white blood corpuscles in action, how they rushed about madly like open-field runners, until they arrived at a focus of infection.

Again, his sincerity appeared in his alertness in turning up a good candidate for medical studies, or adding an able physician to the "San" staff. The Doctor was a kind of fisher of men for the microscope and the stethoscope, and highly successful in surrounding himself with medical men who enjoyed the respect of the profession, such as Doctors J. Stuart Pritchard, Charles E. Stewart, E. L. Eggleston, Paul Roth, the Swiss; Mortenson, a good heart man; James T. Case and J. R. Jeffery.

There was another side—Kellogg the salesman and manipulator, the casuist, the operator, the actor who put on almost too good a show. Kellogg liked adulation.

"I don't care greatly to be seen of men," W. K. Kellogg once remarked. "I let The Doctor take care of the publicity."

Dr. Kellogg was photographed in almost as many different settings and compositions as a popular movie star—with his cockatoo perched upon his shoulder, leaning over to admire an orchid, seated at his piano. No wonder it got under W. K.'s skin. "Advertising," he scoffed.

When he was ninety-one, The Doctor trotted back and forth across a cinder path for the benefit of the photographers. Sweating slightly, a sign of good health, he warned the boys that he could run as long as they had any film. And he was as good as his threat.

The Doctor held out a muscled forearm.

"Feel it—give it a good pinch. I'm like that all over," Kellogg declared, his goatee sticking out aggressively. "Feel that chest."

Pulling on a white dressing gown the health educator assumed a John L. Sullivan stance.

"You've got to live right," he declared.

The sun cast long shadows over the spry doctor and the wilted newsmen before they called it a day.

"Need any more shots of me running?"

No, the boys said; they'd done pretty well, and began to pack up.

"How about a few more of me riding my bicycle?" suggested The Doctor.

So the cameras were unpacked and the session started over again. Dr. Kellogg, now in white knickers and a white pith helmet, slowly pedalled in figure eights, back and forth on the driveway.

Stories and legends gather around such a man. On one Thanksgiving Day, the "San" guests were served something which looked like roast turkey and tasted like roast turkey, but wasn't; while on a raised platform in the dining room The Doctor had placed a live gobbler. A legend on the coop announced "A Thankful Turkey." The turkey ate his grain ration like all the other guests, flapped his wings and gobbled his appreciation.

It was no more than an incident recalling a remote past when Mrs. Ellen G. White died in California in 1915. She had long been senile, though she never lost her awareness, as Elder A. G. Daniels said in his funeral sermon, of "the exceeding sinfulness of sin." An intracapsular fracture of the left femur, sustained in a fall at the door of her study, at St. Helena, California, laid the fundamentalist leader low, and she never recovered. The Adventists gave her three whopping funerals, two in California and an all-out service at the Tabernacle in Battle Creek. Many doctors and nurses came down to the "Tab" from the Sanitarium for Sister White's last earthly visit to Battle Creek, saw again in memory's eye the ample figure of the inspired *religeuse* in her prime, rising at the desk with her Bible in her hand. Again they heard down the lane of memory, faintly and for the last time, the ringing voice which once echoed through the tents and oak-openings of Michigan, calling out "glory, glory" and proclaiming decretals for the guidance of the faithful.

And so the doughty visionist whom Dr. Kellogg had bested in a long and intemperate wrangle, the uncompromising disciplinarian who ruled a church and served well the cause of diet reform, headed at long last for the marble orchards. Visiting Adventists from afar lingered after the funeral among the sleeping fathers of their faith, to reflect upon the thrilling scene when the graves would open and Uriah Smith, M. E. Cornell, G. W. Amadon, D. T. Bordeau, the Whites, J. P. Kellogg and Annette would leap out again, shouting joyously of man's final victory over death.

Throughout Sister White's long and useful life, the question which often agitated the Adventists, "Why Doesn't God Destroy the Devil?" had never been answered satisfactorily. The Devil had even laid his hands in subtle ways upon the authoress of *The Great Controversy*. Ellen White had ever to be especially vigilant against flattery, self-righteousness, arrogance and a narrow sectarian spirit.

Despite the handicap of the disreputable toe-cracking Fox sisters, who created unimaginable difficulties for all subsequent communicants with the invisible world, Ellen White used her prophetic powers successfully to establish an aggressive religion with a special view of world history. Upon her death, a sister in Los Angeles and another in Washington, D. C., tried to assume the post which the venerable mystic had occupied. But they couldn't fill the shoes. And no other sister since has been able to carry the high commission of the Maine farm girl who walked with the Lord, taught that fashionable dress caused catarrh, and promoted the breakfast foods of Battle Creek.

To J. H. Kellogg, Mrs. White's writ had long ago ceased to run. To W. K. Kellogg, she had never been a problem. To C. W. Post, she was no more than an historical anecdote in black bombazine.

When the Wolverine, crack train on the Michigan Central, stood for five minutes longer than usual in front of the Battle Creek station, the conductor on the platform, his watch in one hand, the other raised for the "highball" gesture, it usually meant that Dr. Kellogg was about to take a trip. A hack pulled up smartly. A stocky figure scudded across the bricks, trailing a secretary with hand luggage, files of work, a hamper of Sanitarium foods to assure a prosperous journey. As the white figure mounted the car steps, the word was passed "The Doctor is on board," and the engineer could open the throttle for Detroit and points east.

Settled on the train, Kellogg ordered a table and two or three Pullman pillows. Leaning back he would start dictating at an easy 185 words a minute. The secretary might, if luck was with him, drop off the train with a full notebook at Detroit; if not, he could shift his hopes to Windsor, St. Thomas, or Buffalo. Or he might find himself next morning in New York City, reluctantly attending a meeting of the National Society for the Prevention of Tuberculosis. There Dr. Kellogg would finally wave him back home and himself climb on the train for Washington to attend a Board meeting of the Life Extension Bureau, then back to New York for the Executive Committee meeting of the Race Betterment Conference and a side visit to the Mount Hermon School up in Massachusetts before heading for home again.

Long before Professor I. P. Pavlov's work on his immortal dogs had revised the ideas of physiologists generally about the digestive functions, Dr. Kellogg was alive to the importance of the Russian's researches. With a close associate, Dr. James T. Case, Kellogg travelled to St. Petersburg soon after the Toasted Corn Flake Company was founded, to visit Pavlov's Institute of Experimental Medicine. They observed the dogs hard at work producing a liter a day of "appetite juice." The Battle Creek visitors took notes busily upon the technique of implanting fistulas in various parts of the intestine so that the products of digestion could be collected and studied. Dr. Kellogg saw standing on a table a beautiful dog with a salivary fistula. While the scientists held their breath, an assistant blew a whistle. The saliva flowed. The conditioned reflex had been demonstrated.

At dinner Kellogg met Mrs. Pavlov who told him what it was like to be the wife of a genius who couldn't buy his clothes, fix anything, or manage his own affairs.

"*Mein Mann ist nur ein Knabe, nur ein Knabe,*" she would exclaim, while the demonstrative Nobel Prize winner talked, waved his arms, eyes blazing, face in play, his expression ever changing, a great dramatic artist strayed into the world of science.

Dr. Kellogg found that Pavlov's ideas on the physiology of digestion supplied new support for the Battle Creek Sanitarium diet system and in 1922 established at the Sanitarium a Pavlov Physiological Institute of his own, with permission to use the name. Dr. W. N. Boldyereff, a Czarist refugee from the Revolution and for ten years chief assistant to Pavlov in the Military Medical Academy at Petrograd, came to Battle Creek as Director of the Institute, which had the equipment of a physiological laboratory and an excellent dog yard. The Doctor kept an ugly old chimpanzee with a nasty disposition, who once tore one leg off Professor Carroll Grant's trousers and nearly took the coat off the back of another scientist. But Dr. Kellogg liked the chimp. He could use him for a stunt. The Doctor would toss him a steak, and the intelligent anthropoid would throw it right back at him. Then John Harvey would hand in a banana. The ape would peel and munch it with evident approval.

The Doctor was a public-relations classic. The Extension De-

partment—non de plume for advertising department—produced
national-magazine advertising with a powerful appeal: Build up
your health and meet interesting people while you do it. The Department also got out circulars, catalogues, brochures, publicity
stories, house organs like *The Sanitarium News*, to pep up the
helpers, and *The Battle Creek Idea* for the guests. The newsletter
was filled with chitchat about the patrons: Admiral Byrd, Ruth
St. Denis were arriving. Also expected soon were John D. Rockefeller, Jr., John Burroughs, Richard Halliburton, Ronald Amundsen,
Temple Bailey, Messrs. Kress and Kresge, J. C. Penney, Ed Little
(the Palmolive Soap executive), C. W. Barron, Mrs. Knox of
gelatine fame, Dr. Carrie Chapman Catt, Mrs. E. T. Stotesbury,
Bob La Follette, Dorothy Draper, Dan Gerber and Mrs. Walgreen
(separately).

If the president of a sheet-metal works in Detroit was a fifth-
timer, the fact was reported. When a manufacturer from Cleveland
proudly called himself "a real 'Sanitarium Crank,'" his remarks
were quoted *in extenso*.

A photo division of the Extension Department rolled out the
glossy prints when a high vegetarian checked in from India, or
John H. Patterson put aside the cares of the National Cash Register
Company long enough to catch up on the latest dietary thinking.
President Patterson was "more than strong for all that Battle Creek
stuff," said the *Dayton Daily News*.

One reason why so many top-drawer names appeared on the
"San" register was that The Doctor picked up the check for the
brighter celebrities. Which luminaries were lodged and fed on
the house and which paid their board bill is at this remote date a
matter of conjecture. It is unlikely that E. T. Welch, the prosperous
grape juice man or Arthur Capper, senator and wealthy publisher,
or the President of the International Harvester Company visited
Battle Creek as deadheads. Eddie Cantor and Percy Grainger may
have entertained in the north parlor as a *quid pro quo*. Johnny
Weismuller could swim for his enemas and massage. George Palmer
Putnam and Amelia Earhart could—and did—repay the "San"
hospitality in an unusual fashion. They took Dr. Kellogg for his
first airplane ride, cruising for ten minutes over the tall smokestacks
of the Health City. Then Miss Earhart banked the plane so The

Doctor could push his goggles up with his surgeon's hand and peer over the fusilage for a new perspective on the vast Sanitarium layout.

Dr. Frank Crane, the thinker, came to Battle Creek, stayed six weeks, and wrote a brochure for The Doctor. So, too, did Doctor—later Sir Wilfred—Grenfell, a Companion of St. Michael and St. George because of his medical missionary work in Labrador— with a K.C.M.G. yet ahead of him. Grenfell confessed that he had previously thought the Battle Creek Sanitarium "might be merely a means of advertising patent foods and a new [sic] sect called Seventh day Adventists," but found it free of cant, the best-known simple food protest in America.

One of Dr. Kellogg's major interests was the Race Betterment Foundation, which he created and financed. The Foundation was an expression of Dr. Kellogg's interest in heredity. The Doctor did not maintain that diet, exercise, rest and health education would do *everything!* Several Race Betterment Conferences were held to study degenerative tendencies in American life and to hear papers on "Uneugenical Matings." This last item of business the newspapers of the country translated into the language of reportage as "eugenic weddings" and "human stock shows." It served to foster Battle Creek's reputation as the home of daft theories and added the possibility of "fast" morals.

To such congresses came Luther Burbank, Luther H. Gulick, not the missionary Luther, but the other one, the "physical ed" Gulick, coinventor of basketball—who was touched with vegetarian theories, possibly because he once attended Oberlin College. Gulick rose to ask, "Is there any place in Battle Creek where boys and girls can build a fire and bake a potato in the open air?" And Mrs. Gulick, or *Hutinim*, to use her secret Camp Fire Girl name, put on her ceremonial gown and her honor beads to describe the spirit of the Camp Fire movement. Beaming in the midst of high activity, flanked by Sir Horace Plunkett, Booker T. Washington and S. S. McClure, was host Kellogg in immaculate white, directing the attention of his distinguished guests to relevant aspects of child life, sex, industrial hygiene and other altruistic questions.

Everybody who was anybody attended the biologic banquet

which closed the Conference, except the Minister from Egypt, who was unavoidably detained; Dean Inge, who said, "I have nothing new to contribute on Nature and Nurture"; and H. G. Wells, who just didn't give a damn.

In the expansive 1920's, when The Doctor was pushing eighty, urged on by an optimistic board of directors, he went into a new-construction program. It added to the Sanitarium a four-story dining-room wing, a fifteen-story tower, tallest building in the city, and a multi-million-dollar debt. The move represented a disastrous error in judgment. The Battle Creek Sanitarium had had an idea which made it undeniably different. A part of its difference was the heritage of asceticism. When the doctors went plushy they went broke. Of course, there were other factors, the top-heavy debt and the general economic situation.

There were social changes occurring, too, which made it doubtful if the "San" needed a luxurious new lobby, with majestic columns of Mankato stone, walnut panelling, marble floors, Oriental rugs, rich tapestries, 265 additional rooms, a magnificent new dining room with crystal chandeliers, murals and drapes as baroque as the decorators from Marshall, Field & Company could devise. The whole sanitarium concept was about to be cut down to size by inscrutable forces. The kinds of foods people were eating had changed significantly—toward more dairy products, more fish, poultry, citrus and other fruits, tomatoes, salad greens, toward less starchy foods, fewer calories; all in all, a better-balanced diet. Fewer people needed to go to Battle Creek to be "boiled out," in The Doctor's old phrase; and if they did go, they didn't stay as long, or esteem so highly as did the dyspeptics of the horse-and-buggy days the purely recreational aspects of a "San" sojourn. The frills, the Chautauqua features, were on their way out, at just about the same time and for much the same reasons, as the tented centers of culture. Life was moving on to a new level, acquiring a new mobility. The string trio was playing to a ragtime audience.

People smiled behind their hands and said that it was too bad that Dr. Kellogg had, at long last, become senile. But they anticipated. John Harvey was not ready to be hurried off the stage. There was still one more good fight in him.

XVII

Doctor Kellogg's Last Fight

A BATTLE CREEK vegetarian, one Edward Buckley, once walked to Florida with only a rucksack on his back. It was filled with strength-giving Battle Creek health foods, to prove that the meatless dietary gave Man the endurance necessary for a fifteen-hundred-mile hike. Dr. Kellogg also went to Florida, but by more comfortable means. In 1931 he established a sanitarium there. It had often been proposed to The Doctor that he combine the advantages of Battle Creek diet and treatment with those of the famed Florida climate and sunshine. When he began to show interest, The Doctor received prodigious quantities of mail from chambers of commerce and individuals, offers of property and, it is said, even hard cash.

Glenn Curtiss, inventor and aircraft manufacturer, a former patient interested in spreading the gospel of The Simple Life, presented Dr. Kellogg with a luxurious estate at Miami Springs. The house, equivalent to a fine hotel, was set like a gem in a beautiful tropical setting. The consideration was one dollar.

"That's too cheap," the seventy-eight-year-old Kellogg remarked, and handed Curtiss a ten-dollar bill.

Begun as a private venture, Battle Creek, Inc., the new sanitarium was fully equipped with all facilities, including outdoor gymnasia, enclosed in a scarlet hedge of Turk's cap, hibiscus and poinsettias. Characteristic Battle Creek dishes were features of the menu, vegetable oyster soup with toasted wheat flakes as croutons, nut roasts, sliced Protose, Granose biscuits, Bromose and Caramel Cereal. The sanitarium, an immediate success, was later turned over as a philanthropic institution, under the name of Miami-Battle Creek, to a board of trustees.

The Doctor was seen less and less in Battle Creek after he became interested in Miami. Otherwise his habits did not change visibly as the years closed in around him. He still thought five hours of sleep enough, could walk into an office during a strenuous day, stretch out on the floor and drop off to sleep, wake up refreshed and ready to dictate an address, or turn off a pamphlet.

Pad and pencil were always at his bedside so that J. H. might catch each fugitive idea. The final solution of the problem of flaking wheat came to him, it will be recalled, in a dream. Sometimes he jotted down a suggestion for a magazine article, an inquiry to the Bureau of Chemistry at the Department of Agriculture. Could they send him any new material relating to the bacteriological examination of oysters? What did they have on bran and phytin, or the composition of chick peas? He must remember to send them some of his own potato flour. He still took his morning trot, could rise to an emergency; as when he dashed up to Callender, Ontario, with a dietician and a nurse to consult with Dr. Dafoe on the quintuplets' digestive upset.

The little Doctor continued to write copiously. His literary productivity had always been prodigious. . . . Once he dictated for twenty hours without a break at a Colorado mountain retreat. On another occasion a telegram arrived, stating that two chapters for a book which Dr. Kellogg had promised in two weeks must be in the mail the next day because the date of publication had been advanced. He began work at once. At five o'clock the next morning, the manuscript was finished, the bibliography checked, the typescript proofread and at the post office. Once he dictated for forty-eight hours without sleep. Most, perhaps all, of this writing was impermanent. His method was obviously not that of the lapidary. And time soon dates a popular article on "What is the Matter with the American Stomach?" Dr. Kellogg wrote to exert an immediate influence upon a contemporary audience. His more successful books ran through many editions, with printings of twenty-six to thirty thousand each. Kellogg attained his objective of reaching a mass audience. His books in the aggregate attained a sale of more than a million copies.

Dr. Kellogg was committed to the idea of progress on scientific grounds. He accepted the principle of evolution in the physical world, and by extension, social evolution, too. On philosophic grounds he believed that man is capable of providing himself with a more perfect physical development which would advance his moral, intellectual and artistic accomplishments. But, somehow— the blame seemed to fall on "civilization"—society had taken a wrong turning. On one occasion The Doctor told the American Public Health Association that the human race was gradually going crazy. But the Battle Creek Doctor insisted that man could, if he would, produce his own social and hygienic mutations in the direction of "right living" by the exercise of common sense, assisted by vegetable gelatine, Battle Creek sherbet and a high state of intestinal motility.

The Doctor worked both ends of the life span. In setting up the proper environment for the forty-odd boys and girls he took into his home, he hoped to show that nurture and guidance would produce a uniformly better human being in both a biological and a social sense. Late in life, as a gerontologist, he tackled the problem at the other end. As a result of his insistence that men and women aged seventy-five and over could enter into "the aristocracy of health," a string of Three-Quarter-of-a-Century Clubs sprang up in various Michigan cities, endowed by his Race Betterment Foundation. The Doctor knew how to take the minds of the aged off their body processes and the way their skin itched. He inspired the hope that they might again regain their elastic tissue, and made the Club pledge, "I hereby promise to do my best to attain the age of one hundred years," both a desirable and an attainable goal.

In 1927, the Battle Creek Sanitarium, which already carried one million dollars of existing debt, bonded itself for three million dollars more to build the fifteen-story tower and the four-story wing. During the Depression, as patronage dropped off, there were vacant rooms, cuts in employment. Some helpers, loyal to their vocation, accepted their pay partly in cash and partly in promissory notes. But that was not enough. On January 1, 1933, the world's largest sanitarium defaulted. A Toledo bondholder petitioned for a receivership under Section 77-B of the National Bankruptcy Act of 1933, which was devised as a tonic for sick corporations whose immediate outlook was dim but which were not without long-range prospects. Federal Judge Arthur J. Tuttle placed the "San" in receivership in February. It had almost twelve million dollars in assets, liabilities of $3,237,573, but was unable to get assistance at the banks. Reorganization got under way the next year. Trustees, bondholders and general creditors agreed on a plan. The general creditors, many of whom were "San" employees already accepting part cash and part notes for their salaries, got forty cents on the dollar. Half of this was cash, half was in new bonds. Judge Tuttle signed the order confirming the plan in 1938. A new corporation emerged, the Battle Creek Sanitarium and Benevolent Association.

While Dr. Kellogg grappled with the "San's" financial problems during the days of the national economic storm, Battle Creek College was also sinking in a sea of difficulties. Falling from a peak of enrollment of nine hundred in 1929, it got down to some four hundred plus students. The College closed its doors in 1938. Dr. Kellogg was in financial difficulties, but they were not insuperable. He was buying up Sanitarium bonds, straining his personal credit to do so, to keep control of the health resort from passing to the bondholders, whom he described as a "gambling and night club crowd." He also had the Miami-Battle Creek sanitarium to keep afloat, and the Battle Creek Food Company, too, where he discovered that the manager had been operating a sales agency on his own which siphoned off a substantial part of the Company's profits. With much on his mind, then, Kellogg delayed repeatedly in approving the College budget for 1938-39. Finally, in April, 1938, President Emil Leffler telephoned Dr. Kellogg in Florida and attempted to force the issue.

He said, "We must approve the budget as it has been set up *or* approve it on a reduced basis *or* close the College."

Kellogg suddenly saw a way out.

"We will close the College," he replied. Thus the blue and white struck its colors.

The Battle Creek Sanitarium never again saw the days of 1,390 registered patients and guests and a service staff of 1,800. In the war year of 1942, when Dr. Kellogg greeted the food stringency with the declaration that meat rationing should hold no terrors since the health of the nation would be vastly improved if we had 365 meatless days a year, some three hundred lonely patients rattled around in the vast Main Building. The click of a heel on the marble floor was a welcome sound. It showed that human life was near.

The end of an era could be discerned in the announcement on May 15, 1942, that the U. S. Army would take over the Sanitarium as a general base hospital. Renamed the Percy Jones General Hospital, the huge building acquired a new character along with its new name. Soon the aroma of roasting Army beef drifted from the vegetarian kitchens. Steam tables appeared beneath the crystal chandeliers. It was usless to protest "Sergeant, spare that tree!" as the profane axe fell against the forty-year-old rubber tree pressing against the dome of the Palm Garden. The space was needed. No place for tree.

The price paid for the real estate and improvements, including the city block occupied by The Doctor's deer park and Residence, was $2,251,100. To this sum, ninety thousand dollars was added later. It enabled the "San" to pay off all outstanding debts and left a handsome million in the kitty. Operation of the Sanitarium would not be interrupted, Dr. Kellogg announced. More vigorous than ever, the "San" would re-establish itself on the other side of the street in John Harvey Kellogg Hall, the old cobblestone buiding where the Phelps brothers had hoped to outshine Dr. Kellogg. The Sanitarium also occupied the Battle Creek College Library Building, and miscellaneous cottages.

Dr. Kellogg's statement on the transaction was a masterly job. Four out of six buildings had been retained, he pointed out; all equipment, apparatus, furniture. New therapy was to be introduced. Activity would increase throughout the institution. A new sponsoring committee of eminent scientists would help to make the "San" more than ever "a great university of health." With a million dollars in the bank and the end in sight of bondholder representation on the Board of Trustees, The Doctor was jubilant. He threw himself enthusiastically into plans for the actual physical moving.

"They bought a building," he would repeat, "not the Sanitarium."

The deadline for moving day was midnight, July 31, 1942. The stocky health leader raced down to Washington in the July heat, to wrestle with the War Production Board over priorities. He pled for copper wire and building materials, came home triumphant with an A-1-J priority. The Board in Washington had decided "no priority" before he arrived. But—"after I advised the Board members of the important work done by the institution the priorities were granted quickly." Kellogg was able to tell his associates "all the major obstacles . . . have been removed.

"We will carry on comfortably here, until, in due course, we will go out to the hills and lakes at the east of town and there we will build it all over again," Dr. Kellogg declared, while his staff struggled with pyramids of beds, chairs, dining and dressing tables, working around the clock day after day. Even the city firemen helped, pushing wheel chairs filled with bedding and blankets and lamps. The white-clad Kellogg stood in the portico amid mountains of mattresses, lamps and fixtures, directing and encouraging, riding the storm, pointing the way to call boys and helpers bending and tugging, a pink-and-white general of the great Army of Health, with the systolic and diastolic pressures of a man of fifty-five.

At the very end of the affair, patients were getting their setting up exercises in the old building. There the main desk was still in operation, selling stamps and post cards, answering questions about where the doctors were, the points of tourist interest in Battle Creek, the mileage to Gull Lake, the location of Sojourner Truth's grave. Over at the new location another desk clerk was selling stamps and post cards, trying to explain where the doctors were, directing guests to the points of tourist interest, and describing the location of Sojourner Truth's grave.

The operation was completed on time. Army M.P.'s took over the entrances and clicked their heels in lobbies once graced by William Jennings Bryan, where Herbert Hoover had passed by, where Carrie Nation had distributed souvenir hatchet pins, and old Sojourner sold her "Shadow" photographs. It was promised that a high wooden Army fence of unparalleled ugliness would soon enclose the property.

When the Sanitarium became independent of the bondholders' jurisdiction, maneuverings began in the Seventh Day Adventist Sanhedrin looking toward a supreme effort to win control of the health institution. A new board of trustees was to be elected at the next annual meeting of the membership of the corporation, due to be held in March, 1943. The members, or constituents, paid ten dollars for a year's membership or one hundred dollars for a life membership. Functioning like stockholders, the constituency elected the board. There were over one hundred constituents, originally mostly "San" workers. Dr. Kellogg had, for years, paid for many memberships, and it was the custom to vote The Doctor in as a member of a friendly Board which reappointed him as Sanitarium superintendent year after year. So The Doctor had, in effect, a self-perpetuating Board. But, by 1943, a majority of the constituents had moved away. The Battle Creek group, loyal to Dr. Kellogg, were in the minority.

What started the shenanigans was the one million dollars in the "San" treasury. The Adventist elders noted The Doctor's advanced age, the absence of long-range planning for his succession, the tempting cash assets. So Elder W. H. Branson, Vice President of the Seventh Day Adventist General Conference, sent out a letter to the members of the denomination saying that the "San" needed their help, that the time had come to take it back into the work of the church. He urged the members of the old constituency to get their memberships paid up and attend the meeting. An Adventist slate of directors and officers was prepared for their convenience, and Branson got in touch with W. K. Kellogg.

There were no flies on W. K. Anything he could do to the detriment of his brother did not remain undone. The Kellogg who once said to a man leaving the employ of Dr. Kellogg, "Your happiness is just beginning," got the point instantly. He saw that his brother could be tossed out upon the town if the plan worked.

Abruptly, W. K., the ex-Adventist, who thought of himself as being "about as religious as most people," meaning *not very*, began to talk the Advent lingo of his youth. The Doctor, he admitted sadly, had flaunted the Message of the Third Angel. It was an accusation to move the devout to revulsion, for it meant that J. H. was indifferent to the Saturday Sabbath. W. K. also demonstrated his support of the church plan by writing to the members of the constituency urging them to attend the meeting and vote the straight Adventist ticket. W. K. put up a fund to pay the absent brothers to come to Battle Creek. He covered their railroad tickets, bus or taxi fares, food, lodging and lost time on their jobs. A secret meeting, a kind of skull practise, was held in Kalamazoo.

Naturally, a Sanitarium constituent loyal to Dr. Kellogg received the Branson and/or the W. K. Kellogg letter, and the cat was out of the bag. The old Doctor worked night and day preparing a counteroffensive. He subpoenaed the Washington records of the Seventh Day Adventists, hailed the implacable W. K. into court, white cane, dog and all, and brought the whole plan into the open. There was no claim that The Doctor was not competent, or that he was not the father of the institution, or its dominant figure. What added a special note of bitterness, from The Doctor's point of view, was that at the depth of the Depression, he had turned in desperation to the Adventist church to see if it would take over the "San." There was no interest at that time.

The issue was whether a board would be elected favorable to denominational control or whether its members would be nonsectarian and sympathetic to The Doctor's methods. There seemed to be general agreement, on the surface, at least, that Dr. Kellogg's position would not be disturbed. But he rejected that conception. The Adventists, he said, never had demonstrated that they could run a successful sanitarium and he couldn't either under their authority.

The immediate question was the seating of members eligible to vote. Some four hundred applicants, waiting to present their credentials, thronged the former Battle Creek College Library building. They chatted, banged on the piano, knitted, peered curiously through narrow glass panes at the closed session of the constituents. The hour grew late, and then early. Sandwiches were brought in. Tired candidates from Washington, D. C., Maryland, Florida, Illinois, Tennessee, Missouri, Oklahoma, California and Oregon lolled on folding chairs and munched their sandwiches while rumors swept through the crowd.

The Adventist faction turned out to be able to elect a slate of ten trustees. The Doctor, his back to the wall, struck back with a weapon which had served him well and often—a court injunction. Charging that the meeting which elected the trustees was an improper "rump session," Dr. Kellogg followed the injunction with an amended order served on the members of "a pretended board of trustees." This maneuver broke up the annual meeting on its second day. Dr. Kellogg withdrew to The Residence to think, the church party to the tabernacle to pray.

The court order banning the Adventists from "intermeddling or interfering with property, business or affairs" of the Sanitarium meant that The Doctor had successfully repelled the Church's commandos at least until the judge decided whether he would make the stay permanent. There was nothing more for the delegates to do except collect their expense money and go home. Judge Blaine W. Hatch appointed six interim trustees to operate the Sanitarium pending the outcome of the litigation.

No gaudy lithograph, such as "Custer's Last Fight," remains to memorialize Dr. Kellogg's final battle; yet his, like Custer's, ended in death. The court fight drew heavily upon the nonagenarian's vitality. With his hearing failing so that even with his hearing aid he had to push the device around the table as each board member spoke, his sight so bad that he had to stare at a photograph of himself in order to autograph it, in his last weeks Dr. Kellogg also had a slight facial paralysis. Ultraproud, he stayed in seclusion. His activity, however, was not lessened. He kept in close touch with Sanitarium affairs. Were the guests comfortable? How were the plumbing installations coming along? The Doctor continued to work on several medical papers dealing with hypertension. His interest in exophthalmic goitre and various cachexias remained as keen as ever.

An annoying bronchial attack upset his schedule, then developed into pneumonia. As Dr. James R. Jeffrey of the "San" staff attended him, Dr. Kellogg jokingly remarked, "Well, maybe this is the last time, Doctor." After a three days' bout with pneumonia, the ninety-one-year-old founder of the breakfast food industry died peacefully in his sleep.

The end of the somatic life of Dr. Kellogg presented an opportunity for composing the legal controversy over the "San" and its bulging treasury. The Doctor, say those who knew him well, would never have given an inch or a penny. But his successors made a settlement. The Adventists received $550,000. Three local farms valued at $75,000 also went to the church Conference. It was stipulated that Adventism could not establish an institution similar to the Sanitarium in Battle Creek for twenty-five years. The Sanitarium was placed under the superintendency of Dr. James T. Case of Chicago and his nominees, all individuals who had worked with Dr. Kellogg and would carry on in his spirit.

W. K. Kellogg failed by three months in his fond ambition to live to be older than his brother. He died at Battle Creek, October 6, 1951, also aged ninety-one, but three months younger than the ninety-one years and ten months which J. H. attained.

W. K. and The Doctor had put up twin monuments on their cemetery lots during their middle years, about the time that W. K.'s first wife, the former Ella Osborn Davis, died, in 1912. But the more Will thought about the chummy arrangement the less he liked it. So he tore his monument down and substituted a simple sundial on which a bronze robin tugged a bronze worm out of the bronze earth. One could scarcely think of a more apt memorial for Will Kellogg than an early bird—and an industrious one.

The death of this fantastically rich old man—the none-genuine-without-this-signature Kellogg—removed almost the last pioneer of a unique U. S. industry which arose so curiously out of a religious movement. Of the little band who revolutionized the world's breakfast habits, the most interesting is versatile, clever J. H. Kellogg, brilliant in his attainments, though lacking the ultimate spaciousness of a truly large spirit. He had zest and a magic touch on life. He could bring tears to the eyes of the gentlemen of the Common Council when Battle Creek eyed the Sanitarium as a taxable. He could cozen an elder, cajole a balky patient, wheedle a fortune out of a millionaire—and give it away the next day. From his island cottage in Gull Lake, Dr. Kellogg could raise his eyes to the galaxies and argue with poetry and deep feeling that the design evident in the night sky implied the existence of a great Designer. There should be no mistake: The Doctor had his own code. He was a great protester, willing to go to extremes, to invite opposition, to undergo ridicule if it would advance his purposes. If there *is* a Second Coming, he seemed to say, let us receive Him with healthy bodies.

In special areas, Kellogg's ideas got in the way of his observations as a scientist. His lifelong vegetarianism was certainly not basic biology. This monism, and his attachment to massage, caused the American Medical Association to look at him with a certain reserve. But he ploughed ahead, accepted the odium of over-emphasis.

"I am a reformer," he said. "I have to ask for several things to get one."

As an educator, Kellogg established schools and colleges. As a physician and surgeon, he healed thousands and contributed to the techniques of abdominal surgery. His writings would make a medical library in themselves. He invented scores of health appliances. Just for the fun of it, he even constructed a kind of no-tobacco Turkish pipe. It made billows of smoke out of the chemical reaction of a harmless alkali in solution. Vast food industries were built on his ideas. Kellogg's invention of flaked ready-to-eat cereals might be compared with man's discovery of *lactus Bacillus Bulgaricus*—sour milk—so important in man's food history; the modern flakes and the ancient curds, each keepable, storable, transportable, and so in its own time an extender of the world's food supply.

When two consummate promoters, C. W. Post and W. K. Kellogg, sized up correctly the commerical possibilities of the Sanitarium health foods, the breakfast-food industry left behind the religionist and faddist. The merchandisers took the risks and reaped the rewards, which include the reward of being remembered. An aging generation recalls Dr. J. H. Kellogg. But every space cadet, every interplanetary patrolman under age twelve, every kiddie who munches Kellogg's Sugar Frosted Flakes, and carries a Kellogg fourteen-inch plastic submachine squirt gun, knows the name of W. K. Kellogg. Millions of dollars' worth of advertising and billions of cereal packages glorify his name.

Different as the two Kellogg brothers were, one suspects that in the afterlife, wherever they are, they are in the Same Place. The little Doctor, all in white, cocks a practised eye at the occupancy rate, one feels, and draws up plans to improve the bill of fare. It is a source of gratification to the food inventor when new arrivals say to him that the name of Kellogg is no strange one to them. But what they are thinking of is the W. K. Kellogg Foundation, the W. K. Kellogg Bird Sanctuary, the W. K. Kellogg Institute of Graduate and Post-Graduate Dentistry at the University of Michigan, the Kellogg International Fellowships awarded in twenty-one countries, and—above all—the good name and fame of Kellogg's Corn Flakes.

What could be more natural, then, for a new referral, upon meeting a patriarchal-looking old party from Battle Creek named Kellogg, to ask politely for his autograph, and to add ingratiatingly, while The Doctor's goatee quivers in distress:

"I've often seen your signature on the package, *Mister* Kellogg."

Like Columbus, the United States vegetarian crusaders sought one end, achieved another. Looking for a grain-fed City of God, they found instead a City of Pure Food. All of these worthies are in God's Acre now; each helped to fashion the America we know. Out of all the prophesying and pamphleteering, the preachings, the grinding and the roasting, the advertising and the selling, came fame and fortune for a few, while United States folklore was enriched, too. The effect was to accomplish a wider diffusion of the grain foods—a substantial contribution to the convenience, the enjoyment and the well-being of the world. Out of the argument between the vegetarians and the butchers has come the sensible mixed diet of today.

New problems ahead may be seen in dim outline. Every year the United States population alone expands at the rate of two and a half million, faster than our food supply. Despite the current United States surpluses, food technologists and population experts look ahead to the end of the 1900's with professional anxiety. While it would be unsafe to assume in fifty years a hungry America, living a subsistence diet on plankton, algae and "stick water" recovered from fertilizer plants, we must recognize that we have nearly come to the end of our land. Agricultural research and technology *may* close the gap between what we will have and what we will need. But the pattern of food consumption cannot but change toward less meat and more cereals if it continues to be true, as it always has been, that only about one eighth of the grain fed to animals is recovered as meat, poultry, milk and eggs.

The grains, as W. K. Kellogg said so many millions of times, are great foods. Enriched by man with vitamins and minerals, there are encouraging prospects ahead of other additives. Among them may be mentioned sesame, a tiny seed with a history predating Moses and a name from the Arabian Nights, crowded full of vitamins B, D, E and F, a 92 per cent digestible source of concentrated protein. Amino-acid fortification promises to balance out the vegetable protein in grains, to extend vastly the supply of biologically available high-grade protein. The Past is, indeed, but Prologue. Perhaps we shall yet gratefully erect that statue to Sylvester Graham which James Parton suggested as his due; or raise a national pantheon to honor *all* the philosophers of diet, who, for their own oddly assorted reasons, have urged the world to "browse, well pleased, the vegetable board."

1794. July 5. Sylvester Graham, diet reformer, born, West Suffield, Connecticut.

1811. March 28. Dr. James Caleb Jackson, hydropathic physician, reformer, food inventor, born, Manlius, New York.

1817. The Reverend William Metcalfe, English dissenter, emigrated from Manchester to Philadelphia, founded a vegetarian church, the Bible Christian.

1829. Sylvester Graham appeared in Philadelphia as a temperance lecturer, became acquainted with the Reverend Metcalfe's dietary views.

1834. John Preston Kellogg, father of Dr. John Harvey and Will K. Kellogg, emigrated from Hadley, Massachusetts to Michigan Territory.

1837. January 26. Michigan became a state.

1843. March, through October 22, 1844. The high point of excitement over Christ's Second Coming among the followers of the Adventist leader, William Miller.

1850. Village of Battle Creek chartered.

1851. September 11. Sylvester Graham died at Northampton, Mass.

1852. February 26. John Harvey Kellogg born in Tyrone, Michigan.

1853. Elder James and seeress Ellen G. White made their first missionary trip to Michigan.

1854. An Adventist church established in Battle Creek.

1854. October 26. Charles W. Post, multimillionaire cereal manufacturer and founder of the Postum Cereal Company, born in Springfield, Illinois.

1858. Dr. James C. Jackson took over a floundering water-cure resort in Dansville, New York, renamed it "Our Home Hygienic Institute."

1860. April 7. Will Keith Kellogg, founder of the Kellogg Co., born in Battle Creek.

1860. Denominational name, Seventh Day Adventists, adopted at a Conference in Battle Creek.

1861. Joshua V. Himes visited Dr. Jackson's sanatorium at Dansville, New York, first Seventh Day Adventist to do so.

circa 1863. Dr. James C. Jackson originated Granula, the first cold cereal breakfast food.

1866. September. Adventists opened their first health institution, the Western Health Reform Institute, at Battle Creek, predecessor to the Battle Creek Sanitarium.

circa 1870. Dr. James C. Jackson invented Granula, the first cold breakfast food, ancestor of Grape Nuts.

1875. John Harvey Kellogg graduated from Bellevue Medical College in New York City.

1876. October 1. Dr. Kellogg became Superintendent of the Western Health Reform Institute.

1878. The name of the Health Reform Institute changed to Battle Creek Sanitarium.

1878. Dr. Kellogg began the manufacture of the first Battle Creek "health food," Granola.

1880. W. K. Kellogg employed as bookkeeper to look after business details for Dr. Kellogg.

1881. Elder James White died in Battle Creek.

1891. February. C. W. Post came to Battle Creek to recover his health, became a mental healer, established a medical boardinghouse, La Vita Inn.

1893. Henry D. Perky, dyspeptic lawyer, obtained first patents for a machine to shred wheat.

1894. Contacts between Dr. Kellogg and Perky stimulated Kellogg to conduct experiments aimed at producing a ready-to-eat wheat food.

1894. C. W. Post started to develop a grain "health coffee."

1895. January 1. Post introduced Postum Cereal Coffee.

1895. February. Dr. Kellogg presented Granose, the first wheat flake, to the General Conference of the Seventh Day Adventists at the Battle Creek Sanitarium.

1895. July 11. Dr. James C. Jackson died at Dansville, N.Y.

1896. April 14. U.S. granted patent No. 558,393 to Dr. Kellogg, the first issued for the manufacture of a flaked cereal food.

1898. Grape Nuts was placed on the market by C. W. Post.

1898. The first corn flakes appeared, called Sanitas Corn Flakes, manufactured by Dr. Kellogg's Sanitas Nut Food Co.

circa 1900. Beginning of the Battle Creek cereal "boom."

1902. February 18. The Battle Creek Sanitarium burned down. Rebuilt, 1902-03.

1902. December 30. The Seventh Day Adventist printing plant burned down.

1903. The Battle Creek Sanitarium barns burned down.

1903. The Adventists moved their world headquarters from Battle Creek to Tacoma Park, Maryland, near Washington, D.C.

1903. The Postum Cereal Co. made $1,100,000 net.

1906. The Battle Creek Toasted Corn Flake Co. established, predecessor of the Kellogg Co., now the world's largest breakfast-food manufacturer.

1906. C. W. Post introduced his corn flakes, "Elijah's Manna," later renamed Post Toasties.

1907. January 1. Federal Food and Drug Act became law.

1907. July 4. The Toasted Corn Flake Company plant burned down.

1907. Dr. Kellogg and W. K. Kellogg excommunicated by the Adventists.

1914. May 9. C. W. Post died.

1915. July 16. Mrs. Ellen G. White, Adventist church leader and visionist, died.

1925. W. K. Kellogg began his career of systematic giving.

1930. W. K. Kellogg established the W. K. Kellogg Foundation to handle his benefactions.

1931. Dr. J. H. Kellogg opened the Miami-Battle Creek Sanitarium at Miami Springs, Florida.

1933. The Battle Creek Sanitarium went into receivership.

1942. The major properties of the Battle Creek Sanitarium were sold to the U.S. Army. The "San" moved across the street to the old Sanitarium Annex.

1943. March to August. Annual meeting of the old constituency of the Battle Creek Sanitarium and subsequent controversy over the control of the "San" between forces of Dr. Kellogg and the church elders.

1943. December 14. Dr. Kellogg died, aged 91 years, 10 months.

1951. October 6. W. K. Kellogg died, aged 91 years, 7 months.

SOURCES AND AUTHORITIES

THIS bibliography is selective rather than comprehensive. Citations in support of every paragraph and sentence appear to be fatiguing and unnecessary in a volume designed to bring pleasurable information to the general reader. And too much bibliography can become supererogatory. In this section I have listed only titles which were useful generally, and which are not repeated under the chapter notes. I have consulted, but omitted reference to, the standard biographical dictionaries, medical dictionaries, encyclopedias, numerous works of local history, and various writings of Sylvester Graham and other popular writers on physiology, food and health, including Mrs. Ellen G. White and Dr. John Harvey Kellogg.

Where it seemed desirable, I have been precise. Otherwise, page numbers are not given; also I have omitted volume, number and page where a considerable run of a newspaper or serial publication was consulted.

Among source books which contributed information, a generalization, an idea or insight, may be mentioned (Dr. W. A. Alcott), *Forty Years in the Wilderness of Pills and Powders; or the Cogitations and Confessions of an Aged Physician*, Boston: 1859; S. W. Avery, M.D., *The Dyspeptic's Monitor*, Second Edition, New York: 1830; Pierre Blot, *Handbook of Practical Cookery*, New York: 1868; Pierre Blot, *What to Eat*, New York: 1863; Nahum Capen, *Reminiscences of Dr. Spurzheim and George Combe* (short title), New York: 1881; Mrs. (Lydia Maria) Child, *The American Frugal Housewife*, Boston: 1835; *The Household Manual*, Battle Creek, Michigan: 1875; A. P. W. Philip, *A Treatise on Indigestion and its Consequences*, Philadelphia: 1825; Mrs. M. L. Shew, Revised by Joel Shew, M.D., *Water-Cure for Ladies*, New York: 1844; R. T. Trall, M.D., *The Illustrated Family Gymnasium*, New York: 1857; [H. F. Phinney] *The Water Cure in America*. Edited by a Water Patient, New York: 1848; *Life Sketches of Ellen G. White*, Mountain View, Calif.: 1915.

The following secondary books were examined: L. Jean Bogert, *Diet and Personality*, New York: 1934; E. Douglas Branch, *The Sentimental Years, 1836-1860*, New York: 1934; Arthur Huff Fauset, *Sojourner Truth*, Chapel Hill: 1938; H. T. Finck, *Food and Flavor*, New

York: 1913; H. T. Finck, *Girth Control*, New York: 1923; and the following by Horace Fletcher, *The A.B.-Z of Our Own Nutrition*, New York: 1903; *The New Glutton or Epicure*, New York: 1899; *The New Menticulture*, New York: 1906; Marion Harland, *Marion Harland's Complete Cook Book*, Indianapolis: 1906; *March of the College of Medical Evangelists*, Los Angeles: 1941; *Michigan, a Guide to the Wolverine State*, New York: 1947; Helen S. Mitchell, "Food Fads, Facts, and Fancies," in *Food and Life, Yearbook of Agriculture, United States Department of Agriculture*, Washington: 1939; *Narrative of Sojourner Truth, a Northern Slave*, Boston: 1850; *Narrative of Sojourner Truth; a Bondswoman of Olden Times* (short title), Battle Creek, Mich.: 1881; and the following two volumes by Arthur M. Schlesinger, *The American as Reformer*, Cambridge: 1950, and *The Rise of the City, 1878-1898*, New York: 1933; also Odell Shepard, *Pedlar's Progress, The Life of Bronson Alcott*, Boston: 1937.

In addition to the use made of periodicals, noted chapter by chapter, this book drew on the following: Horace L. Sipple, and Charles Glen King, "Food Fads and Fancies," *Agricultural and Food Chemistry*, Vol. II, No. 7, March 31, 1954; *American Grocer*, Vol. I, No. 3, October 15, 1869, and *ibid.*, Vol. LXXXVII, No. 6, February 6, 1907; A. M. Liebstein and Neil L. Ehmke, "The Case For Vegetarianism," and Joseph D. Wassersug, "The Case Against Vegetarianism," *The American Mercury*, Vol. LXX, No. 316, April, 1950; Helen S. Mitchell, and Gladys M. Cook, "Facts, Fads and Frauds in Nutrition," *Bulletin of the Massachusetts Agricultural Experiment Station*, No. 342; Dr. J. H. Kellogg, "A Great Physician Speaks on Music," *The Etude Music Magazine*, Vol. XLIX, No. 7, July, 1931; Eugene Wood, "Degeneracy of the Breakfast," *Everybody's Magazine*, Vol. XXII, No. 1, January, 1910; "Let Them Eat Cake," *Fortune*, Vol. X, No. 4, October, 1934; and *ibid.*, "The Wonders of Diet," Vol. XIII, No. 2, May, 1936; *Hall's Journal of Health*, Vol. XL, No. 8, August, 1893; *Headlight*, May, 1895; Luther H. Gulick, "The Mistake of Eating Meat," *Ladies' Home Journal*, Vol. XXVI, No. 26, March, 1909; Mrs. E. S. Bladen, "Dinners of Fifty Years Ago," *Lippincott's Magazine*, December, 1902; Ira V. Brown, "Watchers for the Second Coming: The Millenarian Tradition in America," *Mississippi Valley Historical Review*, Vol. XXXIX, No. 3, December, 1952; Dr. Lafayette B. Mendel, "Some Historical Aspects of Vegetarianism," *The Popular Science Monthly*, March, 1904; four articles in *Scientific American* on the then-novel subject of cereal breakfast foods, as follows: Vol. 61, June 30, 1906, and Vol. 62, July 7, July 21, and September 1, also 1906; and Frank Fayant, "The Industry that

Cook's the World's Breakfast," *Success*, Vol. VI, No. 108, May, 1903.

Pamphlet material used but not included in the chapter references includes: Origen Bacheler, *Graham's System Brought to the Test of Scripture* (short title), New York: 1833; *Battle Creek Centennial, 1831-1931*, Battle Creek: 1931; *Battle Creek Illustrated* (Battle Creek), 1889; *Battle Creek for Rest*, n.p., n.d.; Annie Besant, *Vegetarianism in the Light of Theosophy*, Madras, India: 1932; *Friendly Notices of the Sanatorium—Dansville, N.Y.*; ca. 1887; *My Visit to Kellogg's*, Battle Creek: 1922; *The Phelps Medical and Surgical Sanatorium. Souvenir of Opening, October 3, 1900*, Battle Creek: 1900; Henry Martin Stegman, *Battle Creek; its Yesterdays*, Battle Creek: 1931; *Tables of Food Composition in Terms of Eleven Nutrients* (short title), U.S. Department of Agriculture Miscellaneous Publication No. 572, n.p., 1945; *A Trip Through Postumville, where Postum Cereal, Instant Postum, Grape Nuts, Post Toasties, etc., Are Made*, Battle Creek: 1920; Harold A. Wooster, Jr., and Fred C. Blanck, *Nutritional Data*, Pittsburgh: 1949; *Yesterday's Pictures, or Familiar Faces*, n.p., 1913.

CHAPTER NOTES

The first reference to each title gives full information. Subsequent citations follow the shortened form. Editions are those used, not necessarily the earliest. Location of manuscript material is given the first time the item is cited. Key: DN = Catlin Memorial Library of the *Detroit News*; CI = Cereal Institute, Inc.; F = Forbes Library, Northampton, Mass.; ISH = Illinois State Historical Library; JH = The Johns Hopkins University Library; K = Kellogg Co.; LC = Library of Congress; MHC = Michigan Historical Collections of The University of Michigan; NYAM = New York Academy of Medicine; P = private source; UC = University of Chicago; W = Willard Library, Battle Creek, Michigan.

Chapter I

The glimpse of Miss Buck has been preserved because Julian Street and a staff artist for *Collier's* dropped off the Michigan Central to see what was going on in Foodtown. "Michigan Meanderings," *Collier's*, Vol. 53, No. 18, July 18, 1914; 7, 8. Frank Fayant wrote, in the midst of the new developments, "The Great Breakfast-Food Industry," *Review of Reviews*, Vol. 77: 613-14, May, 1903. For a perspective, written a generation later by a professional historian, see "A Dietary Interpretation of American History," by Arthur Meier Schlesinger, *Proceedings of the Massachusetts Historical Society*, Vol. LXVIII, October, 1944-May, 1947, Boston: 1952; 200-202. A popular summary of Battle Creek's contribution to U.S. food processing is "Here's the Latest Exciting Chapter in the Cereal Story," by Robert Froman, *Collier's*, Vol. 129, No. 15, April 12, 1952.

The religious sanction for the "health foods" runs all through the writings of Mrs. Ellen G. White, prophetess of the Second Coming. See *The Health Reformer*, Vol. XIII, No. 9, September, 1878. I also used her *Counsels on Diet and Foods*, Washington: 1938. Tributes to Battle Creek hurry and hustle appeared in *Jabs*, April, 1902, Chicago humorous publication; and in the *Chicago Sunday Tribune*, May 24, 1903; 37.

For the physical setting of Battle Creek and its general industrial development, I followed H. Thompson Straw, "Battle Creek: a Study in Urban Geography," *Papers of the Michigan Academy of Science, Arts and Letters*, Vol. XXIII, Ann Arbor: 1938.

American additions to man's food resources are conveniently listed by Schlesinger, *op. cit.* For information on the history and characteristics of corn, I am indebted to *Indian Corn in Old America*, by Paul Weatherwax, New York: 1954.

Consumption data, dollar value and advertising expense figures were supplied by The Cereal Institute, Inc. The discussion of cereal premiums is based upon personal experience and "Follow Through— Key to Premium Success," by Arthur E. Irwin, *Advertising Requirements Magazine*, December, 1954, and a reprint of Gordon C. Bower, "Do's and Don't's for Premium Buyers," *ibid.*, 1955, but no month given.

The boy who liked to breakfast in solitude so he could read cereal package literature, was the subject of an editorial paragraph in *The New Yorker*, December 3, 1955. "Kicker's" letter to the editor appeared in *The New York Times*, September 7, 1941, Section IV, p. 7. Marketing studies constitute a vast but private and not easily accessible literature. I consulted two, both by Elmo Roper, *A Study of Influences and Motives That Determine Cereal Eating*, n.p., 1954, and *A Study of Attitudes Toward and Habits Concerning Nutrition Among Young Women*, n.p., 1952 [CI]. Eating habits of the younger generation are reported in Mrs. Katherine E. Bridges, ed., and others, *Tested School and Community Breakfast Program Activities*, Chicago: n.d. The other end of the human life span is treated in *A Summary of the Iowa Breakfast Studies on Men Past 60 Years of Age*, Chicago; n.d. The statement made in my text that people of all ages and weights thrive better on an adequate breakfast is true en masse. But Dr. Norman Jolliffe points out that there are subgroups "that feel better with a poor breakfast. These groups should not be made to feel like nutritional lepers just because they are different from most."

The Bible verse from which the Seventh Day Adventists drew authority for their vegetarian practice is Gen. I:29. "Gizzardite," was an epithet referring to the muscular stomach of fowls, and suggesting an excessive preoccupation on the part of the Adventists with their digestive processes.

Dr. Jolliffe's discussion of population growth and food supply appears in his "Recent Advances in Nutrition of Public Health Significance," *Metabolism*, Vol. IV, No. 3, May, 1955; 191-92.

Chapter II

For the account of Cowherd's dilemma I drew upon *The Message*, Henry Stephen Clubb, ed., Vol. III, No. 1, and upon J. Thomas Scharf and Thompson Westcott, *History of Philadelphia, 1609-1884*, 3 vols., Philadelphia: 1884. For the career of the Reverend Metcalfe and his vegetarian flock, I followed *The Illustrated Vegetarian Almanac for 1855*, Henry S. Clubb, ed., and Scharf and Westcott, *op. cit.* Further data was gleaned from the fragile pages of the *American Vegetarian* files, from *Food, Home and Garden*; and Dr. John Harvey Kellogg traversed the same ground in "A Century's Progress in Health Reform," *Good Health*, Vol. 37, No. 3, March, 1902. Also useful was the *History of the Philadelphia Bible-Christian Church*, Philadelphia: 1922. I followed the activities of The American Vegetarian Society through the files of *The American Vegetarian*, and Dr. Isaac Jennings' name appears there frequently.

For the impact of nineteenth-century food reform upon Oberlin— town and college—I found scattered material in *The Graham Journal of Health and Longevity*, 1837-39, *Oberliniana*, by A. L. Shumway and C. DeW. Brower, Cleveland: n.d.; Robert S. Fletcher's "Bread and Doctrine at Oberlin," *Ohio State Archeological and Historical Quarterly*, Vol. XLIX (1940), 61, quoted in *The Health Reform Movement in the United States, 1830-70*, by William B. Walker, typescript dissertation, Baltimore: 1955, 136 (JH).

Thomas L. Nichols (1815-1901), pioneer dietician and hydrotherapist, left a lively memoir of his incarceration, from which I have borrowed, *Journal Kept in Jail*, Buffalo: 1840.

I collected biographical material about the Rev. Henry S. Clubb from the little coterie magazines, *The Vegetarian Almanac, op. cit.; The Phrenological Journal;* also *Early History of Michigan with Biographies of State Officers, Members of Congress, Judges and Legislators,* Lansing: 1888; and Albert J. Edmunds, "Pigs in a Vegetarian Sunday School," *The Open Court,* Vol. XXII (No. 8), No. 627, August, 1908.

For the treatment of Clubb's disaster in the Kansas Eden, I consulted the prospectus issued by the promoters, *The Octagon Settlement Company, Kanzas, containing Full Information for Inquirers,* New York: 1856; Russell Hickman, "Vegetarian and Octagon Settlement Company," *Kansas Historical Quarterly,* Vol. II, No. 4, November, 1933; 377-85. The subject is recapitulated briefly in Stewart Holbrook, *The Yankee Exodus,* New York: 1950. An understandably critical view of the colonizing venture is the personal narrative of a survivor, Mrs. Miriam Davis Colt, *Went to Kansas* (short title), Watertown: 1862. Clubb's vegetarian courtship and domestic felicities emerge from the "Henry Stephen Clubb Papers," (MHC).

I have applied to the Adventist and vegetarian *mystique* the historical background of romantic naturalism, which Hoxie Neale Fairchild studied in *The Noble Savage,* New York: 1928.

Vegetarian activities in Chicago are summarized from files of the *Chicago Vegetarian,* 1898-1900, especially Vol. III, No. 8, April, 1899.

Chapter III

The effects of Sunday breakfast in New England in the nineteenth century are depicted by Albert J. Bellows, M.D., in *The Philosophy of Eating,* Boston: 1870. John Grosvenor tells nostalgically how easy it was to dine too well in New York state in his "Recollections—Schoharie County Foods," *Schoharie County Historical Review,* Vol. XVIII, No. 1, May, 1954. The descriptions of Illinois food appear, in order, in *The Letter Box,* Miss Harriet Austin and J. C. Jackson, M.D., eds., and *The Graham Journal,* II, 323 and 374.

Greeley's travel narrative, *An Overland Journey from New York to San Francisco in . . . 1859,* New York: 1860, appears in extract in Warren S. Tryon, ed., *A Mirror for Americans. Life and Manners in the United States, 1790-1870, as Recorded by American Travellers.* 3 vols., Chicago: 1952, III, 729 *passim.* Parton: see his *Smoking and Drinking,* Boston: 1868; 87. There were helpful hints on table etiquette among "the American peasantry" in *A True Picture of Emigration,* Milo Milton Quaife, ed., Chicago: 1936. The decencies of table manners are treated in (Robert Tomes, M.D.), *The Bazar Book of Decorum,* New York: 1870.

Hitchcock's views are synthesized from his *Dyspepsy Forestalled & Resisted* (short title), Amherst: 1830. The high-pressure hospitality of the pickle bottle is retold from Fredrika Bremer, *America of the Fifties,* London: 1924. Cleveland Amory quotes from William Appleton's diary on a spacious Boston dinner party in *The Proper Bostonians,* New York: 1947.

The Southern Colonel's hospitality was set down by Mrs. Anne Royal, quoted from Tryon, *op. cit.,* II, 271. The American breakfast, pre-Battle Creek, is handled in disapproving detail in *Forty Years of American Life,* by Thomas L. Nichols, 2 vols. London: 1864. There is a wealth of material on frontier food and eating in Carl Wittke's *The History of the State of Ohio,* 6 vols., Columbus: 1941-43.

Pierre Blot was editor of the *Almanack Gastronomique* in Paris. The inventory of baked goods which the Vermont housewife produced appeared in *Harper's Bazaar,* December 7, 1878, quoted by Schlesinger, *loc. cit.*

The U.S. businessman's manner of dining was observed by Mackie in his *From Cape Cod to Dixie and the Tropics,* New York: 1864, quoted from Tryon, *op. cit.,* II, 69. For dining à la Chicago: I have followed Dallas L. Jones, "Chicago in 1833," *Journal of the Illinois State Historical Society,* Vol. XLVII, No. 2, Summer, 1954; 174 and 260. The manners were graceless at Niblo's Hotel in New York, too. See Thomas Hamilton, *Men and Manners in America,* 2 vols., Philadelphia: 1833, 21.

For material on farm diet, I am indebted to Richard Osborn Cummings, *The American and His Food,* Chicago: 1940, and to Bellows, *op. cit.* The encomium to saleratus occurs in William A. Baillie-Grohman's *Camps in the Rockies,* London: 1882; 65. Mrs. White took the opposite view of baking-powder biscuits in *Counsels on Diet,* Mountain View, Calif., 1938; 343.

Dr. Merritt G. Kellogg is a principal source for family data on the cornflake Kelloggs in his *Notes Concerning the Kelloggs,* n.p., n.d. Professor Luther West, a former close associate of Dr. John Harvey Kellogg, supplied background information in a valuable memorandum prepared for the guidance of the author. Merritt G. Kellogg, *op. cit.,* discusses the health and medication of his father. U. P. Hedrick wrote of his Michigan memories in *The Land of the Crooked Tree,* New York: 1948, to which I am indebted for his opinion of dried-apple pie.

Dr. Asa Green describes the food offered in a city boardinghouse in

The Perils of Pearl Street, including a Taste of the Dangers of Wall Street, by a late Merchant, New York: 1834, a work of fiction, founded upon experience and realistic observation. Material on public dinners is drawn from (Frank W. Reilly), *The Health-Lift,* Chicago: 1869, promotional pamphlet for home gymnastic equipment; Parton, *op. cit.;* *Vermont History,* Vol. XXIII, No. 2, April, 1955, 170; and the *Annual Report of The New-York Historical Society for the Year 1954.* F. J. Schlink and M. C. Phillips, *Meat Three Times a Day,* New York: 1946, are my source on the table d'hôte at the St. Nicholas Hotel in New York City and the generous provision of eatables at Harvard College.

For a contrasting nostalgic view of the gastronomic binge of the last century, see H. L. Mencken, *Happy Days,* New York: 1940, and the description of a comfortable kitchen of the 70's, from Wittke, *op. cit.,* V, 338. The gustatory life of the Elijah Thompson family in Michigan is delightfully evoked in *The Country Kitchen* by Della T. Lutes, Boston: 1936. I am especially indebted to the chapter, "Breakfast Old Style," p. 196ff.

Dr. Kellogg's strictures on oatmeal occur in *The Miracle of Life,* Battle Creek: 1904. The gibe of the *New-York Review* is quoted from Vol. I, No. 2, October, 1837; 345.

Chapter IV

Material on Graham appears in Parton's *The Life of Horace Greeley,* Boston: 1872; *The Northampton Book,* Northampton: 1954; Mildred V. Naylor, "Sylvester Graham (1794-1851)," *Annals of Medical History,* Third Ser., Vol. IV, No. 3, Whole No. 121, May, 1942; 236-40; and the files of the *Hampshire Gazette.* Of especial value to this chapter was the *Hampshire Gazette Index. The Historical Records Survey of the W.P.A.* Northampton: 1939. [F.]

The verse on reform is from the *Sibyl,* March 1, 1859, quoted in Bertha-Monica Stearns, "Reform Periodicals and Female Reformers", *American Historical Review,* Vol. XXXVII, No. 4, July, 1932; 678.

Walker, *op. cit.,* says of Tissot's *Onanisme* and Graham's excursion into sexology that "the similarities between their works appear more than coincidental." Despite Father Graham's deplorable literary ethics, he was cheered on by a whole corps of Reverends and the Director of the Massachusetts State Lunatic Asylum. Graham's boast about his fame was printed in the *Graham Journal,* I, 8, quoted in *ibid.* Graham's sense of close rapport with God, which he communicated to Gerrit Smith, is reported in Ralph Volney Harlow, *Gerrit Smith*, New York: 1939; 95.

Graham's views on whole-wheat flour and home breadmaking are a major theme in his writings. See *Lectures on the Science of Human Life*, New York: 1858, and his *Treatise on Bread and Bread-Making*, Boston: 1837. His mistrust of commercial bakers is expressed in *ibid.*, 42-44. The vegetarian argument made from comparative anatomy appears frequently in the *Graham Journal*. In his *Lectures, op. cit.*, iv-vii, Dr. Graham harmonizes his dietetic views with Calvinist theology and, more tentatively, with phrenology, iv and 208. Graham proposed to save men's souls through their stomachs, a method later extended and perfected by the Adventists. See Richard H. Shryock, "Sylvester Graham and the Popular Health Movement," *Mississippi Valley Historical Review*, Vol. XVIII, No. 2, September, 1931; 172-83.

Graham's platform manner is described in the *Hampshire Gazette*. His discourses were "interminable," said the *Boston Medical and Surgical Journal*, in 1838, quoted in Walker, *op. cit.* I am indebted, for information on the rise of popular interest in health and hygiene, to Hebbel E. Hoff and John F. Fulton, "The Centenary of the First American Physiological Society Founded at Boston by William A. Alcott and Sylvester Graham," *Bulletin of the Institute of the History of Medicine*, Vol. V, No. 8, October, 1937.

The story of the riot is summarized from "The Isms of Forty Years Ago," *Harper's New Monthly Magazine*, Vol. LX, No. ccclvi, January, 1880. The paragraph on Mrs. Gove drew upon Hoff and Fulton, *loc. cit.*, Nichols, *op. cit.*, Stearns, *loc. cit.*, and Walker, *op. cit.*

For the atmosphere of a Graham boardinghouse I used a letter from William S. Tyler to Edward Tyler, October 10, 1833, finding it in Thomas H. LeDuc's "Grahamites and Garrisonites," *New York History*, Vol. XX, 1939; 190-91. The spread of Grahamism among collegians is mentioned in the *Graham Journal*.

The transcendental community at Florence, Mass., is treated in *The History of Florence, Massachusetts*, Charles A. Sheffeld, ed., Florence, Mass.: 1895. For information about the many water-cure resorts in the area I have relied upon Dorothy B. Porter and Edwin C. Rozwenc, *The Northhampton Water Cures*. Typescript, n.p.; n.d. (F); Dorothy B. Porter, "Northampton Won Widespread Fame Through Water Cure Establishments," *Daily Hampshire Gazette Tercentenary Supplement*, June 8, 1954; and a pamphlet, *Dr. Edward Denniston's Home for Invalids at Springdale*, Northampton, Massachusetts: 1870.

Typescripts of Father Graham's poetry are deposited in the Forbes Library. Dr. Russel T. Trall's memoir on Graham appeared in *The Water Cure Journal and Herald of Health Reform*, Vol. XII, No. 5, November, 1851. Data was obtained from the obituary of Graham in the *Hampshire Gazette*, September 16, 1851. The notion that Graham got the staggers from eating graham bread was put forward by an anonymous *New-York Review* essayist, I, No. 2, October, 1837, "New Ethics of Eating." Dr. Kellogg's estimate of the significance of Graham to Battle Creek was set forth in an address, quoted in ms. *Early Days of Battle Creek*, by Henry J. A. Wiegmink, 4 vols., pp. 507 (W).

A valuable modern synthesis, to which I am indebted, is Richard H. Shryock, "Public Relations of the Medical Profession in Great Britain and the United States: 1600-1870," *Annals of Medical History*, Vol. II, No. 3, New Series, May, 1930; 316-17. Edward Deming Andrews discusses the triangular relationship of Grahamism, hydropathy and the Shakers, in *The People Called Shakers. A Search for the Perfect Society*, New York: 1953. I used the second edition of Mrs. Nicholson's *Nature's Own Book*, New York: 1835.

Chapter V

I brought together biographical details on Dr. James C. Jackson from the *Dansville Advertiser*, July 18, 1895, an unpublished manuscript *Autobiography* (P), and *Biographical Review of the Leading Citizens of Livingston and Wyoming Counties, New York*, Boston: 1895.

Mrs. Elizabeth Cady Stanton claimed for her cousin, Elizabeth Smith Miller, daughter of Gerrit Smith, the honor of being the first American woman to adopt "the shorts"—"but do not mention it," she said in a letter to cousin Miller, "or Mrs. Bloomer would tear my eyes out." From *Elizabeth Cady Stanton, As Revealed in her Letters, Diary and Reminiscences*, M. Theodore Stanton and Harriot Stanton Blatch, eds., 2 vols., New York: 1922, II, 32. Mrs. Stanton gives a list of other reform-minded ladies who donned the bloomer outfit in her *Eighty Years and More*, New York: 1898; 203.

The development of the dress-reform idea at the Dansville Sanatorium may be traced in the pages of *Laws of Life*, successor to *The Letter Box*. My material on recreation, diet, treatment techniques and atmosphere is largely derived from work done in these files. Sources for the story of Granula are the *Dansville Advertiser*, April 12, 1883; a personal communication from James A. Jackson, the John K. Lippen manuscript, *Recollections of Early History of the Cereal Industry in Battle Creek,* n.p.; ca. 1935 [P]; and the manuscript *Story of the Kellogg Business,* by Horton and Henry, Inc., 3 vols., n.p.; n.d.

Clara Barton's tribute to "Our Home" is contained in an ALS letter to Dr. Jackson, March 3, 1890 (LC). I have consulted the discussion of Fruitlands in Alice Felt Tyler, *Freedom's Ferment—Phases of American Social History to 1860,* Minneapolis: 1944; 172-75. Health, social and moral crusades are all intertwined in the pages of the *Graham Journal,* in *Harper's Magazine, loc. cit.,* in Alexander Milton Ross, *Memoirs of a Reformer,* Toronto: 1893; Stearns, *loc. cit.,* Shryock, *Mississippi Valley, loc cit.,* contributed to my discussion new factual material and illuminating comment.

Dr. Jackson retired in 1879. Two generations of Jacksons carried on; then the Sanatorium ended up ingloriously as a Macfadden "Health-atorium," where noncontagious patrons got slanting table work and wriggled their fingers to piano music.

The Laws of Life, Vol. 9, whole number 99, March, 1866, p. 84, gives as 1861 the date when the first Seventh Day Adventist entered the Dansville Sanatorium. I used *Footprints of the Pioneers,* by Arthur Whitefield Spalding, Washington: 1947, Chapter 21, "Home on the Hillside," in establishing the link between Dansville and Battle Creek. Spalding writes from the special Adventist point of view.

Chapter VI

I have drawn on Spalding, *ibid.,* 170-73, in trying to figure out what went on at the Hilliards', also Dores Eugene Robinson, *The Story of Our Health Message,* Nashville, Tennessee: 1943; 65-69. The problems of diet, holiness and humility are discussed helpfully in Harold M. Walton and Kathryn Jensen Nelson, *Historical Sketches of the Medical Work of Seventh-day Adventists from 1866 to 1896,* Washington, D.C.: 1948, as well as the Advent drive against tobacco. Mother White's opinion of pork may be found in her *Counsels on Diet, op. cit.,* 393. For her consolation that the Israelites also complained, see *ibid.,* 408. An Adventist elder, Dudley M. Canright, advanced the argument of immodesty against hoop skirts in the *Sabbath Review and Advent Herald.*

It is difficult to believe that James White got a charge out of Miss Austin's sacklike suit, but it appears that he did, from H. E. Carver, *Mrs. E. G. White's Claims to Divine Inspiration Examined,* Marion, Iowa: 1877. Mrs. White's instructions regarding the Turkish trousers may be found in her *Testimonies for the Church*, 8 vols., 3rd ed., Mountain View, Calif., n.d., I, 424, 457, 459, 461, 463-65. An entertaining story of how Mrs. White merchandised patterns to the church ladies at one dollar each is told by Canright in his *Life of Mrs. E. G. White*, Cincinnati: 1919; 220, 271-73.

There is an account of Sister White's visions which fixed Battle Creek's destiny as the health hunters' home, in Robinson, *op. cit.* She tells of her adolescent conversion to William Miller's doctrines in *Life Sketches*, Mountain View, Calif.: 1915, and her first vision, too, where she recognized two familiar homely Maine faces, along with more wondrous sights; cf. Revelation, 5. And why, indeed, should not simple farm people and mechanics have believed that they had better varnish the shay for the coming of the Bridegroom, when the Rev. Timothy Dwight, President of Yale College, and a towering figure in the land of steady habits, believed literally in good and bad angels, and Jedediah Morse, the "father of American geography," thought in 1800 that grey squirrels crossed a river by embarking on a shingle or piece of bark, raised their tails for sails, and tacked to the opposite side? Dixon Ryan Fox preserves this bit of cultural history in *Ideas in Motion*, New York: 1935, the essay on "Refuse Ideas and Their Disposal."

Canright, *op. cit.*, tells about how Elder White remaindered some of his wife's old titles. For Gough's interruption of the Millerite meeting: John Lardner, "That Was New York, the Seven Lost Days on Walker Street," *The New Yorker*, Vol. XXXI, No. 49, January 21, 1956. The Millerite excesses are vividly but inaccurately described, according to Adventist writers, in J. B. McMaster, *A History of the People of the United States from the Revolution to the Civil War*. 8 vols., New York: 1883-1913, VII, 135-41; and in *Days of Delusion*, by Clara Endicott Sears, Boston: 1924. For the denominational view of what happened, see Francis D. Nichol, *The Midnight Cry* (short title), Washington: 1944.

The cynicism which followed the Great Disappointment was recorded by a contemporary journal, *Voice of Truth*, November 19, 1845; 528; December 31, 1845; 2; and December 23, 1846; 5-7, all quoted from Whitney R. Cross, *The Burned-over District*, Ithaca: 1950; 314.

Details on the beginning of the health work of Adventism were gathered from files of *The Health Reformer*. The close association of the Whites and the Kelloggs at the Tabernacle is recited in *The Beginnings of Adventism in Battle Creek*, compiled from articles published in *The Enquirer and News*, n.p., n.d. Information on Dr. M. G. Kellogg's career in the south Pacific came from Walton and Nelson, *op.*

cit. Robinson, *op. cit.*, states how the financing of John Harvey Kellogg's education was accomplished.

Chapter VII

Genealogical data on the Kellogg family was drawn from the following mss: L. Schoenfield, *Biographical Sketch of Dr. J. H. Kellogg*, dated Sept. 10, 1941 (DN); Chipman, *Biographical Sketch of W. K. Kellogg*, Battle Creek: 1934 (DN); Anon., *Biographical Sketch of W. K. Kellogg*, n.p.; 1935 (DN); also Horton and Henry, *op. cit.*; and Putney Haight, work sheets and notes for a proposed biography of W. K. Kellogg (P). Among printed works I consulted Merritt G. Kellogg, *op. cit.*; Spalding, *op. cit.*; Sylvester Judd, *History of Hadley*, Springfield, Mass.: 1905; and the *Battle Creek Enquirer and News*, Sunday, October 7, 1951.

For conditions of life and travel in pioneer times I found material in the *Detroit Free Press*, Sunday, November 17, 1907, and in *Calhoun County. The City of Battle Creek—its Early History, Growth, and Present Condition. From the Detroit Post and Tribune*, June 16, 1878. Michigan Historical Collections, 1879-80; III, 347-66.

Horton and Henry, *op. cit.*, give 1850 as the year when John Preston Kellogg became interested in the Second Coming, confirmed by the biographer of W. K. Kellogg, Horace B. Powell, *The Original Has This Signature—W. K. Kellogg*, Englewood Cliffs, N.J.: 1956; 16. Powell says that an elder from Battle Creek converted Kellogg, interrupting him as he was raking hay, to bring him the Advent message. The Powell volume contains new material on the family and W.K.'s spectacular business success. Because of the substantial completion of my ms. before seeing Powell, my use of this recent work is limited.

Sources on broomcorn and corn-broom manufacture: Judd, *op. cit.*; Alice Morse Earl's *Home Life in Colonial Days*, New York: 1931; Richardson Wright, *Hawkers and Walkers in Early America*, Philadelphia: 1927; *Broom-Corn and Brooms*, New York: 1876; John L. Martin, "Broomcorn—The Frontiersman's Cash Crop," *Economic Botany*, Vol. VII, No. 2, April-June, 1953.

John Harvey Kellogg's dream: "How to Beat Old Father Time," Ledger Syndicate, n.p., n.d. His apprenticeship to the printing trade is extracted from the extensive obituary published in the *Battle Creek Enquirer and News*, December 15, 1943.

Old Spot is vouched for by Horton and Henry, *op. cit.*, who are also my source for Will's experience with his brother Albert. Dr. Kellogg's early services to the cause of Adventism may be traced in Spalding, *op. cit.*, Robinson, *op. cit.*, and the *Yearbook of the Seventh Day Adventists*, Washington: 1904, 1905, 1906, 1907, 1908.

For information about Battle Creek College I acknowledge obligation to *Illustrated Atlas and Directory of Free Holders of Calhoun County, Michigan*. Fort Wayne, Indiana: 1894; to a dissertation by Thomas Wilson Steen, *The Vocational Choices of Students Whose Religious Beliefs Limit Their Occupational Opportunities*, Chicago: 1939; and Spalding, *op. cit.*

The paragraphs dealing with Dr. Kellogg's years in New York rest on the *Annual Circular and Catalogue of the Bellevue Hospital Medical College, 1870-71*. New York: 1870; *Second Decennial Catalogue of the Trustees, Faculty, Officers and of the Alumni of the Bellevue Hospital Medical College of the City of New York, 1861-1881*, by Frederick A. Castle, M.D., New York: 1884; and the ms. *Bellevue Hospital, New York, Case Histories, 1881-82* (NYAM). The case of the veteran of Chancellorsville is real. I have imagined that John Harvey Kellogg described his phthisis and wrote the diagnosis in the casebook.

The beginnings of the breakfast-food industry: Wiegmink, *op. cit.* For Granula: personal communication from James A. Jackson.

The *Detroit News*, December 17, 1943, states that Dr. Kellogg attended the Centennial Exposition in 1876, confirmed by Roy V. Ashley. *The Health Reformer*, edited at the time by Kellogg, published material about the Exposition. See Vol. XI, No. 8, August, 1876. The author received the anecdote of Kellogg's "human needlework," from Mrs. Grace C. Rose; information regarding "Ward's Natural Science Establishment" at the Centennial from Roswell Ward.

Chapter VIII

Gibes at the water cures: the verse is from *The Knickerbocker Magazine*, XLI, 254, March, 1853. A writer in the same publication, January, 1850, said when he saw the patients promenading, he thought he was in a lunatic asylum, and when he saw them breakfasting, he thought he was in a penitentiary.

The pejorative on mineral springs occurs in *The Family Health Almanac*, Battle Creek, Michigan: 1876. C. W. Post's communication headed, "Two Thoughtful Letters from Mr. Charles W. Post," was published in a Battle Creek newspaper on or about October 24, 1905.

My paragraph on the sanatorium movement is drawn from *The Sanitarian*, January, 1876.

W.K.'s remark is from Horton and Henry, *op. cit.* Thirteen years and several modest raises later, he began to receive one fourth of the profits from The Doctor's business enterprises.

My treatment of the "San" was developed from a collection of pamphlets: *What Some Noteworthy People Think About 'Battle Creek Ideas,'* n.p., n.d.; *Medical and Surgical Sanitarium, Battle Creek, Michigan,* n.p., n.d.; a group of four with identical titles, *The Battle Creek Sanitarium,* 1902; n.p., n.d.; one by John Wiley, reprinted from *The Hotel Monthly,* May, 1929; and one dated 1930. The three kinds of "San" food service were discussed in *The Sanitarium News Bulletin,* April 24, 1929. Mrs. White's ukase on meat occurs in *Counsels on Diet, op. cit.,* 413. The spiritual life at the "San" is treated in Robinson, *op. cit.* The governance of the staff, as I have described it, is derived from a folder, *Rules for Helpers,* n.p., *ca.* 1880.

For my discussion of the economic disabilities of Adventists, I found valuable material in Steen, *op. cit.* The American doctor who joked about "Lane's Kink," was Morris Fishbein, in *Fads and Quackery in Healing,* New York: 1932.

Kellogg as a collector: the evidence has been surveyed by the author in a glass case in the parlors of the present Battle Creek Sanitarium. My summary of the accomplishments of German scholarship in the '80's rests upon W. O. Atwater, "What We Should Eat," *The Century Magazine,* Vol. XXXVI, No. 2, June, 1888. The glimpse of Kellogg dictating in the Sahara Desert was found in the *Detroit News,* October 31, 1926. The quiet help which Mrs. Kellogg provided on The Doctor's tours is acknowledged in his *In Memoriam,* Battle Creek: (1920?). How the Sanitarium foods spread over the world is told by Kellogg, *ibid.,* and the way he juggled his many food companies is narrated in Horton and Henry, *op. cit.* The *Battle Creek Morning Enquirer* announced, June 6, 1907, the rehabilitation of rhubarb at the "San" after twenty years in eclipse.

In Memoriam, op. cit., was used generally as a source for the contributions of Mrs. Kellogg to her husband's life work. She wrote *Science in the Kitchen,* Battle Creek: 1892, steadily reprinted until 1910, and *Healthful Cookery,* Battle Creek: 1904, and wrote copiously for *Good Health.*

For the whole Battle Creek complex as seen through the eyes of a visiting Adventist from the tall timber, I used *Experiences of a Pioneer Minister of Minnesota,* Minneapolis: 1892. Elbert Hubbard's sketch of Dr. Kellogg's personality occurs in *Selected Writings of Elbert Hubbard,* New York, n.d., II, 321-22. The sampling from *Modern Medicine* is taken from Vol. II, Nos. 1-2, January and February, 1893.

Chapter IX

My description of the vegetarian breakfast of the mid-nineteenth century is based on Shumway, *op. cit.* P. P. Stewart's invitation to the boarders to breakfast on parched corn is quoted from *ibid.*, 16. The "San's" breakfast in the very early days makes bleak reading, from Kellogg's *In Memoriam*, *op. cit.* Ellen White's remark appears in her *Counsels on Diet, op. cit.*, 259. Cecil Woodham-Smith is my authority for associating oatmeal with prison life in England, *circa* 1840, in *The Reason Why*, New York: 1953; 75-76.

Ferdinand Schumacher's services to the American breakfast are given scholarly and extended treatment in *The History of the Quaker Oats Company*, by Harrison John Thornton, Chicago: 1933. See also "Early Days in the Breakfast Food Industry," by Gerald Carson, *Advertising and Selling*, September and October, 1944. The entrenched position of oatmeal on Boston tables is Cleveland Amory's story in *The Proper Bostonians*, New York: 1947; 229. Dr. Kellogg's uncharitable remark on hot breakfast foods is taken from *The Battle Creek Sanitarium System*, Battle Creek: 1908; 137.

The sentiment of Dr. Ross will be found in his work previously cited. Sources on Perky's career: *Denver Tribune*, August 1, 1882; *Denver Post*, July 2, 1906; personal communication from Andrew Ross, who was prominent in the merchandising of Shredded Wheat as well as Kellogg's Corn Flakes; Horton and Henry, *op. cit.*, *Advertising and Selling*, *loc. cit.*; *Chicago Vegetarian*, Vol. III, No. 4, December, 1898; *ibid.*, No. 5, January, 1899; and for material on Shredded Wheat I consulted L. H. Merrill and E. R. Mansfield, "Cereal Breakfast Foods," *Maine Experiment Station Bulletin No. 84* (1902); also Alice Helen Mustard, *Cereal Breakfast Foods: a Study of the Manufacture and Cost on Basis of Composition and Portion*, an unpublished thesis, Chicago: 1926 (UC). Also *Printer's Ink Monthly*, February, 1927; "How They Started," by Albert E. Hasse, *ibid.*, December, 1935; *Printer's Ink Weekly*, January 31, 1924, and November 11, 1938; Lulu G. Graves, "Breakfast Food Facts," *Hygeia*, Vol. V, November, 1927-January, 1928; *The Nabisco Magazine*, Vol. 30, No. 3, May-June, 1943; letter to the author from Samuel N. Holliday. Also various promotional pamphlets: *The Vital Question, Devoted to Natural Food*, Niagara Falls, N.Y.: 1901; *The Happy Way to Health*, New York: 1917; Frank Presbrey, *The History and Development of Advertising*, Garden City: 1929; 408; *Battle Creek Enquirer and News*, October 7, 1951; interview with Roy V. Ashley; memorandum prepared for the author by R. O. Eastman. I have used details from the *Enquirer and News, supra,* in preparing my account of Dr. Kellogg's flaking experiments, as well as information growing out of interviews with Ashley, Eastman and A. F. Bloese. The *Detroit News,* October 7, 1951; Horton and Henry, *op. cit.;* were also helpful.

Dr. Kellogg's recollection of the dream which led to the successful invention of flaked breakfast foods: I used Albert Edward Wiggam, "The Most Remarkable Man I Have Ever Known," *American Magazine,* Vol. VI, No. 6, December, 1925; 14-15, checked against the version appearing in *Good Health,* Vol. 85, No. 9, September, 1950; 205.

The Granose patent, U.S. Patent No. 558,393, was granted April 14, 1896, the first issued for a flaked food. W.K.'s remark about the glory appears in Horton and Henry, *op. cit.,* 97. The younger Kellogg's contribution is a controversial point. He testified in his brother's 1916 lawsuit that they were in it together, both made suggestions. Miss Elsa Johnson supplied information on the part played by Adolph Johnson Co. in the early days of the Battle Creek cereal industry.

My discussion of cereal patents is based upon personal interviews with Andrew Ross and Clarence Jordan; Horton and Henry, *op. cit.;* letters from Miss Johnson and G. H. Lauhoff; also a memorandum he prepared for the author, *The Lauhoff Story of the Cereal Food Industry to 1910.* Powell, *op. cit.,* states that the Lauhoff firm was the only source of flaking rolls in the early 1900's.

Chapter X

Mrs. E. G. White's spiritual wrestling over what to do about Battle Creek was reported in the *Battle Creek Daily Moon,* April 3, 1901. The circumstances of how Battle Creek College was moved away from the cereal city in response to Mrs. White's dictates are summarized in the *Review and Herald,* Vol. 80, No. 21, May 26, 1903; and also in the issues of August, September and October, 1903.

Mrs. White fathered—or mothered—the idea that an angel guided Dr. Kellogg's knife in the operating room, and it appears in the controversial pamphlet, an exposé of the visionist which split Adventism into two camps, *A Response to an Urgent Testimony from Mrs. Ellen G. White Concerning Contradictions, Inconsistencies and Other Errors in Her Writings,* Battle Creek, Michigan: n.d. This "little blue book" was published anonymously, but Canright makes the attribution to Dr. Charles E. Stewart, a close associate of Doctor Kellogg's, in the *Life of Mrs. White, op. cit.,* 194. A *Response* was the immediate cause of the expulsion of Kellogg from the Adventist communion. See also the *Battle Creek Journal*, November 10, 1907.

Mother White's admonition to Kellogg about the source of his success is reported in the *Review and Herald*, Vol. 80, No. 15, April 14, 1903; 19, and his reaction: "He put on the coat of irritation and retaliation." The break between the prophetess and The Doctor was treated at length in the *Detroit Free Press*, January 31, 1909. I have drawn on that story of the affair. The intrusion of economics into the church quarrel is cited from Robinson, *op. cit.*, 258.

The running story of the "San" fire and its afterclap appears in Battle Creek newspapers during late winter and spring, 1902, and I have used the files of that period. I found Mrs. E. G. White's apt metaphor of the sword of fire in the *Review and Herald*, Vol. 80, No. 15, April 4, 1903; 7; also her claim of precognition.

The quotation from the *Detroit News*: January 10, 1922.

The description of the new Sanitarium building appears in contemporary local newspapers; in *The Battle Creek Sanitarium Book, op. cit.*; and "San" pamphlets already cited. The atmosphere of the dedication emerges from *A Brief Account of the Dedicatory Services of the New Main Building of the Battle Creek Sanitarium*, Battle Creek, Michigan: 1904. The *New York Tribune*, May 31, 1904, carried the story of the "gunpowder plot."

Battle Creek College was a stout arm of The Doctor's health propaganda. When a well-stacked senior coed passed along Washington Street, Dr. Kellogg would point out how much better-looking she was than the freshmen. Reason: she had had the benefit of four years of right living; *The American Magazine, loc. cit.* The furore raised over Dr. Kellogg's heretical book, *The Living Temple*, Battle Creek: 1903, is remembered by Ashley and Bloese, and appears in an acrimonious article in the *Review and Herald*, Vol. 80, No. 42, October 22, 1903; 8-9. Purged, the book became *The Miracle of Life*, Battle Creek: 1904, cast pious doubt upon the concept of evolution.

The *Battle Creek Journal* reports the dismissal of W. K. Kellogg and others from the Tabernacle; July 8, 1907. The proceedings against Dr. Kellogg are recorded in Canright, *Life*, 215-16; vividly remembered by Thomas C. O'Donnell who took down the stenographic record, and *The Battle Creek Journal* published details of Dr. Kellogg's excommunication, November 10 and 12, 1907. I have also consulted "Kellogg's Heresy Beginning of End for Adventists," by Bertha V. O'Brien, the *Detroit Free Press*, November 24, 1907. The article traverses the whole controversy.

Chapter XI

The verse and quoted comment are from the *New York World*, September 7, 1902. Charles Dudley Eaves and C. A. Hutchinson, *Post City, Texas*, Austin: 1952, quote C. W. Post on his experience as a mechanic. The biographical notice of C. W. Post's father appears in *History of Sangamon County, Illinois*, Chicago: 1881; 701. Biographical material was also amplified from Eaves and Hutchinson, *op. cit.* The story, unconfirmed, about Post and Lincoln is printed by Francis Bellamy, in *Effective Magazine Advertising*, New York: 1909. Information on Post's career as a militiaman has been extracted from the manuscript, *History of the Governor's Guard*, Springfield: 1933, by Alta Mae Speulda (IHS).

The circumstances of Post's going broke are recited in an article, "About C. W. Post," *Battle Creek Morning Enquirer*, February 6, 1903, which bears internal evidence of emanating from the Postum Cereal Co. as a publicity release. For Post's early life and Texas adventures I also consulted the typescript, *Biography of Charles William Post, Prepared by the Verne Burnett Organization in Collaboration with Marjorie Post Davies and Carroll L. Post*, n.p.; 1947 (P). There is autobiographical data in Post's "*I Am Well!*" *The Modern Practise of Natural Suggestion as Distinct from Hypnotic or Unnatural Influence. Scientia Vitae*. Second edition, Boston: 1895; and in *Charles William Post. A Memorial. Born October 26, 1854. Died May 9, 1914*, n.p.; (1915?). The materials cited in this paragraph throw light upon Post's mental therapeutics period, as does a deposition he made in 1899, quoted in the *New York Tribune*, August 23, 1905; 7, col. 2. For my treatment of this subject I also drew upon the pamphlet, *The $50,000 Verdict Awarded Collier's Against the Postum Cereal Company*, New York: 1911.

La Vita Inn figures in "*I Am Well!*", *op. cit.*; *The Biography, op. cit.*; and *The $50,000 Verdict, op. cit.* W. K. Kellogg's recollections of Post were found in Horton and Henry, *op. cit.*, I, 92.

My sampling of remarkable cures at the mental-suggestion boardinghouse is indebted to Post, "*I Am Well!*", *op. cit.*; and *Collier's*, Vol. XLVI, No. 14, December 24, 1910. The court battle: its annals may be found in *Collier's*, various issues in the latter part of 1910, quoted by Alexander Woollcott, "Rattling a Skeleton," *The New Yorker*, Vol. X, No. 39, November 10, 1934; 38.

The Second Man, by C. W. Post, was published by La Vita Inn Co., Battle Creek, Michigan; n.d. Post's depreciative remarks about Dr.

Kellogg appear in *"I Am Well!"*, *op. cit.* I have used *Good Health's* version of the origin of Postum, Vol. 85, No. 9, September, 1950; 207. Dr. Kellogg made his riposte to the commercial success of Postum and Grape Nuts in *The Battle Creek Sanitarium System*, Battle Creek, Michigan: 1908. The Lasker comment is recorded in "The Personal Reminiscences of Albert Lasker," *American Heritage*, Vol. VI, No. 1, December, 1954; 77.

My paragraphs on the beginnings of Postum manufacture rest on *C. W. Post: a Memorial*, *op. cit.*; the *Battle Creek Enquirer and News*, October 7, 1951, and January 4, 1955. Also *50 Years at Post Products*, *Jan. 1, 1945*, Battle Creek: n.d.; *Battle Creek Daily Moon*, April 4, 1900; and *Good Health*, May, 1897.

I found "White Beaver" in *The Making of Buffalo Bill*, by Richard J. Walsh and Milton S. Salisbury, Indianapolis: 1928; 305, and in Mary Hardgrove Hebberd, "Notes on Dr. David Franklin Powell, Known as 'White Beaver,' " *Wisconsin Magazine of History*, Summer, 1952, Vol. 35, No. 4.

For the pre-Battle Creek history of coffee substitutes I relied, in addition to the works mentioned in the text, upon Horton and Henry, *op. cit.*; *Dr. Chase's Recipes*, by A. W. Chase, Thirty-second ed., Ann Arbor, Michigan: 1866; 90 and 292; Washington Gardner, *History of Calhoun County*, 2 vols., n.p., 1913; I, 366; E. T. Freedley, *Opportunities for Industry and the Safe Investment of Capital: or, a Thousand Chances to Make Money*, Philadelphia: 1859; Andrews, *op. cit.*, 200; Helen Evartson Smith, *Colonial Days & Ways*, New York: 1900; 229.

Postum in paper bags: *Battle Creek Evening News*, May 9, 13-14, 1914. *Ibid.*, May 9, recites the story of Postum's invasion of Grand Rapids. An important source is the *New York World*, *loc cit.*, containing an 8-page section, "Battle Creek, Queen City of Michigan." Eaves and Hutchinson, *op. cit.*, gives the volume of sales for the first years of Postum Cereal Co.

Some legal vivacities over the curative powers of Postum and Grape Nuts are reported in *The New York Times*, December 3, 1910; 2, 2. Post's spectacular advertising is easily encountered in the leading magazines and newspapers of large circulation in the first years of this century. The Postum advertisement about lost eyesight, for example, was published in William Jennings Bryan's *The Commoner*, Vol. VI, No. 1, January 19, 1906. My authorities for the improvisation involved in the financing of Postum advertising are Horton and Henry, *op. cit.*; and a personal communication from James O'Shaughnessy.

Grape Nuts manufacture: my sources were *Hygeia*, *loc. cit.*; the

ms. *The Story of Post Cereals Division, General Foods Corporation,*
n.p., n.d. (P); "Let Them Eat Cake," *Fortune,* Vol. X, No. 4, October,
1934; Fuller, *op. cit.,* III, 271; and ms. notes supplied by Forest H.
Sweet. Grape Nuts packaging is discussed, historically, in *Printer's Ink
Monthly,* Vol. XXI, No. 2, September 30, 1935, and by Owen Winters,
"The Road to Wellville Plays a Return Engagement," *Printer's Ink
Weekly,* Vol. 130, No. 11, March 12, 1925; 33. Grape Nuts advertising
is reviewed in *Collier's,* December 17, 1910. The novel food was popular enough to be listed in the Sears, Roebuck & Co. catalogue, 1902, according to Cummings, *op. cit.,* 108.

C. W. Post's advertising to get endorsers for Postum was published
in *The New York Magazine of Mysteries,* Vol. VIII, No. 1, November,
1904; 73. How the letters were "condensed" was explained in a brochure
entitled *Coffee Ails Disappear by Use of Postum Food Coffee,* n.p., n.d.
C.W.'s homely philosophy on the use of advertising to get the customers
to swallow cereal is quoted from *The Lauhoff Story, op. cit.,* 4.

The food manufacturer's views on welfare work are the subject of
"Architects of Their Own Greatness; How Post, of Battle Creek, Has
Made and Spent Several Fortunes," by Idah McGlone Gibson, *Home
Life,* August, 1912, quoted in Eaves and Hutchinson, *op. cit.,* 22. For
Post's outlook on labor problems I consulted Walter Gordon Merritt,
History of the League for Industrial Rights, New York: 1925; Eaves
and Hutchinson, *op. cit.,* 15-19 *passim;* and *The Square Deal,* Vol. II,
No. 1, August, 1906, and No. 7, February, 1907. The *Battle Creek
Morning Enquirer,* January 2, 1905, reported on the previous evening's
banquet at which Post discussed his domestic affairs with his industrial
family.

The Texas colonizing venture is the principal theme of Eaves and
Hutchinson, *op. cit.* The list of rich men of the period appeared under
the title "American Millionaires," in the *World Almanac,* 1902; See
also Sidney Ratner, *New Light on the History of Great American For-
tunes. American Millionaires of 1892 and 1902.* New York: 1953. For
Goodwin and Elliot at the Post Theatre, I used a contemporary ac-
count in *The Battle Creek Daily Journal,* March 14, 1902; 4. For C. W.
Post's last days and death I have used *The New York Times,* March 4,
May 10, 11, 26, 1914; the *Detroit News,* May 10, 1914; and *Battle
Creek Evening News,* May 9, 13, 14, 1914.

Chapter XII

No organized narrative exists on the boom days in the breakfast-food industry. I have pieced together the story from widely scattered sources: the Kellogg Co.'s trade magazine, the *Square Dealer,* Sept. 1911-December, 1913; Battle Creek city directories; the *Recollections* of Lippen; and personal interviews. My narrative has benefited from correspondence with Earnest Elmo Calkins, and I have consulted his *Louder, Please,* Boston: 1924; the files of Battle Creek newspapers during the first decade of this century; also Horton and Henry, *op. cit.;* *New York World, loc. cit.; Advertising and Selling, loc. cit.;* the *Chicago Tribune, loc. cit.;* Wiegmink, *op. cit.;* Gardner, *op. cit.; Packages,* June, 1903; *Jabs, loc. cit.;* Frederick E. S. Tucker, "Battle Creek, the Health Food City," *National Magazine,* Vol. XVII, No. 1, October, 1902; "When New York Eats," *Current Literature,* May, 1902, quoting *Leslie's Weekly,* n.d.

Chaotic conditions in the food processing industry which led to federal legislation in the interest of the consumer are described in somewhat more detail in "Who Put the Borax in Dr. Wiley's Butter?", by Gerald Carson, *American Heritage,* Vol. VII, No. 5, August, 1956; and in very much more detail in Harvey W. Wiley's *An Autobiography,* Indianapolis: 1930.

Miss Marguerite Swallen assisted me in preparing the description of cornflakes manufacture. Miss Elsa Johnson provided information on early manufacturing methods.

Battle Creek newspapers and city directories, the *New York World, loc. cit.,* and Arthur J. Cramp's *Nostrums and Quackery,* 3 vols., Chicago: 1912, 1921, 1936, provided the background on various hangers-on and ancillary businesses attracted to Battle Creek because of the town's health connotations.

Chapter XIII

The glimpse of Post joking with his men is from Eaves and Hutchinson, *op. cit.* I have taken the fancy of Post on a desert island from Zach Moore, "Making Dreams Come True," *Pearson's* magazine, October, 1909, quoted in *ibid.,* 160-61.

The Ralston Health Food advertisement is label copy, quoted from Dr. William Frear, *Breakfast Foods,* Pennsylvania Department of Agriculture Bulletin No. 162, Harrisburg: 1909.

In summarizing various questions which arose about ready-to-eat breakfast foods, I referred to Merrill and Mansfield, *op. cit.*; *Hygeia, loc. cit.*; C. D. Woods and H. Snyder, *Cereal Breakfast Foods, United States Department of Agriculture, Farmer's Bulletin No. 249*; *Square Dealer*, June, 1912; 18; Mustard, *op. cit.*; Harvey W. Wiley's *Foods and Their Adulteration*, Philadelphia: 1907, 271; and Wiley's *Foods and Food Adulterants, United States Department of Agriculture. Division of Chemistry. Bulletin No. 13, pt. 9*, "Cereals and Cereal Products." Washington: 1898. The results of the Pennsylvania Department of Agriculture's chemical examination of cereal foods is reported in the Pennsylvania pamphlet, *Breakfast Foods, op. cit.*

The inspiration for the picture on the carton front of Elijah's Manna, showing the ravens bringing the prophet his food, may be found in the Bible, I Kings, 17:6. The reason for the change in name was announced in the *Battle Creek Journal*, February 11, 1908. The inappropriateness of both the Manna name, and Sanitas, as applied to corn flakes, is discussed in "Kellogg Success Based on Idea and Advertising," by Patricia Ryden, *Advertising Age*, April 26, 1948; 1, 50-51. The article gives a good general view of the merchandising history of the Kellogg Co.

Chapter XIV

For what is said about corn I acknowledge an obligation to Weatherwax, *op. cit.*, and Conway Zirkle's review of the same book in *Isis*, Vol. 46, Part I, No. 143, March, 1955. There were useful suggestions also in *American Ways of Life*, by George R. Stewart, Garden City: 1954. Corn has been suggested for the U.S. national floral emblem, and the Corn Tassel National Emblem Association, Minneapolis, Minnesota, is whole-heartedly behind the idea.

For the ascendancy of wheat flakes and the tentative beginnings of corn flakes I have followed Horton and Henry, *op. cit.*; and Lippen, *op. cit.*

So far as can be determined now, the first imitation of the Toasted Corn Flakes manufactured by W. K. Kellogg was Blancke's Toasted Corn Flakes, product of the C. F. Blancke Tea and Coffee Co., St. Louis, Mo., which also made a grain coffee called Blancke's Kafeka. The time: summer, 1906. See Otis H. Gates, ed., *U.S. Department of Agriculture. U.S. Solicitor of the Agriculture Department. Decisions of Courts in Cases Under the Federal Food and Drug Act*. Washington:

1934. But W.K. usually accredited Post Toasties, *née* Elijah's Manna, as "the original imitator," and his *Square Dealer* added, referring to the neighbor across the street, "Hell is paved with good imitations."

The trade-mark situation on corn flakes: I have levied upon Horton and Henry, *op. cit.*; also for further orientation in the subject I consulted James E. Shaw, *Trade Marks and Unfair Competition*, Boston: 1952; and William D. Shoemaker, *Trade-Marks*, 2 vols. Washington: 1931. The result of the Kellogg Co. suit against the Quaker Oats Company is reported in *Printer's Ink Weekly*, January 28, 1915.

Mr. Frank Lauhoff gave me the story of the "Diamond in the Corner." I drew on *Advertising Age*, *loc. cit.*, for details of W.K.'s virtuosity in advertising and selling breakfast foods, including the adoption of a pretty "Sweetheart of the Corn," who once pounded a typewriter in the Kellogg Co. offices. In this connection, it may be of some anthropological interest to note that the southwestern tribes had a male Corn God, while the Mandans and other Indians of the Great Plains personified maize, as Kellogg did, in the person of a Corn Maiden.

The legal battle of the Kellogg brothers over the commercial use of their patronymic is summarized in the *Enquirer and News*, October 7, 1951; 13-14. I have also traced this complicated matter through the files of *Printer's Ink Weekly*.

Chapter XV

The chicken story is told in Horton and Henry, *op. cit.*, I, 55. The statement of Howard List, advertising manager of Kellogg Co., was published in an article, "Cereal & Selling," by John A. McWethy, *Wall Street Journal*, Vol. CXLII, No. 89, November 3, 1953; 1. The episode in which Dr. Kellogg overreached himself and lost the valuable Pep trade-mark is narrated in Horton and Henry, *op. cit.* W.K.'s two bestowals of the horse ranch are surveyed in the *Battle Creek Enquirer and News*, October 7, 1951; 13; also in a personal communication from Putney Haight, and in his memorandum, October 22, 1940 (P).

The Shredded Wheat battle may be followed in Horton and Henry, *op. cit.*, and in Kellogg Co. *v.* National Biscuit Co. 305 U.S. 111, 1938. For J. L. Kellogg's business career, I consulted Horton and Henry, *op. cit.*; *Printer's Ink Weekly*, Vol. 111, May 20, 1920; *The New York Times*, May 17, 1942; *Battle Creek Evening News*, July 23, 1915; *Square Dealer*, February, 1911; the *Enquirer and News*, February 7, 1938 and April 3, 1950. Also personal communications from Andrew Ross, interviews with Mrs. Fanny Sprague Talbot, Burritt Hamilton.

W. K. Kellogg's brief autobiography, often quoted, will be found in the *Enquirer and News*, October 7, 1951; 12. For my treatment of the W.K. Foundation I have found useful the *Statement of Mr. W. H. Vanderploeg, op. cit.*; *Kellogg News*, November, 1951; publications of the Foundation—*The First Eleven Years, 1930-1941*, Battle Creek: 1942; and *The First Twenty-Five Years, The Story of a Foundation*. Battle Creek, Michigan: (1955); *Report for 1953-1954*, W.K. *Foundation*, Battle Creek, Michigan: n.d.; also *The New York Times*, September 12, 1955; and the *Enquirer and News*, December 21, 1955.

Chapter XVI

Information on the "San's" contribution to the economy of the city of Battle Creek is taken from the *Detroit News*, July 17, 1927.

Charles Wagner (1852-1918), tweedy French essayist of the peace-of-mind school, published *La Vie Simple* in 1895. It was translated into English in 1901 and became a U.S. best seller, assisted by Theodore Roosevelt, Major J. B. Pond and the Reverend Russell Hermann Conwell, who gave Wagner an honorary doctorate at Temple University.

The quotation from Holbrook occurs in *Yankee, op. cit.* I am indebted to Professor Carroll Grant for the picture of Dr. Kellogg at his own breakfast table. In reconstructing The Doctor's strenuous day, I used "A Private Secretary and a Full Time Job," by R. V. Ashley, *The Shorthand Writer*, Vol. X, No. 3, March, 1914; 107-11. The names are fictional, the atmosphere is as Ashley knew it and as Wiggam reported it in *The American Magazine, loc. cit.* For "San" atmosphere I am indebted to Frank Northrup and August E. Johansen, Mrs. Bertha Stump, Miss Leta Browning, the files of *The Battle Creek Idea*, Julian Street in *Collier's, loc. cit.*; the *Enquirer and News*, January 1, 1927; and pamphlets by Dr. Frank Crane, *A Sanitarium Experience, What the Battle Creek Sanitarium Really Is*, Battle Creek, Michigan: n.d.; Wilfred Grenfell, M.D., *The Soul of Battle Creek*, n.p., n.d.; and Francis Grierson, *A Visit to the Battle Creek Sanitarium*, n.p., n.d.

The infiltration of non-Adventists into the "San" is indicated in the kind of wry humor which emanated in later years from the University of Health; for example, in World War I days, the Home Ec. girls who said, "Don't eat the East Hall toothpicks 'til you've seen the bran"; or the staff bacteriologist who loved his smoke, but remarked sadly after his vegetarian meal, "It really isn't worth while having a cigar after that." The humor affords a measure of the attenuation of the fierce old religio-mysticism about the meatless meal as a way of life. The occasional dietetic derelictions of the "San" doctors are mentioned in the *Detroit News*, October 31, 1926. They must have meditated at times upon John 4:32, ". . . I have meat to eat that ye know not of."

Dr. Kellogg's physical appearance is described by Ashley, *loc. cit.*, and may be studied in the limitless number of photographs still extant. The episode of The Doctor and the photographers is derived from the *Enquirer and News*, December 16, 1943.

The circumstances of Mrs. White's death and her three handsome funerals are fully treated in the *Review and Herald*, July 29 and August 5, 1915, reprinted in a pamphlet, *In Memoriam, Mrs. E. G. White, 1827-1915*, n.p., n.d.

I have used Dr. Kellogg's own account of his Russian experience, in "A Visit to Pavlov's Laboratory," *Bulletin of the Battle Creek Sanitarium, Special Issue in Honor of the 80th Birthday of Professor Ivan Pavlov, with Papers by his Pupils, Friends, and Admirers.* October, 1929; 203-09. Dr. Kellogg owned a St. Bernard dog who ate vegetarian, officially. But Battle Creek knew that Duke got bones and meat trimmings from a friendly butcher, says Powell, *op. cit.*, 87-88. Professor Grant has good reason to remember The Doctor's clever anthropoid.

The tribute of Sir Wilfred Grenfell is quoted from his *The Soul, op. cit.*

Chapter XVII

For details on the Florida sanitarium I have drawn on the *Enquirer and News*, December 15, 1943; and *Good Health*, January, 1944. Dr. Kellogg's activities in the field of geriatrics are recounted in "Battle Creek Number," *The Magazine of Michigan*, Vol. II, No. 3, March, 1930. My treatment of Battle Creek Sanitarium affairs, from the erection of the 1927 addition, through the Depression, receivership, sale to the U.S. Army and final struggle for control, is based upon the files of the *Detroit News*, supplemented by and checked against the *Enquirer and News* for the same period.

The "Message of the Third Angel" is Adventese for the call to honor the seventh day Sabbath of the Decalogue (Exodus 20: 8-11). Revelation 14: 9-11 forecasts, according to Adventist theology, what is going to happen to people who go to church on Sunday.

The question about our future food supply is raised by Dr. Norman Jolliffe in "Recent Advances in Nutrition of Public Health Significance," *Metabolism, op. cit.*; Fairfield Osborn's *The Limits of the Earth*, Boston: 1953; M. K. Bennett, *The World's Food*, New York: 1954, and by a news report by Gladwin Hill, *The New York Times*, Nov. 15, 1956. Sesame is the subject of a *Wall Street Journal* article, June 14, 1955 to which I acknowledge obligation. Milton wrote "browse, well pleased" etc., an appropriate line to encounter where I found it—in *The American Vegetarian*, Vol. IV, No. 6, June, 1854; 131.

Grateful acknowledgment is made to the following sources for the illustrations which have been reproduced in this volume:

Battle Creek Enquirer and News, Battle Creek, Michigan, illustration number 20.

Battle Creek Sanitarium, Battle Creek, Michigan, illustrations numbered 10, 14, 15, 19 and 25.

Brown Bros., New York, N.Y., illustration number 9.

Chicago Tribune, Chicago, Illinois, illustration number 13.

Culver Service, New York, N.Y., illustrations numbered 8 and 24.

Dansville Historical File, Dansville, New York, illustration number 2.

Charles Presbrey and Marguerite Cree Presbrey, New York, N.Y., illustration number 21, reprinted from "The History and Development of Advertising," by the late Frank Presbrey, published by Doubleday & Company, Garden City, N.Y.

Professor Carroll W. Grant, Brooklyn College, Brooklyn, N.Y., illustration number 11, from "Ladies' Guide in Health and Disease," by J. H. Kellogg, M.D., published in 1891, by the Good Health Publishing Company, Battle Creek, Michigan.

Historical Society of Pennsylvania, Philadelphia, Pennsylvania, illustration number 1.

James A. Jackson, Conesus, New York, illustration number 3.

W. K. Kellogg Foundation, Battle Creek, Michigan, illustrations numbered 16 (copyright 1907) and 17.

New-York Historical Society, New York, N.Y., illustration number 18.

New York Public Library, New York, N.Y., illustrations numbered 6 and 12.

Post Cereals Division, General Foods Corporation, Battle Creek, Michigan, illustrations numbered 22 and 23.

Review & Herald Publishing Association, Washington, D.C., illustration number 7.

The Water-Cure Journal, Vol. 12, No. 2, August, 1951, from which illustration number 5 was reproduced.

Yankee Notions, Vol. I, No. 5, May, 1952, from which illustration number 4 was reproduced.

INDEX

289